The Private Chapel
in Ancient Egypt

Studies in Egyptology

Edited by Alan B. Lloyd

Professor of Classics and Ancient History, University College of Swansea

Editorial Advisor: A. F. Shore

Professor of Egyptology, University of Liverpool

Kegan Paul International

The Private Chapel in Ancient Egypt

A study of the chapels in the Workmen's Village at El Amarna with special reference to Deir el Medina and other sites.

Ann H. Bomann

KEGAN PAUL INTERNATIONAL

London and New York

First published in 1991 by
Kegan Paul International Ltd
PO Box 256, London WC1B 3SW, England

Distributed by
John Wiley & Sons Ltd
Southern Cross Trading Estate
1 Oldlands Way, Bognor Regis,
West Sussex, PO22 9SA, England

Routledge, Chapman & Hall Inc
29 West 35th Street
New York, NY 10001, USA

The Canterbury Press Pty Ltd
Unit 2, 71 Rushdale Street
Scoresby, Victoria 3179, Australia

DT
68,8
. B 6 6
1991

Printed in Great Britain by T. J. Press

British Library Cataloguing in Publication Data
Bomann, A.
    The private chapel in ancient Egypt: a study of the chapels in the workmen's villages at
    el Amarna with special reference to Deir el Medina and other sites. – (Studies in
    Egyptology).
    1. Egypt. Chapels. Architectural features, ancient period I. Title II. Series
    726'.4

    ISBN 0-7103-0346-7

Library of Congress Cataloging-in-Publication Data
Bomann, Ann H.
    The Private chapel in ancient Egypt: a study of the chapels in the workmen's villages
    at el Amarna with special reference to Deir el Medina and other sites / Ann H. Bomann.
        p. cm. -- (Studies in Egyptology)
    Includes bibliographical references and indexes.
    ISBN 0-7103-0346-7
    1. Chapels--Egypt. 2. Tell el-Amarna (Egypt). 3. Dayr al-Madīnah Site (Egypt).
    4. Architecture. Ancient--Egypt. I. Title. II. Series.
    DT68.8.B66 1991
                                                                        91-11080
                                                                            CIP

Contents

Acknowledgements

The research for this book was originally undertaken for my dissertation, submitted to the University of Birmingham in 1987. It was supervised by Dr M.A. Leahy, Lecturer in Egyptology at the University of Birmingham, and examined by Mr D.G. Jeffreys of University College, London and Field Director for the Survey of Memphis. Since then it has been revised, corrected and brought up to date in accordance with new information.

I am grateful to Dr M.A. Leahy for his careful guidance, support and encouragement throughout my work, and to Mr D.G. Jeffreys for reading it and giving his helpful comments.

I wish to express my appreciation and thanks to Mr B. J. Kemp, with whom I worked for six seasons in the field at the Workmen's Village and one season in the Main City at Amarna. He offered me the opportunity to study the chapels and gave me access to important material (some of which was unpublished until now) without which this book would have been incomplete.

My appreciation goes to Professor M. Bietak, who spent time discussing with me, while working at Tell el Dab'a, his group of Canaanite temples and generously permitted me to use some of his material.

To Mohammed el Soghayer, Director General for Upper Egypt, I owe thanks for permitting me to examine in detail the private chapels at Deir el Medina. He also kindly showed me his excavations south of the Karnak Temple precinct, which helped me to arrive at some conclusions in this study.

I also wish to extend my thanks to the following: Carol Andrews of the Department of Egyptology in the British Museum for her help and for giving me access to the finds in the British Museum from the excavations of T. E. Peet and C. L. Woolley from the Workmen's Village at Amarna; Dr G. Dreyer of the German Institute in Cairo, who discussed with me his ideas on ancestor worship; Mr P. Lacovara of the Boston Museum of Fine Arts, who provided me with reports and plans of his excavations at Deir el Ballas; Ann Cornwell, whose list of references of **T**-shaped basins from the Workmen's Village Reference Archive in Cambridge helped my research.

I extend my thanks to Fran Weatherhead, who updated her excellent reconstruction of Chapel 561 (Main Chapel), Amarna, which first appeared in *Amarna Reports* III (1986), and which she provided for the cover of this book.

Among Levantine scholars, special thanks go to Jonathan N. Tubb of the Department of Western Asia of the British Museum and Director of excavations at Tell es-Sa'idiyeh, Jordan, and to Dr R. L. Chapman, Executive Secretary of the Palestine Exploration Fund. To the former, I am grateful for the opportunity of working on his site, which has helped to familiarize me with Near Eastern material, and for his advice on the Sea Peoples. To the latter, I am appreciative of the time he spent in discussions with me and for furnishing me with many valuable references pertaining to Levantine history and archaeology.

I am grateful to Mr W. V. Davies, Keeper of the Department of Egyptian Antiquities at the British Museum, for recommending this book to Kegan Paul International, and to Mr P. Hopkins, Chairman of KPI, for publishing it. To Linda Carless Hulin of Caradoc Books I am indebted for her invaluable help in meticulously preparing the manuscript for publication.

Lastly, I wish to dedicate this book to Amarna, B. J. Kemp and all the members of staff and Egyptians with whom I have worked — years of my life which hold a special place in my affections.

London 1988.

List of Illustrations

Abbreviations

AASOR	Annual of the American Schools of Oriental Research.
AJA	American Journal of Archaeology.
AR	*Amarna Reports*
ASAE	Annales du Service des Antiquités de l'Égypte.
BASOR	Bulletin of the American Schools of Oriental Research.
BES	Bulletin of the Egyptological Seminar.
BIE	Bulletin de l'Institut d'Égypte.
BIFAO	Bulletin de l'Institut Français d'Archéologie Orientale du Caire.
CAH	*Cambridge Ancient History.*
COA	*City of Akhenaten.*
IAE	International Association of Egyptologists.
IFAO	L'Institut Français d'Archéologie Orientale du Caire.
JAOS	Journal of the American Oriental Society.
JARCE	Journal of the American Research Center in Egypt.
JEA	The Journal of Egyptian Archaeology.
JEOL	Jahrbericht 'Ex Oriente Lux'.
JESHO	Journal of the Economic and Social History of the Orient.
KRI	K.A. Kitchen, *Ramesside Inscriptions.*
LAAA	Liverpool Annals of Archaeology and Anthropology.
Manuel	Manuel d'Archéologie Égyptienne.
MDAIK	Mitteilungen des Deutschen Archäologischen Instituts Abteilung Kairo.
OINE	Oriental Institute Nubian Expedition.
OLP	Orientalia Lovaniensia Periodica.
Ouvriers	*Les Ouvriers de la Tombe: Deir el Médineh à l'époque Ramesside.*
PM	B. Porter and R.L.B. Moss, *Topographical Bibliography of Ancient Egyptian Hieroglyphic Texts, Reliefs and Paintings.*
Rapport	*Les Fouilles de Deir el Médineh.*
Urk.IV	Urkunden der 18 Dynastie.
Wb	Wörterbuch der aegyptischen Sprache.
ZÄS	Zeitschrift für Ägyptische Sprache und Alterkumskunde.

Introduction

Apart from some of the reports of Bruyère, little attention has been devoted to the private votive chapel in Egypt and its role in the life of the ordinary man. It was not until excavation began again in the Workmen's Village at Tell el Amarna in 1979 that the votive chapel came into a new focus. Owing to the increased interest in exploring the area of settlement archaeology in Egypt over the last few decades, it is possible to examine the subject in a different light. The work of Bietak and Kemp at Tell el Dab'a and El Amarna is among the foremost in this area of research, but valuable information on urbanism is also being contributed by D. Jeffreys and Mohammed el Soghayer at Memphis and ancient Thebes respectively.

The main concentration of field work in Egypt since the nineteenth century has been in the excavation, recording and restoration of state religious and funerary monuments together with the tomb chapels of private officials. This has provided a vast fund of information on the civilization of Egypt, but at the same time has created an unbalanced conception of Egyptian life which has been partly offset by the excavation of Deir el Medina. The exposure of this workmen's village by Bruyère during the years of 1922-1951 shed light on another area of Egyptian society — the ordinary citizen who counted for the greater number of the population of Egypt, and who, until the excavation of the workers' settlement, had been largely neglected.

The early excavations at Deir el Medina were concurrent with those of Peet and Woolley at the Workmen's Village at El Amarna in the early twenties of this century. At this time, the private votive chapel of the ordinary man (to be called *private chapel* hereafter) became known.

The basis for the following study of the private chapel is provided by the two above-named sites. Other chapels, related in origin and development, are also discussed. For two reasons, however, the point of departure for this investigation is the group of chapels at El Amarna. First, the private chapel, which served both a religious and a funerary purpose in the life of the worker and the craftsman, appears in its fully developed and earliest now extant form at El Amarna. Although chapels anterior to those extant at Deir el Medina today probably existed on that site, next to no trace of them remains. Those accessible at Deir el Medina post-date those at El Amarna. Secondly, my work at the Workmen's Village, El Amarna, during six seasons, which included the excavation and recording of the Main Chapel, as well as the re-recording of some of Peet's chapels of 1921, afforded me the opportunity of a closer study.

The history of the work on the chapels in the Workmen's Village at El Amarna commenced with Peet and Woolley, who excavated twenty-five structures, five of which were not chapels. Peet recognized that these five were an anomaly in the chapel plan, and they have since proved to be either a chapel dependency or, in two cases (nos. 540 and 541), buildings with a different use.[1]

This area was then left to drift sands. Fifty-eight years later, work recommenced at the Workmen's Village under the direction of B. J. Kemp, sponsored by the Egypt Exploration Society (1979-86). The initial work consisted of excavation south and southwest of the Walled Village and within the village itself (fig. 1).[2] In 1983 work was once more resumed in the chapel area. This began with chapel 561 (the Main Chapel). Peet had started work on the northern niche of the sanctuary, but had left the excavation of this building unfinished.[3] At the same time work started on replanning some of the chapels excavated by Peet. The first to be accomplished was 'Chapel' 523, a dependency of Chapel 522. The shrine of the latter building was also replanned that season.[4] Two new chapels were excavated (numbered 570 and 571) in 1983-4.[5]

During 1984 it was decided to re-examine more of Peet's chapels. The replanning of Chapel 522 was completed and the re-clearing and re-recording of Chapels 528, 529, 530, 531 and 537 was begun.[6] This proved to be highly valuable. Not only did the re-examination of these buildings produce considerably more information than Peet had recorded, but it also exposed in Building 528 architectural features so far unique in ancient Egyptian religious structures. 1985 saw the completion of the planning of Chapel 537 and the re-clearance of buildings 540 and 541,[7] and in 1986 the recovery of Chapel 556[8] (originally commenced by Woolley in 1922) and dependencies of Chapel 561 were completed.

To obtain the most comprehensive understanding of the chapels, a meticulous archaeological procedure was followed. This consisted in the removal and sifting of Peet's dumps, detailed phase by phase planning as buildings began to emerge, the collection of soil and botanical specimens for analysis, the gathering of faunal remains and other organic material, the reconstruction of painted wall plaster, the recording of objects and the study of pottery associated with the chapels.

Although work has now ceased at the Workmen's Village for the time being, more chapels await excavation.[9] With the increased interest in the settlements of ancient Egypt, future work may expose more of these less familiar cult structures in communities other than those of necropolis workers. However, until that time should arrive, it is hoped that this examination of the private chapel will help to increase understanding of this type of building, which served a vital function in the religious and funerary life of Egypt's ordinary citizen.

Notes

1.   T.E. Peet and C.L. Woolley, *City of Akhenaten* I (London, 1923), 92-108 (hereafter *COA*); T. E. Peet, *JEA* 7 (1921), 179-182.
2.   B.J. Kemp, *JEA* 66 (1980), 5-16; 67 (1981), 5-20; 69 (1983), 5-24. Kemp, *Amarna Reports* I (London, 1984), 14-33, 40-88 (hereafter *AR*).
3.   Peet and Woolley, *COA* I, 101.
4.   Kemp, *AR* I, 25-27.
5.   Ibid., 34-39.
6.   Kemp, *AR* II, 39-50.
7.   Kemp, *AR* III, 60-79.
8.   Kemp, *AR* IV, 70-83.
9.   The stairway to a chapel appeared during the season of 1986 lying east of the Walled Village north of Chapel 521.

Chapter 1

The Topographical Layout of the Private Chapels at El Amarna

The eastern desert in which the ancient capital of Akhetaten was situated stretches for nearly four kilometres from the cultivation to sharply rising cliffs which form a natural arc that once enclosed the city and its outposts. This arc runs for about eight kilometres from north to south. In the southern sector, some one and a half kilometres from the Main City, is the Workmen's Village. It lies in a bay on the south side of one of the several terraces formed during the Pleistocene period which fan out from the eastern cliffs of the Red Sea desert (fig. 1). The bedrock of this part of the desert is a marl ranging from a red terracotta colour to a burnt orange tone. This lies on average some two metres below drift sand deposited either by wind or alluvial action.

The terrace containing the Workmen's Village is situated between the Royal Wadi to the north and the Great Wadi to the south. The bay which encloses the Worker's settlement has a steeply rising escarpment to the west and north, and a terraced gradient commencing to the east and continuing to the south. Running east to a series of terraces fronting the Great Wadi is a broad valley floor. South of this again lies another terrace with a steep ascent. The northwest angle of this terrace and the southwest corner of the bay form a natural entrance to the Workmen's Village which looks out across the level desert to the low lying cliffs which contain the southern group of noblemen's tombs and the entrance to the road leading to the Hatnub quarries.

Across the summit of the broad terrace in which the Workmen's Village lies are a series of ancient patrol routes running in parallel lines approximately north to south to and from the village. Other routes encircle the settlement to the north and southeast in the area where the main body of the chapels are situated (fig. 2). Some of the routes in this part of the site adjoin areas marked out with stones on the desert surface in the shape of a **T**.

The main route of entry to the village is between the southern and northern faces of the two terraces encircling the settlement.

On the southern slope of the main terrace outside the village is a group of buildings called X1, which possibly housed the village guards or watchman.[1] Beyond, on a direct line with the main route from the city to the Workmen's Village, lay a compound for water storage jars known as the *Zir* area. This provided the immediate water supply for the village.[2] Beyond this to the east is an area composed of a platform of marl brick a little over five metres square and of unknown use. This is abutted by a huge quarry, the full extent of which is still undetermined, which supplied the marl for the village.[3] To the north, east and south of this respectively, are located the Walled Village, the chapels, and the animal pens. The quarry, which reached a depth of over two metres, served later as a dumping ground for the village rubbish, which covered a large area south of the village wall.

Situated between the quarry and the southern wall of the village is a group of organically developing chambers (no. 350) cut into the bedrock and which appear to have been the earliest houses of the village before the erection of the orthogonally laid out buildings of the main settlement.[4] Separating it from the southern wall of the Walled Village was a packed mud deposit forming a platform into which were sunk five T-shaped basins, numbered 1 to 5 starting from the west (fig. 3). Nos 1 to 3 lay directly on the axis of the main entrance of Chapel 561, situated at the southeast corner of the Walled Village. Nos 4 to 5 begin to veer slightly to the southeast in a line with T-shaped basin no. 6, which lay before the entrance to Annexe 450, abutting the Main Chapel to its south.

The Main Chapel, which was the last built, acts as a connecting link between the domestic and daily life of the people and their religious activities. The T-shaped basins stretching before the village wall provide the 'bridge' which symbolically joins the two worlds. Behind the Main Chapel are ranged the remainder of the chapels.

Looking to the extreme north of the village is an isolated group of chapels called the 'northern group', nos 551-556. This group is just north and east of the Walled Village (fig. 4). No. 555 lies in isolation west of this group, and is oriented towards the east, whereas the other chapels in this sector are oriented north. The buildings are cut into the gebel of the terrace escarpment enclosing the rear, eastern wall of the village.

South of the northern group of chapels and lying about five metres from the eastern wall of the village are a series of animal pens.[5] These enclosures extend up the steeply rising slope towards the sharp summit of the terrace behind. The boundary between religious structures and pens is broken at the junction between the rising gradient of the terrace and its steep promontory. Here some of the shaft tombs discovered in 1921 appear, and directly to the south the chapels take up a position that runs steadily around the eastern curve of the bay.

The first in this series, still north of the Main Chapel, is chapel 521, followed by 522 with its annexe 523. These are positioned just east of Chapel 561, on the slope above (figs 1, 5), and are cut into the rising gebel. Just beyond this group the convolution of the terrace promontory turns sharply towards the east. Cut into the gebel face of the terrace at this point is chapel Group 524, 526, 527 and 525 as numbered on Newton's plan of 1921 (figs 1, 5). On a line with the axis of Chapel 525 is a shaft tomb sunk into the plateau above (fig. 5).

A space of about five metres separates this group of contiguously built chapels from the succeeding cluster of buildings. These (nos 528-531) (figs 1, 5) are built on a broad lower terrace jutting out from the south side of the naturally formed bay. Beyond these, on the same lower plateau, lies another isolated group of chapels. These are numbered, according to Newton's sequence, chapel 535 with a dependency labelled 534, then 533, 532 and 536 (figs 1, 5). Beyond, the lower terrace gradually fades into the valley floor to the east where chapel 537 (fig. 14) stands alone, furthest east of all the religious buildings so far excavated.

South of Chapel 561 and its Annexe 450 is a group of enclosures numbered 400, consisting of a series of animal pens (fig. 1).[6] A corridor or pathway lead from the platform with its T-shaped basins in front of the village up the side of the hill between the Main Chapel and Annexe 450 and the animal pens on the other side, past Building 523 onto the lower terrace containing chapel groups 528 through 536. A passageway also once existed between the animal pens and the eastern wall of the village which led in the direction of the northern group of chapels.

More animal pens spread to the south of Building 400 covering part of a slope studded with boulders on the southeastern bend of the bay.[7] Stretching between this lower group of pens (which lie adjacent to the quarry and the rubbish dumps and Chapels 527 and 525) are Buildings 540 and 541 (fig. 5), which appear also to have served as quarters for sheltering animals.

On an axis with buildings 540 and 541, and lying south of them on the valley floor below, is another group of chapels numbered 570 and 571 (figs 1, 9). Sunk into the gebel rising north of 570 is a tomb shaft. This last group of chapels is on a direct line with the quarry and the *Zir* area.

The topographical layout of the Workmen's Village has certain parallels with the workmen's village at Deir el Medina. Both are set in an area surrounded by cliffs and low lying hills distant from their respective main cities. The houses in the case of Amarna are situated in the lower level of the bay and at Deir el Medina they stretch across the valley floor. In both cases the majority of the chapels and tomb shafts are ranged along the surrounding escarpment overlooking the domestic area of the site. One principal route led to the village from the main city or supply depot. Other subsidiary roads passed across the top of the terraces or cliffs.

The Workmen's Village at El Amarna was a self-contained settlement. The plan shows fully developed domestic quarters with accommodation for raising animals. An area was set aside for maintaining a constant water supply which would have been brought from the main city. This suggests that grain, oil, and possibly wine, and other items would have been delivered as well. The votive chapels provided for the religious and cultic needs of the settlement. From the material evidence at hand, it is seen that the inhabitants of the village were supplied with the necessary facilities for maintaining everyday life both worldly and spiritual.

Notes

1. Kemp, *JEA* 66 (1980), 8.
2. Kemp, *AR* I, 78-80.
3. Ibid., 81-88.
4. Kemp, *JEA* 67 (1981), 10, 13; fig. 4.
5. Kemp, *AR* III, 34-49.
6. Kemp, *AR* I, 40-51.
7. Kemp, *AR* III, 50-59.

Chapter 2

The Architecture of the New and Replanned Chapels at El Amarna

The chapels in the Workmen's Village at Amarna date from the latter part of the Eighteenth Dynasty. This includes the reigns of Akhenaten, Smenkhkare and Tutankhamun. One source for dating is the ring bezels bearing the cartouches of these monarchs that were found distributed in the workers' settlement.[1] Two bezels with the cartouche of Akhenaten came from within the Walled Village from the excavations of 1921 and 1922, and one from Long Wall Street 6 from the excavations of 1979. The rubbish dumps outside the Walled Village produced more ring bezels, the higher proportion of which belong to Smenkhkare and the lesser proportion to Tutankhamun. However, within the village nineteen bezels bearing the name of Tutankhamun were found and only two of Smenkhkare. Since the preponderance of bezels belong to the two last named kings, it suggests that the village was more heavily populated and active during these reigns than during that of Akhenaten. This would imply that the majority of chapels were constructed during the reigns of Smenkhkare and Tutankhamun and the minority probably during the latter years of Akhenaten's lifetime. It might be argued that the discovery of the bezels in areas outside the chapel confines is not evidence for dating those buildings. It is logical, nevertheless, to envisage the occupants of the village as responsible for constructing the chapels during their residence. Although Amarna was not totally deserted by the reign of Tutankhamun and there is evidence of post-Amarna habitation of the village even several hundred years later, by 'squatters',[2] their desultory way of life certainly could not be responsible for the ordered construction of the chapels.

Another source for dating, although only tentative, is the wine label dockets from jars found in the village.[3] The majority of the labels are from the latter years of Akhenaten's reign. Allowing for storage and reuse of jars, the main activity in the village was in the final years of Akhenaten, and more especially the reigns of his successors.

Given this sparse epigraphical information, the construction of the chapels can be placed within a limited period of history of around eight years. The next problem is attempting to establish a relative chronology of the chapels at El Amarna within this narrow space of time. This entails the examination of architectural features, details of wall decoration and texts, of which few examples survive, and, lastly, of objects found within the chapel context.

The Amarna chapels follow a fairly standard plan, but within its framework a refreshing individuality is expressed, which seems to vanish with the chapels of the Nineteenth and Twentieth Dynasties at Deir el Medina. The almost predictable regularity then apparent can be traced in the style of the chapels assigned to the later phase at Amarna.

The chapels to be analyzed in this Chapter are those which have been newly excavated and those that have been re-cleared. The plans are referred to mainly when the physical details are not available for examination, as in the case of the remainder of the un-cleared chapels at Amarna discussed in Chapter Three.

The new buildings are Chapel 561 and its Annexe 450, Chapel 570 and Chapel 571. The replanned chapels are Chapel 522 and its annexe 523, Chapel Group 528-531, Chapel 537 and Chapel 556. The first group to be examined will be the newly excavated chapels, followed by the replanned buildings. A discussion of the possible chronological sequence of construction will follow the examination of the remaining chapels in Chapter Three.

Chapel 561

This chapel (the Main Chapel),[4] whose main axis is oriented east to west, was one of the largest among this series of buildings. Its outer measurements from the flight of stairs leading into the forecourt to the shrine are 18.63 m. and its width taken from the outer hall inclusive of the left annexe or side chapel is 7.29 m. (figs 6-7a). The outermost flight of stairs abutting the forecourt of the chapel were built of boulders and cobbles sunk into a marl matrix (fig. 7a). The flanking walls of the stairs showed traces that it was once plastered in marl and gypsum. Only two steps and a threshold remain, the rest having been rubbed out. These were once plastered in Nile mud and gypsum. To the right of the stairway is a cobble and mortar pavement abutting the forecourt wall and which had continued also once on the left side of the stairs. This was washed out, however, by alluvial action, i.e., by flash flooding, long after life had ceased in the village.[5]

Forecourt

The forecourt, whose outer measurements are 8.50 m. wide by 3.43 m. deep, was a rough construction of boulders sunk into a marl matrix. The marl brick tumble associated with the forecourt wall to the north suggests that several courses of brick were laid upon the boulders, a common method of construction for buildings in the village. The exact height of the forecourt wall is difficult to determine, since the brick courses were completely mulched and could not be counted.[6] It is reasonable to assume, however, that it rose over a metre in height so as to preclude a direct view of the inner confines of the chapel. Since no roofing fragments were present in this area, the court would seem not to have been roofed. The floor, which was heavily gutted, still retained patches of hard-packed marl which had been laid as a surface directly on the desert floor. In the southeast corner of the forecourt large fragments of a *zir* were found,[7] suggesting that water for some of the chapel requirements was kept here. *Zir* emplacements in the forecourt of some of the chapels at Deir el Medina have been noted.[8]

The forecourt, the inner face of which was plastered in Nile mud and then coated with a gypsum whitewash, was the last part of the building to be constructed. This has been determined by the presence of traces of gypsum plaster on the south side of the main entrance wall to the outer hall of the Main Chapel, which were covered by the forecourt wall. It was not unusual to build a section of a building and then whitewash it before adding on the remainder of a wall or another sequence of the building, as will be seen later.

To the east of the forecourt was the principal entrance to the Main Chapel, which is marked by the remains of two brick pylons 45 cm. long × 20 cm. wide. These were plastered in alluvial mud and gypsum. Set between them was a step of stones and mortar followed by the impression of a stone which had once formed the threshold. On either side of these were the remains of a low balustrade of alluvial mud, marl and gypsum plaster. When it had been repaired anciently, it had been extended beyond the distance of the stairs. Traces of gypsum plaster were still visible on the threshold and step. Before them on the floor were a few patches of red paint.[9] During the excavations around the western area of the chapel, small lumps of hematite came up in the spoil.[10] This was a mineral used for red paint and may have been residue left from wall painting. In the case of the forecourt, splashes of red paint could have fallen on the pavement below during the painting of a cavetto cornice, which may have surmounted the pylons.

Two post holes serving as supports for flagpoles lie on either side of the step near the pylons. The northern one still contains fragments of wood and accommodated a post about 8 cm. in diameter.[11] It is clear from the southern hole that the post was sunk into gypsum before the masonry around it was completed. Another hole at the north end only of the threshold suggests the presence of a door pivot, indicating that the entrance to the Main Chapel had only a single door panel.

Outer Hall

Beyond the main entrance in the outer hall, which measures 4.40 × 6.10 m., were two benches, set against its north and south walls. The usual method of constructing a bench was to encase a fill of rubble or stones and marl in marl brick on the top and sides. The top surface accommodates two courses of bricks laid on their broad sides. The brick is invariably marl for bench construction at Amarna, with the exception of alluvial brick inclusions in part of the outer casing of the benches in Chapel 537. The bench was then plastered in marl, alluvial mud or layers of both followed by a coating of gypsum. The dimensions average 25-30 cm. in height and 32-44 cm. in depth. The base of the benches in the outer hall of the Main Chapel was made of specially selected cobbles with flat surfaces. The benches had been repaired or renewed with fresh plaster at least once. The first phase had showed a coating of Nile mud and gypsum and the second phase an application of marl plaster. Both types of plaster were tempered with straw.

The floor of the outer hall was of hard packed marl. This material was usually employed for creating floor surfaces in the chapels at Amarna. They were often re-surfaced, presumably when they had become pitted and worn with use, and there may have been as many as four additional layers.[12] In the outer hall, at least two major layers were distinguishable. Traces of Nile mud plaster coated with gypsum suggested that one of the renewal phases may have involved an additional surfacing of alluvial mud and gypsum throughout. Alternatively, the alluvial mud could have been used for random patching with a finish of gypsum. Embedded in the floor were botanical and faunal remains.

Almost in the centre of the hall was a large burnt patch which had turned the mud floor to a terracotta colour. Much ash was still present. Impressions of two jar stands and a basket ring were pressed into the floor. Contained within the hall were also a pottery altar stand with a bowl bearing encrusted grains of incense on the floor nearby, a small pottery dog's head,[13] a bronze spearhead, a standard holder in the shape of a lotus, a basket ring and a small grass brush. The significance of these finds will be discussed in Chapter Five.

The outer hall, whose walls were of marl brick, like those of all the chapels at Amarna, were plastered with alluvial mud and coated with gypsum in the interior. There was no evidence of wall decoration in this part of the building. Unlike the forecourt, the outer hall was roofed, its collapsed roofing material lying within this area. A doorway in the southwest wall of the outer hall led to Annexe 450, and in the northeast wall another doorway led to the left annexe or side chapel. As will be seen below (Chapter 5, 72, fig. 23.1), a side annexe on the left of the main building, for a subsidiary chapel and abutting chambers is a frequent characteristic.

Inner Hall

The inner hall was entered by a step made of two limestone slabs. The larger one (fig. 7) was a re-used threshold from another building. The gypsum filled door jamb sockets are not spaced widely enough to accommodate the doorway into the hall. The door pivot hole associated with the southern jamb was not filled, which leaves an open question whether this part of the building had a single panel door or not. However, it seems doubtful that doors were contained either in the doorway leading into the inner hall or into the sanctuary, for the following architectural reason. Two brick piers, between which the limestone threshold lay, abutted two screen walls. Screen walls can range from 14 to 90 cm. in height in these chapels. The top-most course of brick is usually convex, as here, indicating that the wall finished at this point. The eastern wall of the inner hall opposite also contained a pair of screen walls at a slightly higher level than those in the western wall. An additional feature of these two walls were the remains of cavetto cornices projecting from the summit of the walls forming a sill. The screen wall permitted what light was available inside the dimly lit chambers of the chapel to pass from one hall into another. To include doors within these two walls would defeat the 'window' aspect of the screen wall, but would allow for privacy if required.

Sunk into the hard packed floor of the inner hall was a small rectangular limestone dais. It consisted of two pieces of stone plastered in gypsum, which displayed the smoothing marks of fingers. It was placed on the long axis before the flight of stairs leading to the pronaos and sanctuary. On it were fragments of a blue-painted jar.[14]

The walls of the inner hall appeared to have been replastered at least once during the lifetime of the chapel, since gypsum was usually the finishing coat. The order of application in the hall was marl with a coat of gypsum, an alluvial mud layer, followed by a second coat of gypsum. The thickness of each was marl, 2 cm., alluvial plaster, 1.6 cm., and gypsum, 2 mm. These thicknesses are about the mean average for the respective plasters on walls in the chapels. An exception to this is the depth of alluvial plaster on the southern pier to the entrance of the pronaos in the Main Chapel, which is 3 cm.

The north and south walls of the inner hall were decorated with paintings and hieroglyphic texts in black. The texts were set in vertical registers with a red dividing line on a background of yellow ochre. The scant remains of text seem to be chiefly concerned with funerary subjects.[15] From the north wall came a painted head of a man wearing a black wig. The remnants of the face, which still retained the eye, was a reddish to orangeish-brown superimposed on a yellow ochre background. On the same background colour was preserved part of a woman's face with half the eye and lips still visible. Her skin was a lighter brown than the man's, containing a pinkish hue. The face was outlined in an orangeish-brown. Part of her headdress was still apparent, consisting of a background of white with a horizontal band of turquoise above one of blue. This was surmounted with a chevron pattern depicted in black with vertical lines at intervals below. A vestige of the lady's shoulder was outlined in red. What may well have been a sistrum and part of the woman's equipment was depicted on the same yellow background in red lines.

The inner hall produced part of a paddle painted white, probably from a model boat. This area of the chapel contained the greatest number of potsherds. Out of this quantity came one of the more significant vessels in the group called 'hearths'. This was a shallow bowl upon the interior of which was a line drawing in black ink of a boat.[16] The boat is one of the several sacred barks generically known as *wiỉ*.[17] Near this bowl lay a large lump of resinous incense about 1 cm. thick.[18]

Pronaos and Sanctuary

A flight of stairs set between balustrades ending in a return, a common feature in many of the chapel staircases,[19] led to the pronaos and sanctuary. The balustrades were surmounted by a rounded coping of marl. The whole structure was plastered in alluvial mud and gypsum. The pronaos, which stood 65 cm. above the level of the inner hall, formed a narrow transverse hall before a tripartite sanctuary. The surface of the floor still retained a pristine coat of gypsum. A limestone slab, nearly square and also whitewashed, was set on the floor before the central shrine and on the same axis as the dais in the inner hall.

Some 43 cm. above the floor of the pronaos on the north wall were the remains of a broad band consisting of black and red lines forming a *serekh* pattern. This same design was present in some of the chapels at Deir el Medina and is found in paintings from some of the Theban tomb chapels (Chapter 4, 52).[20] It was customary to depict paintings above it, but in the case of Chapel 561 none survived. Wall paintings and architectural embellishments that did survive in the rubble in this part of the chapel were substantial fragments of cavetto cornices, torus moulding and sufficient wall paintings to be able to identify a winged solar disc and two Nekhbet vultures with outstretched wings and with plumes and *šn* signs grasped in either claw.[21] The cavetto cornices and torus moulding had once framed the entrances to the three niches in the sanctuary. The cavetto cornice was constructed in brick, plastered, and then painted green, red and blue. The torus moulding was made from bound bundles of grass, plastered in marl, coated with gypsum and painted with red lines in imitation of the lashings of the torus. Although Kemp believes that these emblems were placed on the west wall of the interior of the sanctuary, on the basis of the height calculated from the number of courses of brick in the collapsed wall,[22] my belief is that the solar disc surmounted the central shrine and the vultures were placed over the two side chapels in the eastern wall (Chapter 5, 57).

The width of the three shrines in the sanctuary varied. The largest, southern one measured 1.55 m. The northern shrine was 1.23 m. wide, whilst the central shrine was the narrowest at 1.21 m. The partition walls and the northern and southern outer walls of the sanctuary were two courses of brick thick. With the exceptions of the main entrance to the chapel, the partial overlapping of the southern wall of the outer hall with that of the inner hall and the outer wall of the side chapel, the outer walls of the Main Chapel are only a single course of brick thick.

Within each shrine, brick benches abutted the back wall, were plastered in alluvial mud and gypsum and averaged a depth of 77 cm. Projecting from the edge of the top of the benches was a single course of bricks forming a cavetto. Around the outer edges and the rear of the benches, including the edges of the shrine floors, were an abundance of scratch marks. A little wooden plaque, 11.3 cm. high × 9.0 cm. wide and 1.4 cm. thick, was found between the limestone slab and the central shrine.[23] Upon it was depicted the god Wepwawet in black outline standing on a standard with two streamers. A man painted in red outline was shown worshipping before the god. On the reverse side were two men running, each holding a rod in their hand. The foremost figure also held a palm frond painted in black. The plaque was rounded on the top with holes in the bottom edge and is believed to be part of a military standard.

The Annexe and Passage Behind the Main Chapel (figs 6 and 7)

The annexe on the north side of the Main Chapel was divided into two sections. To the west was a subsidiary chapel entered by a door in the north wall of the outer hall of the Main Chapel. This side chapel was itself divided into two — a shrine room and an outer room. The shrine room, directly accessible to the Main Chapel, had a bench built in the same manner as those in the main sanctuary. Painted on its back or eastern wall were the remains of another *serekh*-type dado, which abutted the top of the bench. The colours in this case were alternating red and blue. The wall upon which the design was painted intercepted the northern wall of the inner hall, which shows that the latter had not been completed when this side chapel was being built. The complete annexe with its two main divisions was thus built contemporaneously with the main body of the chapel and not added later. Against the north and west wall of the shrine room was a bench 30 cm. high × c. 33 cm. deep. A connecting door led into the adjacent chamber, where another bench spanned nearly the whole length of the north wall. The floors of both chambers were of hard packed marl. This outer chamber had once borne decorations of a grapevine and trellis. Remains of text in black hieroglyphs on a white ground were also among the surviving wall decoration. Among the vessels found in the side chapel were a *zir* bearing an incised cross near its base lying before the shrine niche, and a large jar stand in the westernmost end of the outer chamber.[24]

The outer half of the annexe adjacent to the side chapel, called the North Annexe, was mostly cut into the gebel. Its walls were of stone, marl mortar and brick with a rough coat of marl plaster. A few traces of gypsum appeared on the inner face of its western wall. It consisted of one unit whose roughly-laid mud floor had a sloping gradient split into two levels by a dividing course of bricks c. 30 cm. high. Abutting the inner face of its eastern wall were two brick steps. The wall was only c. 50 cm. high, the top course of brick being worn to an uneven height. Adjoining this was a passage which led around the outside of the sanctuary wall of the Main Chapel. The area directly beyond the wall measured 1.36 × 1.71 m. and then formed a narrow corridor behind the sanctuary, its lowest measurement attaining a height of only c. 50 cm. Appearing in the marl floor and below it, in a trial trench dug by Peet in 1921, were the remains of the foundations of buildings earlier than the Main Chapel.[25] Two parallel foundation walls 5 cm. apart lay east of the sanctuary and ran under it and the small revetment wall abutting the large retaining wall that extended beyond the breadth of the Main Chapel. How far these foundations extended under the sanctuary is hard to determine, but they did not go beyond it, since the floor of the inner hall was laid directly on bedrock. They may have continued as far as the pronaos, which as already noted lies at a greater height than the inner hall, and the higher level in the adjacent annexe may also have formed part of an earlier structure. The vestiges of foundations lying to the north of the Main Chapel and running north to south showed that it had once joined the revetment wall to the north. Kemp has suggested that these foundations could have belonged to a small dwelling, such as Building 350 south of the Walled Village,[26] which existed before the latter was constructed. In any case, this information provides evidence for a chronology of the chapels (Chapter 3, 35).

Over the passage floor behind the chapel a secondary floor had been laid. The extent of the plaster on the rear of the sanctuary wall of the chapel did not reach its foundations and exposed several courses of bricks that had not been rendered. The space between the plaster and the original floor of the passage was *c.* 30 cm. The succeeding floor, composed of a make-up layer and presumably surfaced with mud (excavated by Peet), probably continued to the eastern wall of the North Annexe.[27] This would have left only 20 cm. of the wall to step over in order to enter the chamber in this part of the annexe.

Roofing Material

Although some roofing material came from the sieving of the 1921 dumps and a few fragments from the re-clearing of other chapels, the main and abundant evidence for roofing practices and style is provided by the Main Chapel. Careful differentiation of the fragments according to the areas in which they were found in the building allowed the distribution of the materials used, the quality of workmanship, and the method of construction employed in the various parts of the chapel to be determined. Results show that the sanctuary, pronaos, inner and outer halls, and the annexe were covered by a flat roof, with skylights in the sanctuary and inner hall.[28] The outer hall and annexe may have had skylights too, but no evidence of such came from those areas. The forecourt, as already mentioned, was hypaethral.

The materials used were wooden beams and poles, mainly from the acacia tree,[29] reeds, bundles of grass tied with fibre, and matting made from string. These provided a structure for varying depths of plaster in either one, two or all of the usual materials of marl, alluvial mud and gypsum. The beams (up to 14 cm. in diameter) were the first step in forming the roof. Between them were placed poles up to 3 cm. in diameter and often split in half, as were sometimes the beams. The materials laid over the basic framework varied.

In the outer and inner halls the main choice was bundles of grass tied in a manner similar to the binding on torus moulding, where the lashings are set horizontally and diagonally at intervals. Other methods used here were reeds laid haphazardly, reeds mixed with grass, grass laid over a layer of reeds, or simply grass and reeds tied in bundles. Marl plaster was then applied over this, averaging a depth of 10.5 cm. The ceiling or interior part of the roof usually received a coat of marl, alluvial mud and gypsum plaster averaging a depth of 7.5 cm. The beam casings were usually only coated in alluvial mud and whitewashed. The pronaos exhibited the most meticulous craftsmanship. The choice of material here was reed bundles tied carefully in rows, the impressions of which in the plaster resembled fine pleated linen.

Circular skylights were used in both the inner hall and the sanctuary. Two were found in the former and one in the latter area. These were circular constructions of mud which appeared to have used the shoulder of a large jar as a mould.[30] These apertures received a final coat of alluvial mud and gypsum. Although only one was found in the sanctuary, presumably there were two more whose remains were demolished in the roof collapse. These would have been placed either over each shrine or just before their doors in the pronaos, so that shafts of light from the sun or beams from the moon could light up the wall painting or any small statues or stelae.[31] The two in the inner hall would have served the same purpose.

The poorest craftsmanship appeared in the annexe. In the subsidiary shrine, roughly laid grass bundles were superimposed over the usual wooden framework. Five separate applications of plaster formed the upper part of the roof. The first was the thickest, whilst two others were added to give a more even surface, the fourth was a very thin, smooth layer of marl and the fifth was a thin coat of alluvial mud. This indicates that the roof exposed to the sky here had been surfaced in Nile mud, whereas marl was usually used. Here the exterior depth of plaster reached a maximum of 20 cm., while the ceiling plaster consisting of marl and gypsum was only 4.5 cm. thick.

The crudest construction was in the eastern section of the annexe. Rough, twisted poles were employed, and matting of rope in a lozenge pattern was laid over beams. Applied over this were four layers of plaster reaching an overall depth of 18 cm. The third deposit was alluvial mud, whilst the last layer was marl, which suggests a renewal of the roof in this section of the building.

Annexe 450 (figs 6, 8)

This consists of a group of dependencies on the south side of the Main Chapel. The main entrance to the annexe was from the west via a side court *c.* 5.80 × 4.20 m. The doorway in the west wall was preceded by a **T**-shaped basin. Other doors were situated in the north wall leading into the outer hall of the Main Chapel and in the southeast corner of the court. The construction was of stone in a marl matrix and brick with a floor of hard packed marl.

Another court entered by the door in the southeast wall of the side court was constructed of the same masonry as the latter. The floor with remains of hard packed mud rose steeply in the east. This area served as a court (fig. 6, area i) to two brick-built chambers lying to the north (fig 6, areas ii, iii). The doorway to the one on the west had a threshold of stones, and measured 2.25 × 2.60 m. The interior of its eastern wall had a batter of boulders and marl. The floor consisted of loose pieces of gebel. A worked stone with a hole in the centre, together with some coprolite, came from this enclosure.

The adjacent chamber to the east, measuring 3.05 × 2.68 m., was entered by a door in its northeast corner that once had a wooden threshold forming a step 28 cm. above the floor level. The floor, which lay above the level of that in the preceding chamber, was made of heavily pitted hard-packed mud. A circular depression near the southeast corner could have been a jar stand. In the northwest corner was a cylindrical oven, 85 cm. in diameter, with a hole in the bottom for stoking the fire. Its clay construction had turned light grey with heat. Nearby, and projecting from the north wall, was a stone whose top was worn into a concave circular depression. It was sunk into the marl and stood 25 cm. from the floor and may have been used as a stand or a support.

Both eastern and western enclosures had been roofed. The one to the east smashed the oven when it collapsed, scattering the installation.

Two steps of stone and marl in the east of the inner court (fig. 6, area i) led to two other enclosures (fig. 6, areas iv, v). The one to the north had a heavy deposit of ash and organic matter, under which was gebel and possibly the remains of a hard packed floor. This may have been another open court, which at certain times may have had a temporary shelter of grass matting, which was present in the section face before completion of excavation in this area. The adjacent enclosure was entered by a doorway in its north face. This contained a rich organic deposit, mostly of decayed coprolite. Stretching from this area to the revetment wall lying behind the Main Chapel were a series of small dependencies, each with an independent character (fig. 6, areas vi-x). Adjoining the corridor behind the chapel was a small passageway giving access to four garden plots constructed of cobbles and marl brick and plastered with marl (fig. 6, area ix). These were cut directly into the gebel, and measured from 55 to 40 cm. in length and 31 to 43 cm. in depth. Partially overlying the plots to the west was an oval, bin-like construction of cobble and marl. Adjacent to this group was a narrow, steep passage forming the northern wall to two small enclosures (fig. 6, areas x, vii, viii). The chamber to the east was 1.57 × 0.84 cm. and gypsum plastered with a few scratch marks in its floor. In the north wall was a circular construction. A narrow door connected this enclosure with the western one which was entered from the narrow passageway by a door in its northern wall which was later blocked by stones. This enclosure measured 1.56 × 1.03 m. and had numerous scratch marks in the centre of its floor.

Completing this series of buildings was an enclosure with a semi-circular wall in the southeastern corner (fig. 6, area vi). Its entrance lay in the northwestern corner, and to the left of the door were a group of stones forming a *zir* emplacement. Another entrance to this chamber, which had later been blocked with stones, lay in the outside wall in the southwestern corner. Left of this blocked entrance was a well-preserved oven with a circular aperture on top and a stoking hole in the bottom. Abutting the eastern wall (which formed part of the revetment wall) and at a higher level than the floor of the main chamber containing the oven, was a niche measuring 1.17 × 0.84 m. (fig. 8, area xi). The corner in the northeast was rounded, and three marl bricks lay in a row on the floor before the opening. Adjoining the southern wall of the niche on the outside was a semi-circular wall of stones.

The southern wall of the niche, abutted on its exterior by a semi-circular stone wall, extended beyond this amalgamation of buildings to the east and formed a right angle with another wall running perpendicular to it that extended towards the outer corridor wall of Building 523.

Chapel Group 570 and 571

These two chapels lying along the base of the southern slopes of the 'chapel' hill both have their axes aligned east to west (figs 9, 9a). They represent a second phase of building. The first consisted of a series of small rectangular garden plots and the walls of other buildings. Large patches of alluvium and hard packed surfaces, presumably rubble from earlier building, were part of this earlier phase. During the second phase the walls marking out plots and/or other buildings were either filled over or incorporated into the chapel walls. The earlier phase has been clarified by the excavations of 1986,[32] in an area beyond the eastern wall of the Walled Village and just below the tomb shafts and chapels on the escarpment above. These exposed the conflation of agricultural and animal husbandry activities. Well-preserved and defined garden plots marked out a grid of small squares abutted by rectangular and oval plots; nearby, isolated plots lay south of a series of animal pens. The plots contained alluvial mud superimposed with ash. The ash, in some cases mixed with alluvium and reaching in places a depth of 50 cm., spread beyond the limitations of the small plots, towards greater walled areas.

From this it seems probable that agriculture was the chief activity carried out on the ground later occupied by Chapels 570 and 571,[33] and that the existence of earlier chapels is unlikely.

Chapel 570

The essential features of this chapel are an approachway, a forecourt or outer hall, an inner hall without benches, and a sanctuary with a single naos. The right-angled wall abutting the wall of the forecourt to 570, together with the outer hall and forecourt wall of Chapel 571, created a bent-axis approach to Chapel 570. In the southeast corner of this entry was a brick construction resembling steps.

The forecourt was rectangular and *c*. 2.30 m. deep. Its northern side projected beyond the width of the inner hall. A doorway in its southeast corner with a brick threshold led into the inner hall, which in this case was devoid of the usual bench. A burnt patch appeared in the southwestern section of the chamber. A door in its eastern wall led directly into the single shrine. A brick pedestal abutted the threshold. This and the walls were gypsum plastered. The eastern wall of the sanctuary was robbed, but from the remaining walls the dimensions suggest that it had a bench to the rear.[34] The depth of the sanctuary walls running west to east was 1.75 m. By comparison, the central shrine in Chapel 561 measured 1.62 m. from the inner edge of the threshold to the interior rear wall, and, as already mentioned, was equipped with a bench. The presence of bricks with grooves on one side and gypsum on the other confirmed that the sanctuary had been vaulted,[35] an unusual feature in the Amarna chapels.

Traces of gypsum plaster on the exterior of the southern wall abutting the northern wall of Chapel 571 suggests that the former was built before or at the same time as the latter. Problems concerning the chronology of these two buildings will be discussed below (see below, p. 16-17).

To the north is a rock cut tomb with a shaft cut into the base of the escarpment, measuring *c.* 2.00 × 1.10-1.75 m. and *c.* 1.30 m. deep.[36] It was roughly rectangular, with its long axis oriented east to west. The interior of the tomb was roughly hewn and seems never to have been occupied.

A marl brick wall extended north from the northeastern corner of the sanctuary of 570 incorporating a containing wall of one of the earlier garden plots. Perpendicular to the southeastern corner, another wall of brick, stone and marl mortar ran towards the east. On its northern face were two buttress-like features, possibly framing a doorway or entrance. This wall was originally associated with the earlier agricultural phase, but was retained at a low height during the chapel period.[37] It may have served simply as a boundary wall to the chapel area in this part of the site. Contained within the area marked out by these two walls was an oval enclosure abutting the north end of the former wall (fig. 9). Within it were vestiges of alluvial mud. This feature is typical of garden plots already described lying to the east of the Walled Village. The plot appears to be contemporary with the chapels, suggesting that others could have continued east of 570, where substantial patches of alluvium and sherds were present,[38] differing in consistency from the alluvium and rubble to the west. Other gardens may have extended to the north in the unexcavated ground.

Chapel 571

This chapel, which is more consistent with the plan of a private votive chapel than is 570,[39] underwent alterations to some of its internal features during its lifetime.

Vestiges of what appeared to be a stone bordered pathway on a graduated level led to a large forecourt primarily constructed of stones in a marl matrix, except for the north wall which was of brick. Two boulders marking out a doorway and step in the east wall led to the outer hall, part of whose north wall was shared with the forecourt of Chapel 570. The southeast corner of the outer hall was pierced by a narrow door giving access to a dependency consisting of four small chambers, each of which were connected by doorways. Another entrance into this southern annexe may have existed in the southwestern corner of the outer hall, but the evidence is inconclusive. The western end of the annexe projected into the forecourt and shared part of its southern wall. Its eastern wall abutted the southern exterior wall of the inner hall. Ashy patches appeared on the packed floor of the outer hall and the second chamber from the west in the annexe. The second chamber from the east in the annexe contained an offering stand around which was a small collection of lancet-shaped leaves.[40]

A doorway in the eastern wall of the outer hall, containing a limestone slab that was part of a doorway pivot or jamb, gave access to the inner hall, which measured *c.* 4.20 × 3.85 m. Benches ran against the north, south and west walls. The southern bench connected with the niche, which was incorporated as a unit into the inner hall. The benches were approximately 38 cm. deep, and the one to the north still retained much of its original surface of gypsum.

The northern side of the inner hall included an architectural feature unusual in Egyptian practice. Although the entire north side of Chapel 571 abutted the southern side of Chapel

570, here in the inner hall (and as far as can be determined also in the sanctuary) the wall was not shared, as elsewhere in the building, which was the usual practice. Instead, it possessed a wall separate from that of Chapel 570, between which was a fill of rubble or packed marl (Chapter 6, 86; fig. 9). On the fill at the westernmost end of both walls, and near the corners of the respective chapels, lay the hind limb of a goat. The implications of this assemblage is discussed in Chapters 5 and 6.

Three burnt patches appeared on the hard packed marl floor of the inner hall, and just in front of the bench forming the sanctuary were two pottery offering stands. Small fragments of blue and turquoise faience lay between them. In the vicinity of the stands was a limestone block pierced with a hole typical of a tethering stone. Near it lay the remains of a piece of rope.

The bench for offerings in the naos of the sanctuary was 3.18 × 1.20 m., and from the remains of plaster near it, displaying traces of a painted border, it must have been decorated with the same motif as the rest of the inner hall. The bench had two building phases, the last of which contained two niches of unequal division.[41] The southern niche, which was 55 cm. wide, incorporated the remains of the stone foundations of a partition wall. The larger niche, which was *c.* 2.25 m. wide, still retained some of the gypsum plaster that covered the remains of the foundation wall of a second partition. Thus the initial phase consisted of a tripartite shrine. These internal adjustments to the sanctuary suggest a change in the ritual or dedication of the chapel.

The chronology proposed by Kemp for this complex of buildings is that Chapel 570 was the first constructed, succeeded by Chapel 571 and then the rock cut tomb.[42] His theory is chiefly based upon the presence of gypsum plaster on the exterior southern wall of 570, which was concealed when Chapel 571 was built. In addition, he points out that the precedence of chapel construction can be determined also by the walls abutting the marl brick boundary wall extending to the east behind the two buildings. He believes the aforementioned wall could have been retained from the earlier phase and that the brick wall that presumably formed the robbed rear wall to the sanctuary of 570 abutted the long boundary wall first. This is inferred from the essentially brick construction of Chapel 570. Furthermore, it is suggested that part of the boundary wall ran under Chapel 570 and may have constituted the demolished walls below the floor of the chapel's inner hall (fig. 9). Lastly, because the back wall of the sanctuary of Chapel 571 abutting this boundary wall is mostly of stone and marl, it is a later addition. The tomb is placed last in the sequence because it seems unfinished, in contrast to the completed chapels.

Despite these valid points, some puzzles remain which concern the structure and projected use of the buildings, the latter point being dealt with more fully in Chapter 5.

First, on the basis of the traces of gypsum on the southern exterior wall of Chapel 570, it is likely that it was the first of this complex of buildings to be built. However, the painted shrine wall in the Main Chapel was partially covered by the inner hall wall and the forecourt wall, behind which lay the gypsum plastered southern wall of the main building (see above, pp. 8; 11), so it does not necessarily indicate that a space of time elapsed between building stages. Both chapels could have been constructed contemporaneously. It might be wondered why a wall should be painted if it is soon to be covered up during the course of building.[43] The answer is that there is no logical reason for it, but it does occur in the Main Chapel. While completed walls were being painted, new ones could be in the process of construction.

The brick wall forming the back wall to 570 belonged to the second or chapel-building phase, and marked out with the eastern boundary wall the large area behind the two buildings. This area must have been delineated before the two chapels were appended to it. While 570 was being built, the rear wall to 571 could have been started. The use of stone and marl in its wall is not necessarily indicative of a later stage of building, although it does not rule out the possibility. Chapel 556 (see below, p. 23) incorporated a stone and marl wall into the eastern inner hall wall (fig. 15), which is an integral part of the building.

Extended use of stone and marl could have been employed for extra strength, durability and support as a revetment. The changes in ground level may have dictated the choice of materials. This appears to be the case with Chapel 531, where the ground begins to drop to the south and east. Chapel 571 is placed on more of the incline of the valley floor.

The abutting walls of the two chapels are on the same alignment as the eastern boundary wall, more especially the northern wall of 571. The boundary wall, instead of linking up with stump walls under the inner hall of 570, could have provided the basis for the hall wall of 571. The excavation of the floors and walls of this building is needed to resolve this point.

The plan of Chapel 570 is singular because it is the only chapel known in the Workmen's Village not to have had the benches which are a typical feature of the private chapel. Could 570 then have been a subsidiary chapel to 571? It lies on the left side of the larger building and possesses only one niche, features common to a side chapel. Another problem is the rubble fill between the two walls, which I interpret as deliberate, rather than the remains of crumbled walls. The fill was similar to the material placed in the interior of benches (see above, p. 9). It must have served as a cushioning between the two walls. Whether this fill attained the full height of the walls or only to where the hind limb of the goat lay can never be answered. It is clear that these double walls were not built for the same purpose as the thickened double walls in the sanctuary of 570. The latter accommodated a vaulted ceiling[44] and one of the interior walls lay off the axis of the filled double walls. In addition, no double walls lay to the exterior of the respective halls.

The articulated goat limb between the two walls is also puzzling. That it was placed there after the denudation of the walls seems unlikely. This leaves two other possibilities. First, that it might just have been part of the general fill between the walls. The other is that it was placed there for the purpose of sanctifying the two chapels. The hind limb of a goat appears in several instances in the Workmen's Village in connection with a chapel or T-shaped basin, and in a significant context suggesting a cultic purpose (to be dealt with more fully in Chapter 5, 59). If this were the case, then the two buildings were associated and could have been built contemporaneously or at least within a close period of time.

In addition, some questions arise concerning the construction of the outer hall and forecourt of 571 and 570. Dividing these two enclosures was a single course wall, which when excavated was in a badly deteriorated state. Could this wall have contained a door which would have connected the two buildings? No traces of a threshold appeared, but the wall was denuded, especially to the west. The solidity of the stone and marl masonry of the outer hall wall of 571, and its rounded right angled turn at the north forming the forecourt of 570, suggests that the two areas were built as one wall.[45] If a door did connect these two areas, then 570 would, because of its plan, have been a side chapel to 571.

If the small rectangular enclosure with the presumed brick step-like feature in its southeast corner was an entrance to 570, this could have been added later. A separate entrance would have been provided. Based on this hypothesis, 570 would have been a proper tomb chapel, for which its plan is the more typical. At this time, the rock tomb could have been cut out and the sanctuary of 571 altered from a tripartite shrine to essentially a single niche with a side compartment.

The foregoing is not conclusive, but offers an alternative interpretation of the chronology and architectural plan of this group of chapels.

THE REPLANNED CHAPELS

Chapel 522 and Annexe 523

When Peet excavated the latter, he observed that it was not like the other chapels. However, since he was uncertain as to which class of building it belonged, he continued to group it with the chapels as 523. He wrote 'We reach 521 and 522, followed by a group of rooms hardly constituting a chapel, to which number 523 was given'.[46]

The photographs taken of these buildings in 1921 show the walls at a greater height with more of the benches intact than is the case today.[47] The small annexe to the left of Chapel 522 no longer exists,[48] but more of the stairs leading into the outer hall of 522, which had not been dug before, were freshly excavated in 1984, along with part of the forecourt and approach stairway leading to it.

Chapel 522 (figs 5, 7, 10)

A flight of stairs with eight steps oriented west to east at a slight angle to the main entrance to 522 led to the forecourt. The steps were of brick laid on a foundation of cobbles and boulders set in marl. The bottom step was of cobble and marl construction, and lay below the balustrade, which enclosed the main set of stairs. The balustrade, which was surmounted by a rounded coping plastered in alluvial mud and gypsum, had the usual returns, the southern one of which abutted the north wall of Chapel 561. A revetment wall of cobbles and marl mortar, *c.* 90 cm. high, formed a terrace and forecourt to 522. The revetment was reinforced by a bank of sand and gravel and under which, near the corner of the stair, was a deposit of wood shavings. These may have been a result of paring the ends of beams and poles for the roof of chapel 522, as well as planing wooden doors for the exterior or interior of the building. The terrace was not completely excavated, but extended towards the north and served as a forecourt to Chapel 521, which has been completely robbed out since the excavations of 1921.[49]

The forecourt of 522 had a packed marl floor and was marked off from the forecourt of 521 to the north by a low stone and marl wall 27 cm. wide running east to west. Abutting its north side were the remains of narrow walls forming rectangular compartments. Alluvial mud and gypsum plaster appeared in one compartment and beyond this to the east was more alluvial mud, ash and fine organic matter. Presumably these were the remains of garden plots.

The usual style of staircase with four brick steps fronted the entrance to the outer hall of 522. In the southern corner of the return of the staircase was a circular hole with a gypsum lining retaining the impression of a wooden pole. In the opposite position to the north was a circular depression, but with no remains of gypsum. Chapels 522 and 561 are the only ones known to have possessed holes for flagstaffs.

The outer hall had benches which had been gypsum plastered. These were set against the north, south and west walls. In the northeast corner of the hall, a door led to a trapezoidal annexe, now vanished, which according to Newton's plan (fig. 5) had a partition wall. Peet's only reference to the annexe was 'a shapeless room between 521 and 522, containing a limestone tank'.[50] Only a few bricks remain of the dividing wall running perpendicular to the north wall of the inner hall of 522. The western section of the annexe had two entrances, one in the west wall that opened onto the forecourt and the other that led into the outer hall of 522.

Four circles appeared on Newton's plan in the eastern section of the annexe. These may have been large stones. There is no evidence that a shrine or ovens were contained here.

The entrance to the inner hall of 522 was marked off by two piers abutting two (probably screen) walls. The floor was packed marl and at a slightly higher level than the outer hall. Before the entrance to the sanctuary was a low, broad, brick dais, gypsum plastered, measuring 104 × 77 × 10 cm. The sanctuary was set off by two brick piers, probably abutting another pair of screen walls. The shrine was a single naos with a rectangular brick bench asymmetrically placed. Its western side once had a cavetto cornice. Peet saw these shrines with the cavetto as divided into an upper and a lower niche. The back wall below the cornice served as the lower compartment and the upper surface of the bench was the floor to what would have been the upper niche in a normal shrine.[51]

Objects from this chapel included a wooden *s* bolt, a wooden disk and a copper chisel (for references to these objects and those from other chapels, see *COA* I, 101-108).

Annexe 523

Attached to the south wall of 522 is a complex of three rectangular enclosures with an L-shaped corridor lying to their south (fig. 11). Some walls present in 1921 had disappeared by the time they were replanned in 1983.[52] Marl brick was used throughout, except for part of the L-shaped enclosure and the western wall which were of stone and marl. The western wall also served as the revetment wall to the passage behind the sanctuary of 561. The floors of at least two of the enclosures were of brick coated in marl plaster. The western enclosure had remains of an inner partition. The central chamber had a smaller compartment in the northeast corner. Bricks laid with their axes north to south in the southwest corner of the central enclosure formed a threshold. The easternmost enclosure had a gypsum coated floor, which still retained the finger marks from smoothing. It, too, had an inner partition. A brick projection from the eastern wall and a ridge continuing from it across the floor marked the division.

Fragments of decayed organic matter from coprolite or fodder embedded into the floor surface of several of the enclosures suggests that animals may have been sheltered there.

Chapel Group 528, 529, 530, 531

These chapels form a self-contained group, owing to their relative isolation from other chapel groups and the contiguity of their plan. They are positioned on a terrace projecting out from the southern face of the hill and overlooking Chapels 570 and 571 in the valley below. To the north of these buildings the gebel rises sharply.

Building 528

Peet described this area as a possible forecourt (fig. 12) of 529, but because it had its own niches he believed this to be improbable.[53] It was joined to Chapel 529 and had a door in its eastern side leading into the outer hall of the chapel. In plan it formed the forecourt to 529, but with its unusual additional architectural features, it should be placed outside the category of the standard forecourt. These unique features, to be described, may signify an extended ritual use supplementary to 529 and possibly 530 and 531. However, because it has since proved to be a forecourt and not a complete chapel, it has been labelled Building 528.

The north wall, which was cut into the gebel behind, contained an elaboration of special features. A bench spanned its entire side, except where it was interrupted by a rectangular construction projecting from the centre. East of the projection, the bench, which was between 52 and 56 cm. high, was better preserved than its western counterpart. It had a fill covered in marl mortar with a coat of alluvial mud plastered with gypsum. Sunk into the top of the bench were seven receptacles, with another on the short continuation of the bench against the east wall. These containers were of marl mortar and had raised rims. All of them were then plastered in alluvial mud and gypsum. Three, somewhat smaller and shallower than the remaining ones, were set close together and separated slightly from the others by a small projecting buttress. On the bench west of the receptacles was another independent group of miniature containers set into a compartment formed by two narrow walls of small stones set in marl adjacent to the central projection. Flanking the projection on its east side was another small bench containing the remains of three more receptacles.

On the bench west of the central projection were found the remains of only four receptacles, together with traces of the small compartment which had once housed the four small containers. There was only one receptacle in the bench that abutted the west wall of the central projection. The plan of the eastern bench suggests that the western could once have accommodated the same number of containers as its neighbour. In the northwest corner of 528 was an oven which cut into the bench. Peet believed this to be a later addition,[54] which it proved to be. It could in that case have demolished a sixth and seventh receptacle on the western bench and another if the bench continued on the west wall. The wall is fairly eroded at this point, but there is enough projection to allow the possibility. An earlier fireplace was traced on the floor near the present oven and was oval in plan. It may have been a hearth of the type found in Chapel 556. The oven resembles the two found in Annexe 450. It was cylindrical, and had a clay lining plastered in marl mortar.

The central projection had two separate levels, described as lower and upper niches by Peet.[55] One section contained a jar emplacement 30 cm. in diameter, but it is no longer visible. Kemp suggested that the lower portion consisted of a small flight of stairs, because of the front step and balustrade walls enclosing this section, and that the jar stood in the upper portion.[56] Chapel 1221 at Deir el Medina (fig. 19) had a central portion in its sanctuary with similarities which could support Kemp's theory.

Before the centre projection was a **T**-shaped basin with an eroded miniature flight of stairs abutting the crossbar. The basin was constructed of marl brick and filled with alluvial mud, which was probably added when the basin was no longer in use (Chapter 7, 283). A paved area enclosed by walls of a single course of marl brick to the east and west linked the basin and the centre projection.

Dark alluvial mud, forming a rectangle around most of the basin, was divided into small garden plots by little stone walls, traces of which still remain. A semi-circular wall of mortar suggests some other arrangement within the garden. This extension of alluvial mud beyond the confines of the plots, and the filling of the **T**-shaped basin, indicate a second phase to the ornamental garden. The floor of the courtyard, which was *c.* 8.00 × 7.00 m., is preserved across the northern section, and in its western half was overlain in limited areas by a small deposit of ash. Beyond the limit of the original floor was a wide strip of more ashy deposit. In the floor were two circular holes, a patch of compacted earth and a circular patch of alluvial mud. The two holes could be remains of jar stands. The patch of alluvial could be fill to an earlier post hole for a standard (Chapter 5, 62).

The entrance to the forecourt was in the west wall and was approached by a pathway of packed marl enclosed by parallel walls of stone set in marl. Oriented parallel to these to the north were the remains of what appears to be a garden plot wall.

The foundation of a wall consisting of a single course of brick with no buttress marked out the limit of 528 in the south. This wall may have been only a few centimetres high, because of its insecure construction.

The east wall of the court formed the front of Chapel 529. It was interrupted by a small step of stones set in mortar lying parallel to the north wall of 529. South of the step was a small rectangular projection, which may have formed part of a now denuded bench. Beyond this was the entrance to the outer hall of 529. In the southeast corner of the court were two bricks set at right angles, probably the remains of a companion bench to the one in the north.

Chapel 529 (fig. 13)

The outer hall of this chapel, oriented on an east to west axis, had benches set against all four walls (fig. 13). Newton's plans suggest that the other chapels in this group may have had the same features in their outer halls. Evidence of this had vanished by 1984. The other chapel that can approximate this feature is 525 (fig. 16), the bench on its north wall is much wider than those against the other walls. The average width of the benches in 529 is 30-33 cm. The original floor of the outer hall was of packed marl which had been resurfaced later. By adding the new surface, the floor was raised by 10 cm. and a ramp of bricks plastered in marl covered the threshold entrance to accommodate the new level. On the floor was a burnt patch. One step from the outer hall led into the inner chamber. It was interrupted by probably two screen walls abutted by brick piers. The wall on the north side is all that remains. Within the hall were two isolated brick piers which had supported a roof. They were braced at the level of the foundation with a single row of bricks. Only the southern row is visible.

The floor of the pronaos was raised 14 cm. above the level of the inner hall, forming an inset between the two piers. On the north wall of the pronaos was a small edge which may have been another bench. In 1984 the bench was only 20 cm. wide, but Newton's plan (fig. 5) shows it having the same width as the benches in the inner hall. Because of the overall symmetry of this chapel, another may have been on the south wall.

The shrine consisted of two unequal side chambers, the largest to the south, and a centre niche now denuded. The 1921 plans and report showed that three steps preceded the centre naos.[57] The steps, now vanished, started parallel with the north and south compartments and reached the central niche, which was set further back. This arrangement of stairs inside the shrine is so far unique at Amarna.

Peet observed a limestone doorpost with a painted inscription of the name Amun and traces of a scene in red, yellow and black on the northern buttress of the doorway going into the sanctuary.[58] In 1984, wall painting fragments of a vine and trellis and a human face were found in the sanctuary foundations. The sanctuary and inner hall, at least, were decorated. In 1921, a wooden pedestal and a disk and horns[59] were discovered in this chapel. On the pedestal appeared the name *Nḥmmȝˁtyw*, described as a *sḏm ˁš* (Chapter 5, 62).

Chapel 530 (fig. 13)

This chapel, also oriented east-west, had a simple forecourt set out in a single course of brick lying at a slight angle to the main axis of the chapel. Its overall width was roughly equal to that of the chapel. The brick threshold in the entrance to the forecourt was in the northwest corner. Another brick threshold in the east wall led into the outer hall, which, as suggested above, may have had surrounding benches.

The inner hall, which is in a slightly less dilapidated condition, had benches on its northern, western and probably southern walls. Burnt patches appeared on the floor of this and the outer hall. The inner hall was a single unit with pronaos and shrine. The brick piers to the east had no dividing screen walls, but like Chapel 529 had a single row of brick abutting and supporting the two piers at foundation level. This foundation course of a single row of bricks formed the edge of the raised floor (which was one brick high) in the area of the pronaos.

Superimposed on this floor was a rectangular brick dais, gypsum plastered and set before a nearly square naos measuring 1.00 × 1.10 m. The total length of the southern wall of Chapel 529, including the forecourt, formed the north wall of 530, which was added on to the former. Finds from this chapel included a stone bowl, an **L**-shaped limestone object and a rectangular stone trough.

Chapel 531

The main body of 531, on an east to west axis, was *c*. 1.70 m. shorter than 529 and 530 and is also considerably denuded (fig. 13).

It had two forecourts, one of the standard type and the other with added features. The southern half of the outermost court still lies under a dump from 1921, but continued the line of the west wall of Chapel 530 and shared its southern wall of a single course of brick with a buttress. On the surface of the floor was a patch of ash.

The second forecourt formed a smaller enclosure than the first. It consisted of an entry followed by a narrow path bordered on either side by parallel walls of stones set in marl. These in turn continued to form two small rectangular garden plots with an additional small square in the southeast. These were filled with dark alluvial soil.

The northern garden was set against a single course of brick stretching from the western wall of the outer hall to the western wall of the second forecourt. This wall then formed a space between it and the outer hall wall of Chapel 530.

The pathway led to a low brick platform with outward turning edges set before the entrance to the outer hall, which may also have had benches against all its walls.

Spanning the exterior wall of the outer hall to the south was an enclosure with foundations of boulder set in marl. Another enclosure adjacent to it may have extended further to the east, since the outer wall of the enclosure continued the line for a few centimetres beyond its eastern wall.

The inner hall had benches on the north and west walls; the southern bench is no longer visible. The hall was separated from the pronaos and shrines by two walls of a single course of brick, with no piers. Only remains of the northern wall exist. Peet reported that this wall had a rounded top and was only 14 cm. high.[60]

In front of the door leading into the shrine was an inverted, truncated conical piece of limestone measuring 12 cm. in height and 40 cm. in diameter. The shrine consists of three naoi. The two to the south are of equal dimensions of 85 × 70 cm. The other extended to the north and abutted the naos of 530, sharing its southern wall. This is especially evident where the back wall to the northern niche is extended to meet the south wall of the shrine in Chapel 530.

The exterior face of the back wall to the sanctuary, together with part of the southern wall of the chapel, were reinforced by a secondary wall of stones set in mortar. This was probably added to strengthen the building, which is on a lower gradient on the terrace and more exposed to elemental erosion than 529 and 530.

Chapel 537

Of all the chapels, 537 lay the furthest to the east beyond 570 and 571 on the valley floor (fig. 14). Its axis was aligned east to west. Very little of the plan remains. It consisted of part of a forecourt or outer hall constructed of both marl and alluvial brick. To the east was a line of boulders that may have formed a broad platform before the entrance to the next chamber, whose walls were aligned with the remains of a bench also constructed of marl and alluvial brick. This was the only chapel to employ alluvial brick in its bench construction as well as its walls.

On the slope rising to the east of Chapel 537 was a shaft dug into the gebel.[61] Owing to the relatively isolated position of 537, it would seem that the shaft, a few metres beyond, was associated with this chapel.

Chapel 556

This chapel is the easternmost in the northern group situated north of the northeast corner of the Walled Village (fig. 15).[62] Woolley started excavating it in 1922 and only completed the sanctuary and inner hall. In 1986, these chambers were recleared and the remainder of the building was excavated. The approachway to the chapel, which was delineated by a series of boulders, ran from the north to the south and veered to the southwest.

Part of this boundary wall appears to have been aligned to the western wall of the outer hall of 556, which was also shared by Chapel 553. The flight of stairs belonging to 553 (figs. 4, 15), which led to its inner hall, was contained within the limits of the larger outer hall and was in direct alignment to the boulder wall. However, if the boundary wall was included in the outer hall, it would have created an asymmetrical plan — an uncommon feature of a main chamber in an Egyptian cult building.[63]

The outer hall was entered from the south. Its dimensions from south to north were 6.60 m. and its width from west to east ranges from 6.70 to 8.50 m. Two square brick bases set on either side of the long axis to the building are all that survived of two pillars which would have supported a roof. A gypsum plastered bench, 41 cm. wide and 26 cm. high, was set against part of the north wall and continued along the east and southeast walls near the main entrance. Traces of it remained to the southwest of the door and against the west wall. In the northeast corner, near the bench, was a hearth of the same class as those found in the houses inside the Walled Village.[64] However, in addition, lodged in the angle formed by the rectangular projection of the hearth, was an appendage with a small circular depression. West of the door leading into the inner hall of 556, sunk into the floor, were four circular impressions aligned north to south. Presumably these were jar stands. Nearby was the neck of a vessel lodged in the floor, also intended as a pot stand. Scratch marks appeared in this area.

The inner hall of 556 was a simple, long rectangular room with gypsum coated benches set against its western, eastern and southern walls. Parts of a limestone threshold with a pivot hole lay dislodged near the door. The eastern wall of the hall was built of cobbles, boulders and marl. It was plastered in marl, alluvial mud and gypsum. This part of the building, including the sanctuary, was cut into the gebel, thus the stone and marl wall in the inner hall at its base at least acted as a revetment wall. The western wall of this hall was shared with Chapel 553. Upon the packed marl floor were alluvial mud roofing fragments with impressions of grass tied in bundles. Some of the fragments were only 2 cm. thick. The floor and walls of this hall had been gypsum plastered.

The sanctuary was at a slightly higher level than the inner hall and was separated from it by a wall containing a doorway with one step. Beyond was another step with small brick piers on either side leading to the shrine. This consisted of a single naos with a bench whose interior was robbed. On either side of the bench and *c.* 10 cm. above the level of the sanctuary floor were platforms. These extended the length of the sanctuary. A small buttress was in the northwest corner and a brick projection abutted the east wall. These two areas would have been compartments serving the central shrine, since no partition walls were present. The whole of the sanctuary, including its floor, was whitewashed.

An L-shaped annexe was attached to the eastern wall of 556. It extended from the inner hall to the southern wall of the outer hall. Its wall, running from north to south, consisted of large boulders whose inner faces were fairly flat. This part of the annexe wall Kemp assigns to a rebuilding in the post-Amarna period, which replaced the original brick wall and probably the entrance to the enclosure. In the northwestern corner were the remains of two large storage jars. In the northeastern corner was a small rectangular brick compartment identified as a box oven. This contained a large collection of at least sixty-four pottery bread moulds.[65] Within this group were two types. The first was the familiar long cylindrical mould, while the second, an usual type, was hemispherical with a small, thick squat stem, resembling a crude form of goblet (fig 24a). Some of these lay strewn beyond the box oven. One of the hemispherical moulds, less crude than the others and displaying traces of decoration, lay in the vicinity of the jar emplacements in the outer hall.

Along the long axis of the enclosure and adjacent to the boulder wall were a series of four garden plots still retaining alluvial mud and marked out by miniature cobble and marl walls. In the extreme south of the enclosure, in the eastern corner, was an oven.

A deposit of limestone chips lay to the north of the L-shaped enclosure. It can only be conjectured that these stone fragments may have been the residual waste from the preparation of building stones.

Discussion

From the foregoing analysis of the excavated and recleared chapels at Amarna a fairly consistent plan emerges.

The layout included a forecourt, an outer and inner hall, a pronaos and sanctuary. The forecourt could be a simple enclosure approached by a stairway or path, or it could contain specialized features that made it a unit on its own. The outer hall in most cases contained benches aligned against facing walls, three walls or, rarely, against four walls. The inner hall entrance usually consisted of a step set between two piers abutting screen walls. Benches were often present and were placed against either two or three walls. Either the inner or the outer hall could have two columns. The shrine in the sanctuary was the most variable element in the chapel. This is especially true with the uncleared chapels in the northern group (fig. 4). The shrines could number from one to three, and they could be symmetrically divided.

Annexes or dependencies could be attached to either the left or right side of the main building. The annexe to the left was more likely to be used for cult purposes as in the Main

Chapel and possibly 570/571, whereas it was more usual for the dependency on the right to serve for domestic and storage facilities, as seen in the Main Chapel, 522, 523, and 556.

The building materials were uniform in all cases. These were stone, marl, alluvial mud, gypsum and limestone for some architectural features. Marl was the chief material used for wall construction and was easily extracted from local desert quarries in the vicinity of the Workmen's Village. The colour ranged from an orangeish red to a brownish pink. This material was shaped into bricks whose average size was 35 × 15 × 10 cm. The marl brick walls were set either on the desert floor or on a foundation of stones sunk into a marl matrix. The walls could be one or two courses thick. When alluvial brick appeared, it was usually incorporated into a staircase and is seldom present in a wall or bench (see above, p. 22).

The plastering of the interior walls varied according to their location. The more sacred areas, such as the inner hall and sanctuary, were often plastered in marl, followed by alluvial mud and gypsum. Over this were applied wall decorations. On the other hand, some of the dependencies, especially those concerned with storage or animal shelters, received a coat of marl only, sometimes whitewashed or not plastered at all.

In most instances, the floors were of hard packed marl and whitewashed. A variant was marl brick plastered in marl and whitewashed.

The constituents for roofing material were reeds, grass, matting, wooden poles and beams. It is assumed, the Main Chapel being the paradigm, that the roof of a chapel extended from the outer hall through the sanctuary, including the left annexe if it had a shrine or magazine. The domestic enclosures could have a roof or a temporary device of matting and poles. Areas containing an oven were not always roofed, as shown by the presence of the oven in the southeast of Annexe 450. Probably in all cases skylights were in the sanctuary and inner hall. The roof was presumably flat in all the chapels, with exception of the sanctuary of 570.

Garden plots were connected with many of the chapels, suggesting that they played a significant part in the cult. On the other hand, very few chapels were directly associated with a tomb, except 570, possibly 537, and one of the northern group to be discussed later.

Notes

1.   I.M.E. Shaw in Kemp, *AR* I, 124-132.
2.   Kemp, *AR* III, 33; *JEA* 69 (1983), 13. J.H. Taylor and A. Boyce in Kemp, *AR* III, 139-142.
3.   M.A. Leahy in Kemp, *AR* II, 65-74.
4.   Kemp, *AR* I, 14, 15.
5.   A substantial deposit of sand and gravel, forming almost a gully in the desert floor below, stretched from the northeast to the southwest passing before the forecourt steps.
6.   Kemp, *AR* II, 28.
7.   Personal observation while excavating. The vessel type was confirmed by P. Rose.
8.   B. Bruyère, *Les Fouilles de Deir el Médineh* (Cairo, 1931-32), pl. I: C.V. 1, 1211 (hereafter *Rapport*).
9.   Kemp, *AR* I, 19, 2.5.
10. W.S. Smith, *A History of Egyptian Sculpture and Painting in the Old Kingdom* (Boston, 1949), 255. A. Lucas and J.R. Harris, *Ancient Egyptian Materials and Industries* (London, 1962), 346-348. Hematite is also called red ochre.
11. Kemp, *AR* I, 18, 2.4; 19, 2.5.
12. H. Hecker in Kemp, *AR* III, 80-81. Dr Hecker recognized at least four surfaces. Some of these may have been microlayers deposited in one application. His use of the term *gypsum* for these layers should be altered to *marl* or *mud*, and it is only this material that is laid to 1-2.5 cm. in depth. Gypsum, at the most, attains a thickness of about 5 mm.
13. The figurine is *c*.3 cm., and in my opinion is the head of a jackal-like dog. The snout is too long and narrow to be a cynocephalus ape, an the ears are long and pointed.
14. P. Rose in Kemp, *AR* III, 105, no. 54029.
15. Kemp, *AR* II, 18-28. G. Robins in Kemp, *AR* II, 110-132.
16. Rose in Kemp, *AR* III, 102-103, 105, no. 57281.
17. A.H. Gardiner, *Egyptian Grammar*[3]: (London, 1969), 499, P.3.
18. Personally observed during excavation. The specimen was a dark resinous brown. It has not been officially

identified, but similar fragments have been burnt on site as a testing sample and the scent is similar to frankincense.

19. Examples from Amarna include nearly all the chapels in the northern group and most of the chapels in the southern group, see figs 4, 5, 6, 7, 10, 13, 15.

20. Bruyère, *Rapport* 1935-40 fasc. I, pl. XXIV; op. cit. 1930 pl. XIII, 1. N. de G. Davies, *Two Ramesside Tombs at Thebes* (New York, 1927), pls XXXI, XXXVIII, Tomb of Ipy. On top of each red vertical line is the addition of a blue spot.

21. Kemp, *AR* II, 25; 26, 2.6.

22. *AR* II, 25-28.

23. Kemp, *AR* I, 28, 2.11.

24. Rose in Kemp, *AR* III, 101-102; 104, nos 56481, 57042.

25. Peet and Woolley, *COA* I, 99.

26. Kemp, *AR* II, 8. Kemp, *JEA* 67 (1981), 10, 13, fig. 4.

27. Peet and Woolley, *COA* I, 99.

28. Kemp, *AR* II, 8-11.

29. Identified verbally by Prof. C. Renfrew.

30. Kemp, *AR* II, 11, 1.9.

31. Peet and Woolley, *COA* I, 104. Two stelae present in Chapel 525.

32. Kemp, *AR* IV, 47-54.

33. Kemp, *AR* II, 31-35.

34. Kemp, *AR* I, 37, 3.3.

35. A.J. Spencer, *Brick Architecture in Ancient Egypt* (Warminster, 1979), 141-142, pl. 53B.

36. Kemp, *AR* II, 36.

37. *AR* II, 33-35.

38. *AR* II, 34.

39. Bruyère, *Rapport* 1931-32 pl. I; 5, 1198, 1211 and surrounding group; *Rapport* 1930 pl. XXIV. These can be compared with the plan of Chapel 570 and represent the more usual tomb chapel at Deir el Medina.

40. Although these leaves have not yet been officially identified, they resemble those from the olive. Renfrew in Kemp, *AR* II, 188: olive stones have been found in the Workmen's Village.

41. Kemp, *AR* II, 29.

42. Kemp, *AR* I, 38; II, 35.

43. Note especially the concealed *serekh* pattern behind the inner hall wall. See p. 11.

44. See n. 35.

45. The north wall of Annexe 450, which forms the southern wall of the forecourt to Chapel 561 is similar in construction to the wall of the outer hall of Chapel 571. The north wall of Annexe 450 was built in one stage. See figs 6 and 9.

46. Peet and Woolley, *COA* I, 101.

47. Ibid. I, pl. XXVI, 3.

48. Ibid.

49. Ibid., pl. XXVII, 4.

50. Ibid., 102; pl. XXVII, 3.

51. Ibid., 102.

52. Ibid., pl. XXVII, 3.

53. Ibid., 105.

54. Ibid.

55. Ibid.

56. Ibid.

57. Ibid.

58. Ibid., 95, 105.

59. Ibid., 100-101; 105.

60. Ibid., 105.

61. Ibid., 106.

62. Kemp, *AR* IV, 70-79.

63. The normal shape of the halls composing an Egyptian temple is rectangular or square. See A. Badawy, *Ancient Egyptian Architectural Design: a study of the harmonic system*, (Berkeley, 1965), 19-39.

64. Kemp, *AR* III, 6, 1.4.

65. Kemp, *AR* IV, 76-77.

Chapter 3

The Architecture of the 1921-1922 Chapels which were not replanned

Fifteen of the twenty-five buildings dug by Peet and Woolley in 1921 and 1922 that were classed as chapels or dependencies, or structures that have since been shown to have had another purpose, were not recleared during the excavations of 1979 to 1986. These consist of chapels 551-555 lying to the north of the Walled Village (fig. 4) and south of these numbers 521 (no longer extant), 524, 525, 526, 527, 532, 533, 534, 535 and 536 (fig. 5).

Today, these chapels are completely filled with drift sand and the only sources of information are the brief reports of Peet, the plans of Newton, and the glass negatives of original photographs.[1] This method of reporting on a building is never as satisfactory as examining it *in situ*, since it is inevitable that questions will arise which can be answered only tenuously. The methods employed in excavating and recording a building in Peet's day lacked the detail with which to furnish a proper understanding. Certain parts of a structure are necessarily left unexplained and open to supposition until such time when the building is re-examined. A prime example of this is Building 528, which presented a totally different picture after it was re-excavated in 1984 (compare figs 5 and 12).

In the following analysis, the chapel architecture will be examined as far as possible in the same light as the excavated group, noting distinctive features. The information gained from all the buildings will be assessed to determine whether a chronological sequence and architectural development can be traced.

The Northern Group

With the exception of Chapel 555, which is oriented east to west, all other chapels in this group are oriented north to south.

Chapel 551 (fig. 4)

The chapel had a long rectangular forecourt. It rose into tiers and was divided into three parts, through which passed a pathway with low walls. To the left of the path, in the first section of the court, was a garden divided into six small plots. The dividing walls of the garden were about 7 cm. in height, which was the average of the plots excavated east of the Walled Village in 1986. Peet and Woolley could not identify this feature,[2] which was to become abundantly familiar in the later excavations. The garden was further enhanced by a semi-circular line of stones, which almost certainly was the containing wall to another plot.

In the second part of the court was a stairway of five steps. To the right of these, the court was divided into two subsidiary divisions. In the centre of the western part of this court was a circular stone with a diameter of 22 cm. that may have been a column base.

The third division of the court to the north had two steps, which may have been an extended continuation of the preceding flight. A circular stone vessel, 22 cm. high, was in the northwestern corner and a compartment with an entrance from the inner hall lay to the east.

On the other hand, the forecourt could have extended only as far as the garden or to the second flight of stairs. It could have formed the outer hall, which would have been roofed. Perhaps the suggested stone column base could have been part of a supporting pillar. The three compartments to the east may have been magazines. This suggested boundary to the forecourt is nearly in alignment with the southern wall to the outer hall of 556, which was roofed. The stone vessel was situated in a parallel position to the three jar emplacements in Chapel 556.

The inner hall lay beyond this area. A bench was set against the western and southern walls, and the eastern wall had a bench, 38 cm. high, that was abutted by a rectangular plastered trough. A flight of four steps led from the inner hall to the sanctuary. The shrine consisted of a bench with rectangular shafts, each of different dimensions, sunk into the masonry. The bases of the pits were 54 cm. above the floor of the shrine. The doorway to the shrine bore a torus moulding surmounted by a cavetto cornice. The cavetto was painted red, blue, green and yellow with a black outline. The torus roll was painted in the same way as the one in Chapel 561. A dado of blue and black ran at the same level as the stair balustrade across the wall, and a broad band, colour not stated, ran near the outer edge of the door jambs.

The roof on the interior of the shrine had a vine pattern which continued downwards to a yellow cavetto and white torus roll moulding. The vine pattern in the side chapel of 561 came mainly from the walls and may have also decorated the ceiling. Below these designs was a lotus pattern in blue and white with a border, under which were yellow and red spots shaped in flames with a chequer pattern in red, blue and white. Designs similar to these were found in the inner hall of 561.[3]

Finds recorded from this chapel included a jar stopper and a fragment of a blue glazed ring bezel (for references to these objects and those in the following chapels see *COA* I, 107-108).

Chapel 552 (fig. 4)

The area before this chapel was divided into two sections and may have formed a forecourt or a forecourt and outer hall. The dividing wall was aligned with the outer hall wall of 556. In my opinion, from the evidence of Chapel 556, both 551 and 552 possessed outer halls as extensive as the former building. The walls when excavated were 35 cm. high, but Peet noted the presence of boulders with traces of brick courses above.[4] Nearby was brick rubble, possibly part of a collapsed wall, which, if so, suggests that they were originally much higher.

Two whitewashed tanks were sunk into the floor of the first part of this area. These lay on either side of a passage. The one to the west was square and that to the east was rectangular. Two square brick bases, which may have formed altars or columns,[5] stood to the west in the second section of this area. It seems more likely that these were altars rather than columns, since they were set closely together and would normally lie on either side of the passage. The reconstructed figure resembles the two altars in the Chapel of Hathor of Seti I at Deir el Medina.[6] These, however, were placed before the pronaos, whereas those in 552 are in what I believe to be the outer hall.

Behind the altars was a broad bench, 55 cm. high, adjacent to the outer wall of the inner hall. It was divided by a staircase of ten steps leading to the next chamber. The eastern portion of the bench extended beyond the limits of the inner hall of 552 and encompassed at a slight angle the length of the western half of the southern wall of the inner hall of 553.

Five engaged columns were set against the exterior of the southern wall to the inner hall. Three lay to the west of the stairway and two to the east. A bench was set against part of the western wall of the inner hall, as well as the southern and eastern sides. No comment was made by Peet concerning the small projection from the north end of the western bench. Here, too, the bench ended in a right angle. Just beyond was a small projection from the western wall which may have been the remains of a partition wall. This may have extended further into the hall to enclose the western part of the shrine and separate it partially from the central naos.

The shrine, which had no pronaos, consisted of three niches, each of an individual asymmetrical plan. The one to the east abutted the central niche and its staircase, as well as the eastern bench in the inner hall. This niche was 25 cm. above the floor and on a line with the niches of Chapel 553. The remaining two extended further north and were aligned with the shrines of 551 and 554. A bench was set against the back wall of the shrine and remains of a cavetto cornice and torus roll appeared 67 cm. above the floor. Decorated wall plaster was also present.

The central shrine was entered by a platform attached to a staircase of seven steps. This, too, contained a bench.[7] The western shrine was a small rectangle with a bench, the whole of which was set into a larger chamber forming an **L**-shape. In the angle of the staircase and the niche was a compartment 70 cm. high. West of this was a single limestone square pillar, 45 cm. high.

The inner hall produced a rectangular limestone basin and an **L**-shaped piece of limestone; a similar object came from the outer hall.

Chapel 553 (fig. 4)

No formally laid out forecourt appears with this chapel or 556, of which the outer hall is shared by both buildings (Chapter 2, 22). A rectangular trough or depression abutted the west wall of the outer hall. A flight of stairs of four steps led to the inner hall, which had benches on its western, southern and eastern walls. The sanctuary had no pronaos, and led directly off the inner hall. It had a tripartite shrine symmetrically planned. The principal niche appeared to be the easternmost compartment, which was emphasized by a flight of stairs. Instead of the usual bench or double niche, it contained a brick pedestal, 48 cm. high, set directly onto the floor. A square depression was sunk into its top, which Peet and Woolley suggested may have accommodated a square column.[8] The central niche was 56 cm. above the floor of the inner hall, with a bench set against its rear wall, while the westernmost niche contained none. Peet and Woolley's report did not indicate whether the western compartment originally had a bench, but fragments of a cavetto cornice and torus roll were mentioned in association with the western and eastern niches, and a limestone cornice with the entrance to the central niche.[9] These may have composed part of the entrance frame, rather than an embellishment to the niche bench. Two limestone offering tables, whose provenance within the building was not recorded, were associated with this chapel.

Chapel 554 (fig. 4)

This chapel was dismissed with barely a comment by Peet and Woolley, although there are some features in the area before the inner hall that deserve some remark.

The right angle formed by cobbles to the east may be all that remains of the forecourt. This line may have formed the edge of the central passageway, as well as the wall to a garden plot. Alternatively, the line of stones running east to west could have been the remains of part of the outer hall wall, and the vestiges of the half rectangular feature beyond could have been a badly denuded bench. The short projection from the western wall is probably all that survives of the outer hall wall in this area. A rectangular structure similar to the one in 553, and situated in a comparable position, abutted the western wall.

The inner hall was provided with benches along its southern, eastern, western and part of its northern walls. Two square column bases, resembling those in 556, were placed symmetrically in the hall before a double flight of stairs. This double stairway, and a smaller independent one, led to three shrines with no pronaos. The eastern niche may once have contained a bench, although no remains of one were reported after it was excavated. The central niche contained a platform or bench, and the western one may have had the usual double niche.

The western niche, although damaged, was of the same dimensions as the central one. It is not certain whether another shrine abutted the western niche, completing the full length of the northern wall. The arrangement of the sanctuary is similar to the plan of the shrine area in Chapel 521 to the south (fig. 5). No location was given to the two limestone offering tables found in this building.

Chapel 555 (fig. 4)

This chapel is isolated at a distance from the others. The forecourt was rectangular, with its length oriented north to south. A semi-circular line of stones enters the area in the west. Only a shell of what once may have been a shallow outer hall formed by the remains of an angle to a brick wall lay to the south. This introduced the inner hall, with benches against all its walls except the eastern one. The shrine was also badly denuded, but appeared to have had two niches. The division to the west had what may have been two small rectangular compartments adjacent to a bench 45 cm. high. Cut into this was a shaft 1.60 m. deep with a stairway. The shrine partly covered it. Without re-examining the structure, it cannot be determined whether the shaft existed before the shrine was built or if it was added later. Two limestone offering tables and a rectangular limestone slab with two bars on its underside came from this building. Their provenance was not noted.

The Southern Group

The orientation of these chapels is as follows: those with their axes aligned east to west include chapels 521, 522, 532, 533, 535 and 536; those aligned north to south are 524, 525, 526 and 527.

Chapel 521 (figs 5 and 7)

The forecourt lay on a terrace and was delineated by a line of stones or a low wall. Part of this was revealed during the excavations of 1984. As pointed out above (Chapter 2, 18), it is likely that it had garden plots.[10] It had no outer hall. The inner hall was entered between two pylons or piers. The hall was broad rather than the usual long, rectangular plan. Benches were set against the southeast corner, the southern wall, and part of the western wall. The pronaos projected into the inner hall and introduced three main shrines. A fourth compartment or shrine, separate from this group, was entered directly from the inner hall. Benches adjoined the back walls of the tripartite shrine. The fourth niche was badly denuded, but may have contained a bench.

Of the group of three, the central shrine was the broadest, rising 65 cm. above the floor with a depth of 85 cm., a width of 1.25 m., and a doorway of 66 cm. The bench had the usual cavetto and torus roll, with the lower niche reaching a height of 17 cm. from the floor. Before it was a stone step, 31 × 28 cm., and 19 cm. high. A stone step also lay before the shrine. A small platform, or step, of brick and stone lay west of this step and abutted the wall of the shrine. The fourth niche was 1.20 m. deep and broader than the other group. Two plain limestone offering tables, a slate palette with remains of green pigment, a rough wooden doll, a piece of wood with three painted panels, and part of a rectangular board with a rounded top came from this building; the provenance was not noted. Near the eastern wall was an ivory ear stud,[11] an object common to the site (for references to these objects and those in following chapels see *COA* I, 101-106).

Chapel 524 (fig. 5)

The forecourt was set out with a brick wall and was probably entered by a short flight of stairs. On the western side was part of a wall, isolated from the main wall, which Peet thought could have been the remains of an earlier court. Alternatively, it could have been part of a garden plot.

The entrance to the outer hall may have been flanked by pylons. Benches lined all but the northern wall. In the northwest corner a doorway led to an annexe that ran the full extent of the inner hall and shrine. In the northeast corner of the hall, a step, which Peet described as having a 'rolled' top,[12] led to a series of steps cut into the gebel on the eastern side of the chapel, forming a passage to the hill rising behind.

The inner hall rose 15 cm. above the outer. Situated in the north end of the inner hall were four gypsum plastered brick pedestals, 25 cm. high, set 90 cm. away from the three shrines that opened directly into the hall. Two of the pedestals abutted each other before the central shrine. The remaining two were before each of the other niches.

A platform, 4 cm. high and 32 cm. wide, ran before the full length of the three shrines. The central niche, whose floor was depressed 6 cm. below the height of its threshold, had a small brick pedestal before the niche. The usual cavetto cornice had once formed part of the lower niche, commencing 38 cm. from the floor. The western and eastern niches also contained a lower niche set off with a cavetto cornice. The eastern shrine was 1.10 m. in depth, which must have been approximately the same as the other two. The central shrine was broader than the western and eastern ones.

The only object mentioned from this chapel was an alabaster finger ring. A small fragment of papyrus, written in hieratic mentioning the name of the Aten, was discovered in the corridor between this chapel and building 523.

Chapel 525 (figs 5 and 16)

The forecourt of this chapel was irregular in plan. Its western wall was formed by the eastern wall of 527. Its southern wall, which is only partly preserved, was formed of large boulders and cobbles which were aligned with the stones delineating the southern side of the pathway leading to Building 528. The court of 525 was extended to the east by a line of stones at some distance from the main body of the chapel. The northern part of the court wall, which abutted the eastern wall of the chapel, appeared to have been built of brick and was provided with a door, which led towards the hill to the rear, where a tomb shaft lay on the same axis as 525.

The entrance to the chapel appears to have had a short flight of stairs set between the usual balustrade and ending in a return. However, Newton interpreted this feature as a wall ending in finials with a cavetto cornice. Since the section in the plan showed the stump of the wall as higher than the normal height of the balustrade in the chapels (fig. 16), Newton may have been correct in his reconstruction, which may have represented a modification of the pavilions attached to the pylons of the Sanctuary in the Great Temple to the Aten.[13]

On either side of the stairway were pylons forming the entrance to the inner hall. This chapel was not provided with an outer hall. A continuous bench lined all four sides of the hall. It was the deepest on the north wall, forming a dais. Eight steps set between a balustrade divided this wall into a doorway to the pronaos. Directly in front of the central shrine was a truncated, inverted conical pedestal 33 cm. high with a diameter of 34 cm. On either side of the stairs, which were on the same axis as the pedestal, were two columns that supported an entablature inscribed with hieroglyphs containing fragments of a *ḥtp dì nsw* invocation to Amun.[14] This had been surmounted by a cavetto cornice and torus moulding.

The shrine may have been tripartite. The western niche was 87 cm. wide. The eastern compartment was partially destroyed and may have had the usual bench. Peet remarked that the chapel was abnormal, since the shrine was in actuality a platform that could have been a lower niche with up to three niches above it. According to Newton's plan, this composed only part of the eastern division, the remaining area forming a side compartment.

Two stelae were described as leaning against the back wall and western section of the western niche. In addition, a large boulder with a flat surface was set before the flight of stairs, and a stone **T**-shaped basin was situated in the inner hall.

Chapel 526 (fig. 5)

What Peet called an inner court to this chapel,[15] I have termed a forecourt. It was an asymmetrical space formed on its western and eastern sides by the walls of Chapels 524 and 527 respectively. A short flight of stairs formed its entrance, and abutting the eastern side of the stairs and the western side of Chapel 527 was an oblong dais, two bricks high. In its northeastern corner was a hollow gypsum plastered enclosure, measuring 40 × 25 cm. The northern part of the forecourt was bounded on its western side by a wall joining the eastern wall of Chapel 524 and the western wall of the inner hall of 526. In the northeastern part of the forecourt was an irregularly shaped enclosure with a doorway in its southeastern wall. This enclosure abutted a flight of steps leading up the side of the hill. What appear to be the remains of earlier walls projected from the western and eastern walls of the court. Peet did not comment on these features. No outer hall appears with this chapel, the inner hall following directly after the court. It was entered by a flight of steps, which adjoined on its eastern side a rectangular compartment built of bricks set on their sides. This may, once again, be the remains of a garden plot. Peet did not refer to another small rectangular projection set in the western corner of the stairs.

Two brick steps led to the main shrine, which contained the usual bench. No comment was made on the projection in the southwestern part of the shrine and the circular form in the niche. A hazard guess is that the former could be a buttress and the latter a low pedestal. To the east of the main niche was a shallow, L-shaped compartment, which was entered by a door, 52 cm. wide, from the inner hall. The objects reported from this building included a rectangular wooden label inscribed in hieratic and a blue glazed earring.

Chapel 527 (fig. 5)

A row of stones to the south may have been part of a pathway wall that eventually linked up with Chapel group 535 and 533. However, because of their size, they may have marked out what remains of the forecourt, as suggested by Peet. To the north were a flight of steps leading to the outer hall or possibly the forecourt, whose walls were of boulder and brick construction. The floor was packed with mud and stones. Abutting the wall in the east was a rectangular enclosure, entered from the northwest corner, which contained a limestone basin with a diameter of 40 cm. Associated with it were reeds and charcoal. The reeds may be the remains of a roof.

Rough stone steps formed the entrance to the inner hall. West of the steps was a rectangular projection abutting the southern exterior wall of the inner hall. Although it is not referred to, it may have been a trough. The interior of the inner hall was lined with benches on the eastern wall and southwestern corner.

Little of the shrine remained before excavation, but traces of a large niche lay to the east. The upper part of it started 70 cm. above the lower niche. A passage 1.40 m. long, to the west of the niche with a floor, was cut into rock 45 cm. higher than the niche. In this area were fragments of painted plaster.[16] This arrangement seems to resemble in part the sanctuary of Chapel 552 in the north. If the speculation about 527 is correct, these two chapels are the only ones to contain an L-shaped compartment running behind the shrine.

No objects were reported from this chapel.

Chapel 532 (fig. 5)

The forecourt to this chapel was unspectacular, forming almost a passage. Its north wall was shared with Chapel 533. To the south a line of stones or boulders marked out the foundation of the southern wall. A flight of stairs to the east, with four steps set between balustrades, led, with a drop of two more steps, into the inner hall. No outer hall was apparent.

Benches were set against the north and south walls of the inner hall. Screen walls ending in piers divided the inner hall from the pronaos. On the central axis of the pronaos was set a rough stone block 27 cm. high. A narrow staircase, with three remaining steps, rose beyond this to the niche. The niche, of which little remains, once extended beyond the rear walls of Chapels 533 and 536. It was of stone and brick construction.

No objects were reported from this chapel.

Chapel 533 (fig. 5)

The building was approached by a stone-lined pathway abutting the forecourt, which was entered by a descending flight of three steps laid in an irregular plan. On the same axis as the steps was the entrance to the inner hall, from which projected two short walls with out-turning ends. The northern projection appeared to form an enclosure in the northeastern corner, and then continued in a broken line to the western wall of the forecourt. This wall may have been continuous, like the one in Building 528 that divided the forecourts of 529 and 530. It is not improbable that this part of the court had garden plots. Part of a projecting wall appeared in the southeastern section of the court, which formed a short passage that set 533 apart from 532. Its eastern and southern walls abutted and shared the walls of 532 respectively. In the southeast corner the wall was destroyed, and it seems more likely that this passage was in fact a dependency of 533. Peet made no detailed comments on this area or the forecourt in general. Because of these marked off areas, it is doubtful that this chapel had an outer hall.

The inner hall was on a broad plan like chapel 521. Benches abutted the northern and western walls. The sanctuary protruded into the hall. It contained three shrines of unequal division. The northern compartment may not have been a shrine and did not appear to have a bench. The central and southern shrines were given more prominence, since they were set on a slightly raised floor. The central niche followed the usual plan, with a bench attached to its rear wall. The southern niche was badly denuded. A small projection from the rear wall may be the remains of another partition wall, which, if so, would suggest that the sanctuary was tripartite. The platform did not join the south wall. This would have left a corridor between the platform and the outer wall of the inner hall and sanctuary.

No objects were reported from this building.

Chapel 535 and Building 534 (fig. 5)

Peet stated that 534 was not completely excavated and that it was doubtful that it was a chapel.[17] It consisted of a small enclosure with an oven (which abutted the northern wall of the forecourt of Chapel 535) and appeared to be a dependency of that building. Its entrance was in the west wall and independent of 535. From the evidence in 556, this was not unusual. It was observed that no apparent interconnecting door led from the outer hall to the dependency.

Chapel 535, contrary to 533, reverted to the plan of the elongated rectangle. The forecourt, which lay on an extended east-west axis, had part of a wall projecting from its western side. This may have been the remains of a pathway that led to the court. Similarly, this chapel did not have an outer hall. Two pylons appeared to have flanked the entrance to the inner hall, which was lined with benches on all the walls except the east. A flight of steps, set between balustrades ending in returns, led to the pronaos before the sanctuary. This part of the chapel was completely demolished, except for its outer walls. Building 534 produced a grey stone figure of a female and the chapel had a limestone offering table; provenance was not recorded.

Chapel 536 (fig. 5)

A border of stones forming the remains of a forecourt ran east to the main part of the chapel. A square projection lay in the northeast corner, which could have been a receptacle or a platform. No description was provided by Peet. A projection of a line of bricks from the western wall of the chapel may have been the southern part of the forecourt wall. Further to the south, a semi-circle of stones suggests the vestiges of a garden plot.

Chapel 536 did not have an outer hall. From the plan, there is no entrance to the inner hall in the main axis of the building, which is the case for all known private chapels. Instead, a bench spanned the full extent of the western wall, which should have accommodated a door. The aperture shown in the plan in the southern wall leaves no option but to climb down a bench. This is unlikely. The bench against the northern wall appears to be severed in the east. The possibility of an entrance just beyond here, via Chapel 532, is also unlikely. Little survived of the stairway that led to the pronaos and the shrine, which were also mostly destroyed.

A subsidiary enclosure consisting of a foundation of boulders and brick was adjacent to the southern wall of 536. It was narrow and divided into two compartments with a small enclosure attached to its western wall. Peet suggested that it could be another shrine.[18] In view of the plans of several of the chapels (figs 9, 15), it is more likely that it was a dependency.

No objects were cited from this chapel.

Discussion

The evidence reviewed here, taken with that of Chapter 2, allows the identification of both characteristic and atypical features of these buildings. To recap, the private chapel essentially consisted of a forecourt, an outer hall, an inner hall, a pronaos and a sanctuary. It could have an annexe, usually accommodating a subsidiary shrine on its left side, and a group of dependencies consisting of magazines, animal enclosures or working areas for domestic concerns on the right. Lastly, a chief characteristic of the chapel was the use of benches. In essence, the private chapel reflected in miniature an Egyptian temple, but whereas the latter exhibited an imposing formality, the former had an informal simplicity.

The forecourt could be furnished with garden plots and receptacles sunk into the ground, presumably for containing water. On the other hand, the court could be a simple open area with no special additions. The outer hall could have had a bench set against one wall, all four walls, or in some instances none. Benches could be absent from the inner hall or could abut at least three walls, which was more usual. Not all sanctuaries had a pronaos, and sometimes it would be included within the main body of the inner hall. The shrine was the most variable feature in the chapel, but in general it was uni-cellular with a side compartment, or tripartite.

The orientation of the chapels could be to the north or east. The ground level usually rose steadily from a few centimetres outside the building to over 50 cm. with the commencement of the sanctuary. An exception is Chapel 533, where one steps down into the forecourt. Evidence from several chapels indicates that probably all the inner halls and sanctuaries bore wall decorations, including side chapels. It cannot be determined whether this occurred in some of the outer halls.

Within this architectural scheme, certain variations can be detected. Chapel group 532-536 did not include an outer hall, nor did 521 or Chapels 525-527, and possibly 554. Chapels 521, 533, 552 and 554 are distinguished by broad halls. Chapel 536 is the only building not to have an entrance on its long axis. Sanctuaries protrude into the inner halls of Chapels 521, 533 and 571. There were square pillars in the inner halls of 529 and 554 and in the outer hall of 556.

Shrine divisions also varied:

> a single naos: 570, 530 and possibly 532 and 551;
> a single naos with one or two compartments: 522, 526, 556 and 571 (second phase);
> symmetrically arranged tripartite shrines without an attached fourth compartment
>   or naos: 524, 529, 561, 571 (first phase);
> the same, but with a fourth addition: 521, 554;
> tripartite shrines asymmetrically arranged or with atypical features within the shrine:
>   552, 553;
> atypical shrines: 527, 531, 533, 551, 552, 553, 554.

Chapels with a left annexe include 522, 524, 561, and chapels with dependencies on the right ranging from the simple to the complex are 531, 533, 536, 556, 522 (523), 561 (450).

Chapels associated with a tomb are 555 and 570, and chapels with a tenuous association are 525 and 537.

Any relative chronology depends on architectural and topographical considerations, as well as on fragments of wall decoration or objects. From a topographical point of view, these buildings, because of their religious and funerary associations, would be sited in the more remote parts of the village, on hill slopes and terraces that had not been occupied by domestic dwellings, but would still be visible and in easy access to the settlement. As suitable ground became scarce, the chapels would begin to encroach upon the village, and land formerly used for another purpose would be reclaimed for cult reasons, such as Chapels 561, 570 and 571. The former occupied the remaining available ground nearest to the Walled Village, which could still be a suitable site for a cult building.

These make it possible to unravel a coherent system within the maze of chapels lining the hills of the Workmen's Village. The initial chapel building may have started in the north with chapel group 551-556, determined by the irregularity of many of the internal features of the buildings suggesting an earlier phase (to be discussed in Chapter 6), as opposed to the more regular plans of many in the southern group. As building continued, it may have moved gradually south along the escarpment east of the Walled Village.

Chapel 533 and its group would have begun at the same time as the construction in the north, and followed by or contemporary with it was group 525-527 and 528-531. The last to be built would have been 570 and 571, and then 561 contemporary with 522. Chapel 522, as already noted, was built either at the same time or just after 561, because its outer staircase abutted the north wall of the Main Chapel (Chapter 2, 18).

The atypical arrangement of most of the sanctuaries in the north, together with other features such as a single flight of stairs to a side naos, receptacles sunk into shrine benches, the use of the broad hall, and the extended forecourts and outer halls are among modified features appearing in 532-536 which may have been the first to be constructed in the south. Assuming that the topographical reasons given for the chronology are correct (siting the first chapels at a distance from the village), the foregoing makes sense. Another architectural point for recognizing the earlier and later buildings can be seen in the development of dependencies and annexes. On the premise that the earlier buildings have been identified, it will be noticed that none have a left annexe attached to the outside of the main building, except possibly 524. In fact, a fourth niche or a naos, not part of the main shrine, was incorporated within the sanctuary. The side chapel, like that attached to 561, seems to be a later development. In addition, the dependencies of the earliest buildings are less complex, consisting of a simple enclosure often within the main building or abutting its outside wall. In the later chapels, a series of enclosures constitute the dependencies, and the addition of animal shelters, and probably slaughter courts directly attached to the chapel precinct, began to appear with 561 and 522. For the earlier chapels, this activity may have been carried out in Buildings 540 and 541, which Kemp identifies with animal keeping.[19]

Another source of information for attempting to establish a relative chronology may be found in a few fragments of wall decoration and objects with traces of iconography. The fragments of wall plaster from the Main Chapel depicted part of the face of a man and woman superimposed on a yellow ochre background. The style of wig and headdress, including the use of background colour, is in keeping with post-Amarna and Nineteenth Dynasty art under the traditional Egyptian religion. Fine examples, similar to this, can be found in the tomb of Tutankhamun and Tomb No. 1 of Sennedjem at Deir el Medina. The inference here is that the Main Chapel may have been constructed during the brief reign of Tutankhamun.

This pictorial evidence is in contrast to two other examples of decorative art. The first comes from Chapel 525 and is the stela of Ptahmay which portrays him before the deities Shed and Isis. He is depicted in the Amarna style kilt, with protruding belly and slightly elongated head.[20] Although the god Amun was named in this chapel, the iconography depicted on the stela does not utilize the traditional form of art. Instead, the Amarna style is present in the company of Amun. If, indeed, the Workmen's village did house many of the artisans who cut out the royal tombs and the northern and southern tombs of the nobles, they would have been schooled in the Amarna style art that was applied in the tombs during the reign of Akhenaten. This, however, did not mean that the workmen had to change to the new religion, but they would have had to employ the style and technique in which they had been trained. Chapel 525, therefore, could have been constructed towards the end of Akhenaten's reign.

The second piece of evidence came from the resifting of one of Peet's dumps, which was located in Square T18 (fig. 8), superimposing the unexcavated ground which in 1984 still covered the easternmost section of the dependency to Chapel 561. This was a brick bearing the fragments of a wall painting. Although quite worn, it depicted the chin and neck of a man or woman. The flesh was slightly pinkish and the features were outlined delicately in red, like the sistrum depicted in 561. Apart from the unconventional colour and outline for a human figure, the salient point is the style of the features, which resembled the familiar form of Akhenaten or Smenkhkare.

The dump could not belong to Chapel 522 and its annexe 523 since those had already been cleared. Therefore, it could only have belonged to one of the group of chapels dug by Peet lying further east. The most logical site would be the group of chapels composing 524 or 526. These are in the same area as 525 and the Ptahmay stela.

In conclusion, the evidence derived from the foregoing points suggests that the first stage of chapel building was probably more concentrated during the latter years of Akhenaten and the short reign of Smenkhkare. These buildings would include those groups lying the furthest from the village. The later buildings such as the Main Chapel and 522 would probably date from the end of the reign of Smenkhkare and the early years of Tutankhamun, when chapel construction was beginning to cease. The Main Chapel, especially, foreshadows in its plan the regular features to be found later in many of the Nineteenth and Twentieth Dynasty chapels at Deir el Medina. With it appears the streamlined tripartite sanctuary, free of atypical features.

Notes

1.   These are the property of the Egypt Exploration Society.
2.   Peet and Woolley, *COA* I, 107.
3.   Kemp, *AR* II, 27, fig. 2.6.
4.   Peet and Woolley, *COA* I, 107.
5.   Ibid., 108, fig. 16.
6.   Bruyère, *Rapport* (1935-1940), fasc. I, 102, fig. 54.
7.   Peet and Woolley's reference to the design painted in the central shrine of Chapel 552 is not clear. He refers to p.94 for the description, which does not appear there, unless he means the same style of design which appears in Chapel 551 described on p. 107. The only reference to the paintings in Chapel 552 is on p. 100, which he states consists of representations of offerings of a loaf, a lotus and other objects no longer recognizable. These appear in a niche, which is presumably the central one if the shrine with a staircase leading to it is described on p. 108 is the compartment meant.
       Peet and Woolley, *COA* I, 94, 100, 107, 108.
8.   Ibid. 108.
9.   Ibid.
10.   This is not included in the report in *AR* II, 13, but is my personal observation while excavating in this area in 1984.
11.   Peet calls the ivory ear stud a lip stud (Peet and Woolley, *COA* I, 102), but no representations of Egyptians in painting or sculpture have been portrayed wearing lip studs, whereas the pierced ear for inserting studs or earrings appears frequently during the New Kingdom, and was introduced during the Twelfth Dynasty of the Middle Kingdom. Ivory ear studs and studs with rosette designs are common objects to the Workmen's Village.
12.   *COA* I, 103.
13.   J. Vandier, *Manuel d'Archéologie Égyptienne II, Les Grandes Époques: L'Architecture Religieuse et Civile* (Paris, 1955), 859, fig. 416 (hereafter *Manuel*).

14. Peet and Woolley, *COA* I, 95.
15. Ibid., 104.
16. Ibid., 105.
17. Ibid., 106.
18. Ibid.
19. Kemp, *AR* III, 60-79.
20. Peet and Woolley, *COA* I, pl. XXVIII, 3.

Chapter 4

A Comparison of Chapel Architecture at Deir el Medina with El Amarna

Among the first to start excavations at Deir el Medina were Schiaparelli in 1906 and Baraize in 1912.[1] Schiaparelli confined his work to a chapel of Seti I, north of the enclosure wall to the main Temple of Hathor. Baraize excavated a small chapel on the interior of the northwest angle of the enclosure wall. From 1922-1951, the major work at Deir el Medina was undertaken by Bruyère, who identified at least thirty-two cult buildings, apart from the Temple of Hathor. These varied in plan from a small court before a shrine, in some instances cut into the cliff, to the usual basic tripartite plan, with or without benches, and finally to what he saw as a miniature temple. The terminology applied to these was diverse: *Chapelle Votive, Chapelles des Confrèries, Chapelle, Chapelle Religieuse, Temple*.[2] The nature of the cult seems to have dictated the plan of individual buildings.

Unlike the Workmen's Village at Amarna, with its gently sloping cliffs and terraces, Deir el Medina was situated in a deep valley with a sheer rock face to the west and sharply rising hills to the east. The choice of location for cult buildings was therefore limited. The Temple of Hathor would seem to have been the focal point around which the chapels were located. The buildings which Bruyère called *Chapelle Votive* (abbreviated to C.V. in the text) were situated to the south and southwest of the main temple. Many of these lay on the lower slopes of the cliff face, whilst others were on a narrow terrace cut into the rock at a higher level. A small group called *Chapelle* were confined within the main temple enclosure, and another group identified as *Chapelle Religieuse* and *Chapelle* stretched beyond the enclosure to the north along the cliff escarpment. To the east was situated the building recognized as a small temple. This was set into the hills of Qurnet Mura'i.

Of the twenty-nine buildings discussed below, I was able to re-examine twenty-seven. Two are no longer visible, so only the plans and reports could be consulted. Of the remaining three which make up Bruyère's thirty-two, 1120 is labelled P 1120 on the plan,[3] and is only a tomb shaft; no. 1224 is situated with the tomb chapels on the western escarpment and should be classed as one from this group;[4] no. 1220 is a domestic structure probably associated with C.V. 1193.[5] For these reasons, these buildings are not included in the assessment.

While excavating these chapels, Bruyère reconstructed most of them. Although the intention of preserving them is commendable, at the same time it is difficult to assess certain parts of the buildings, since the reconstruction must be distinguished from the original structure. Many of the walls and stairs have been totally renewed, in some cases with material from a different part of the chapel. For instance, bricks from vaulted ceilings were reused as fill for staircases. This was apparent in the Temple of Hathor of Seti I. Much of the reconstruction is today deteriorating, with wall and stair collapses occurring in many of the buildings. None of the original floors are visible, being neatly covered over with gravel and sand. Features including column bases, ovens, and receptacles sunk into the ground, which appear in the plans of Jourdain and Robichon, have either vanished or are located in a different place. Without re-excavating some of the buildings, features called *fosse* or *silo* by Bruyère, which are now partially filled with sand and debris, cannot be re-assessed properly in comparison with the recent excavations at the Workmen's Village at El Amarna. Very little of the original plaster and wall paintings mentioned in the reports survives. However, I was able to obtain useful information which may be compared with that from Amarna.

Besides reviewing the buildings in their natural setting, the relevant reports and plans have also been consulted. Unfortunately, these contain discrepancies. In some cases, the plans do not match the report, or the plans are not consistent with each other. This will be pointed out where appropriate. Detailed measurements were not provided; most of those given here are my own, and are all taken from the interior. When Bruyère's measurements are quoted, these will be identified accordingly.

THE CHAPELS AT DEIR EL MEDINA

The first in the series to be discussed are those buildings lying west and southwest of the main temple (figs 17, 18, 19, 20). These are the chapels identified by Bruyère as *Chapelles Votives* and which he identified by C.V. plus a number or a number alone. For clarity, all of this group will be prefixed with C.V. plus the relevant number where given in the report.

The Chapels West and Southwest of the Main Temple

C.V. 1 (fig. 17)

This chapel lay southwest of the main enclosure wall, to which its long axis was parallel.[6] The sanctuary lay to the northwest. The chapel was situated on the level valley floor just before the escarpment to the sheer cliffs rising to the west.

The plan included a forecourt, outer and inner halls, a pronaos and sanctuary, and a side annexe. The length of the building, inclusive of the forecourt, was approximately 19.15 m. The average brick size was 33 × 15 × 9 cm. The forecourt had two entrances to the north, one to the south and possibly one to the east. Little of this part of the wall is visible and the plan shows a ragged aperture which may not have been an entrance. On the north side near the entry was a *zir* emplacement.

The outer hall was reduced in size to that of the inner hall and appears to form almost an antechamber to the latter. The inner hall had two benches set against the north and south walls. That to the north was 39 cm. deep, 30 cm. high and 3.03 m. long, whilst the southern one was 36 cm. deep and 1.65 m. long. According to Jourdain's plan, twelve limestone seats were originally sunk into the benches, seven to the north and five to the south. Bruyère stated that there must have been fourteen: eight to the north and six to the south. Some of these seats may be those now lodged in the Turin museum, which are inscribed in ink or engraved with the names and details of workers from the village, of which more will be said in Chapter 5. Of the three that remain, none are inscribed.

Beyond the inner hall were the pronaos and sanctuary. The pronaos was 4.40 × 2.00 m. Its entrance wall was a single course of mudbrick divided by a doorway consisting of two piers and a step. Fragments of mud plaster with gypsum coating are still present. The sanctuary had three niches and benches set against the back walls. Their measurements averaged 0.61 × 1.13 m. The partition walls of the shrines were a single course of brick ending in finials. The thresholds were of brick.

Abutting the south or left side of the chapel was an annexe which could be entered by the forecourt, outer and inner hall, and sanctuary. The width of the doorways averaged between 61 and 63 cm. What appears to be a blocked entrance, 66 cm. wide, is visible in the south wall of the pronaos. The annexe was divided into three compartments with interconnecting doors. Tomb shaft no. 1240 was adjacent to the south wall of the dependency, and its association with C.V. 1 is not proved. Questions concerning this are reserved for Chapter 5.

C.V. 2 (fig. 17)

This chapel lay to the southwest of C.V. 1,[7] with its sanctuary to the west. Only the shell of the building survives, but the plan includes an irregularly-shaped forecourt, outer and inner halls, a pronaos and sanctuary.

A series of terraces and stairs led to the forecourt. In the outer hall was a rectangular pit or fosse. These features could be the remains of foundations from earlier houses or chapels dating to the Eighteenth Dynasty. Bonnet and Valbelle conducted excavations on houses south of this chapel which dated to Tuthmosis I.[8]

The inner hall had two jar emplacements near the north wall. No benches appeared in either of the two halls. The pronaos was entered by four steps set between balustrades with convex coping. It was 1.78 m. wide, and today is level with the sanctuary. At its southern end was a sunken rectangular area. The sanctuary was divided asymmetrically into a large and small compartment.

C.V. 1211 (fig. 18a)

Bruyère also named this chapel *Chapelle à Trois Loges*.[9] It was situated apart from the other chapels of this group and with the tomb chapels on the lower slopes of the western cliff face. Its sanctuary was oriented to the east, and the plan consisted of a forecourt, inner hall, pronaos and sanctuary.

The forecourt was approached from a passage lying behind the houses of the village and before a row of tomb chapels. A group of five *zir* emplacements were situated near the entrance and in the court itself. The court was entered by a flight of stairs. Tomb shaft 1272 was sunk into the centre of the court, beyond which lay the inner hall or antechamber. No benches were present. A rectangular pit was sunk into the floor to the south.

Beyond the pronaos were three symmetrical niches, all of which, including the pronaos, had vaulted ceilings. The walls were mud and gypsum plastered. Various gods and other subject matter were depicted in simple red lines in the niches. On the north wall of the northern niche was the sun god Re surmounted by the sun disk encircled by the serpent. On the opposite wall were the remains of the head of a man. The central niche showed the deceased and the bark of Soker, coupled with a representation of five bed legs in the shape of bulls' feet and a headrest. Only the traces of the figure of a man remained in the southern niche.

The partition wall between the central and southern niche had a large aperture, which Bruyère described as a low rectangular door.[10] Today, it appears to be more the work of vandals than as part of the original plan.

A rectangular enclosure abutted the southern wall of the chapel and contained two shafts. Bruyère suggested that it may have been quarters for lodging priests.[11] This will be discussed more fully in Chapter 5.

C.V. (fig. 18b)

No number was assigned to this structure by Bruyère.[12] It was situated northeast of C.V. 1211 and west of C.V. 2. The sanctuary lay to the west. Nothing, apart from an outline of its plan in brick and stone, remains. It consisted of an irregularly-shaped forecourt, into which was sunk tomb shaft 1260, and a nearly square antechamber set before a pronaos and shrine. The shrine may have been tripartite, and in its northeastern corner was a rectangular depression.

What appear to be dependencies to this chapel abutted it to the north and to the east. These consist of an irregularly-shaped enclosure adjoining two large shafts called *silos*, followed to the east by three small compartments also called *silos*, near tomb shafts 1257-59.

C.V. 1212 (fig. 19)

This chapel is also named *Chapelle du Dessinateur*.[13] The plan was simple, incorporating one court, a pronaos and sanctuary. The sanctuary lay to the west. The whole building abutted the southern end of C.V. 1213. The hall, which may have been an unroofed forecourt, had doorways on the south and north walls leading to C.V. 1213. It was 3.82 m. long with a bench (47 cm. deep × 38 cm. high and 2.00 m. long) set against the south wall. The pronaos was defined by a wall of a single course of brick 0.77 × 3.40 m. The sanctuary consisted of a bench set against the back wall and rising in four tiers. A niche was set into its central axis.

C.V. 1213 (fig. 19)

Known also as *Chapelle du Djebel*, it lay on a north to south axis.[14] Access to the chapel was through the court of C.V. 1212, which led to the outer hall. Beyond was the inner hall, pronaos and sanctuary.

The outer hall was 5.70 m. wide × 4.35 m. long. Benches ran along the eastern, western and most of the southern walls. The average dimension was 49 cm. deep and 38 cm. high. Two column bases now in the hall do not appear on the plan of Jourdain and Robichon. These may have been removed from the entrance to the pronaos, where remains of pillars were reported. Two large jars were aligned on either side of the north wall of the inner hall. No benches appear in the inner hall. A flight of four steps set between piers led to the pronaos, which was defined by screen walls abutting the respective piers.

A bench was set against the back wall of the sanctuary, measuring 2.90 m. long × 1.05 m. wide × 0.65 m. high. A partition wall of a single course of bricks divided the bench, forming a cubicle 0.95 m. long. Bruyère suggested that the shrine may have once been tripartite. Although the evidence is not apparent today, it is possible, since the shrine can easily accommodate three niches 95 cm. in width. Where the central niche would have been situated were the remains of some limestone facing against the back wall, which Bruyère suggested could have been the remains of a stela. The sanctuary was whitewashed.

The chapel, whose sanctuary was cut into the gebel behind, lay on a direct axis to a hypogeum of two chambers numbered 1189. No mummies were found in its chambers. It was reached by a passage leading off the outer hall of C.V. 1213 and east of the outer wall of the inner hall and sanctuary. This continued around the rear of the naos until it joined the stairs leading to the subterranean chambers. Associated with this chapel were limestone fragments of libation vases and basins; one bore the cartouche of Amenhotep I.

C.V. 1215 (fig. 19)

Its long axis was oriented north to south, and it consisted of a single elongated hall and sanctuary.[15] The outer hall, or possibly the forecourt, was 10.23 m. long × 3.84 m. wide. Bruyère's measurements for this area were 8.20 m. long × 8.80 m. wide. These neither correspond with the shape of the enclosure on the site nor with the plans of Jourdain and Robichon. Within the hall was a rectangular pit of mudbrick with traces of gypsum that also coated the bottom, now filled with debris. The dimensions are today 1.95 × 1.15 m., with an original depth provided by Bruyère of 1.75 m. The hall was without benches. A small buttress projected from the eastern wall.

The sanctuary was provided with a four-tiered bench, before which was a low platform upon which had once been a jar. The bench contained a single niche set into it, like C.V. 1212. Fragments of paintings, including ceiling decorations, came from this area.

C.V. 1216 (fig. 19)

On the same axis as C.V. 1215, it consisted of one hall, a pronaos and sanctuary.[16] The hall was 5.65 m. long × 4.45 m. wide, with a bench set against most of its eastern wall. Two low, square, limestone platforms were set in either corner of the southern wall. Bruyère suggested that these may have been part of two small chambers incorporated into two pylons. The chapel may have had pylons, but the bench to the southeast was set between the outer wall of the hall and the platform, which seems to rule out the practicability of a chamber. Two jar emplacements appeared in the northeast of the hall. The pronaos was entered by a flight of four steps, flanked at the top by a column on either side. The corridor of the pronaos was sectioned off, creating a central passage. Two rectangular receptacles were sunk into the floor of the corridor to the east and to the west. The former, which is no longer visible, is reported to have been constructed of brick and plastered with gypsum.

Stela fragments with representations of Thoth and Seshat came from this chapel.

C.V. 1190 (fig. 19)

The chapel lay on an east-west axis with a plan consisting of a small court, inner hall, pronaos and sanctuary.[17]

An L-shaped passage fronted the court or outer hall, in the northwest corner of which was a jar emplacement. Beyond was the inner hall with benches set against its north and south walls. These averaged 58 cm. in width and 42 cm. in height. In the doorway to the pronaos was a limestone threshold, in which was sunk a pivot hole and architrave grooves, indicating that a single panel door had been used here. At the north end of the corridor of the pronaos were stairs leading to a hypogeum. The sanctuary was tripartite. Before the central shrine was a flight of four steps between a pair of level balustrades, instead of the usual sloping rail with a return. A bench spanned the back wall of the shrine. No benches appeared in the southern or northern shrines, the latter of which projected in an L-shape beyond the depth of the other two. Fragments of stelae, door jambs, and wooden ex-votos came from this chapel.

Adjoining the southern wall of C.V. 1190 was an enclosure entered from the east, numbered 1217 by Bruyère. It consisted of a T-shaped basin with a rectangular depression or receptacle lying west of it. North of the basin were the remains of a brick promontory abutting the chapel wall. C.V. 1190 is the only known chapel to have a dependency containing a T-shaped basin sunk into the floor.

Another dependency of C.V. 1190, numbered 1218, lay to the east of the L-shaped passage off the forecourt. This was an enclosure containing a small cubicle to the northeast and a bench set in the southwest corner. Before the bench was a feature called an oven by Bruyère, but which, according to the plans, resembles more the outline of a hearth.[18] This structure is no longer present.

C.V. 1221 (fig. 19)

The chapel was situated half way up the escarpment on an east-west axis, and consisted of an outer hall, pronaos and sanctuary.[19] A bench, no longer present, was set against the north wall of the outer hall.

The pronaos was marked off by two screen walls containing four features resembling small, rectangular receptacles sunk into the masonry. The partition wall of the one to the north is no longer present. These were mud plastered and whitewashed and may have been ablution basins. The compartmental dimensions of the trough to the south were 60 × 40 × 15 cm.

A bench of four tiers was set against the sanctuary wall. An incurving, stepped niche was sunk into the central axis of the wall. In the northwest corner, another niche on a level with the summit of the bench was cut into the cliff face. What may have been dependencies, or another chapel, abutted the north wall of C.V. 1221. These were divided into three contiguous enclosures, with a small socle abutting the back wall of the westernmost chamber.

C.V. 1193 (fig. 19)

The chapel was situated on the same terrace near C.V. 1221 and was oriented north-north-east. It consisted of a simple plan of an antechamber and sanctuary.[20] The sanctuary may have been tripartite, but nothing remains of the partition wall that surmounted the bench, before which was a low platform, shown on the plan. Remnants of a wall decoration depicting a deity appeared on the west wall. To the rear of the sanctuary was an irregular enclosure, the access to which is not readily apparent. To the east of the chapel were a series of steps leading to an upper terrace and a hypogeum (numbered 1194) on the same axis as C.V. 1193, with which it may be associated.

C.V. 1198 (fig. 19)

The chapel lay on an upper terrace above and east of C.V. 1193.[21] It was aligned on a north-south axis, with little surviving of its simple plan of forecourt, inner hall, and two rock-cut shrines. The plans of 1929 and 1931-32 of this chapel are inconsistent. The earlier plans showed two irregularly shaped shrines, with a tiered bench in the westernmost shrine. The inner hall was vaulted, and to the east a passage led to a speos, numbered 1199. To the west of the sanctuary was a brick-lined chamber with a vaulted ceiling. The later plans showed no vaults, and the two rock-cut shrines were shown as nearly rectangular without benches. The once-rounded shrine to the east was now brick-lined, and the corridor to the east no longer led to the speos. The chapel is in a ruinous state today, and it is therefore difficult to determine which plan is correct.

C.V. 1222 (fig. 20)

The chapel lay on the same terrace as C.V. 1198 and was on an east-west axis.[22] It comprised outer and inner halls, a pronaos and sanctuary. It was approximately 11 m. long and 6.80 m. wide. The main entrance to the outer hall was in the east, and a second entrance was to the south. The eastern entrance may have had pylons, but the irregularity of dimensions and layout seem to preclude this suggestion. The one to the south contained a small compartment and was shorter than the pylon to the north. Access to the southern entrance was by means of stairs leading to a small enclosure. Directly within the hall in the southeast corner was a jar emplacement. Of two column bases axially aligned, only one remains, in the southwest corner of the hall. The hall was vaulted and Bruyère quoted measurements of 5.50 m. long × 4 m. wide. Traces of wall decoration still remain on the north wall.

The inner hall was also provided with a jar in the northeast corner. A rectangular shaft, cut through the floor and covered by a stone slab, connected with a subterranean chamber which may once have been a tomb. This was numbered 1244. Neither the outer nor the inner halls possessed benches. The sanctuary was divided symmetrically into three niches. The southern walls to the inner hall and the sanctuary were reinforced with several courses of brick. The former had three, and the latter four.

An enclosure, abutting the north wall of the chapel and serving as a court to tomb 215, was entered from the southeast off the irregularly shaped walk-way that served both C.V. 1222 and C.V. 1223.

C.V. 1223 (fig. 20)

On the same terrace east of C.V. 1222 was situated C.V. 1223 on a north-south axis.[23] Little survives of its plan of an outer hall, once vaulted, pronaos and sanctuary.

A flight of five steps, not indicated on the plan, led from the pronaos to the tripartite sanctuary. Benches were set against their back walls. The average depth of the shrines was 1.24 m., and the benches were between 55-63 cm. deep and 23-25 cm. high. The central shrine was 86 cm. wide, that to the west was 79 cm. wide, and that to the east was 64 cm. Traces of wall decoration depicting a seated goddess, probably before the deceased were on the west wall. A sycamore was shown on the back wall. The painting was executed in crude red outlines on a gypsum background. The interior of the figure was shown in yellow ochre.

Chapel Northeast of the Village Enclosure Wall (not numbered; fig. 21a)

The chapel abutted the northeast corner of the village enclosure wall, and was aligned on a north-north-west to south-south-east axis.[24] The plan consisted of a single, long hall with a sanctuary oriented to the west.

The building, which is no longer visible, was reported to be 10 m. long by 3.50 m. wide. Benches were set against the north and south walls. The north bench in the plan showed eight and a half seats against Bruyère's report of seven. A column base was set on the central axis near the sanctuary. Two low screen walls, 75 cm. high and 1.25 m. long, separated the pronaos from the hall. These had a cavetto cornice and both were decorated with scenes of a man in a kilt leading a bull. The sanctuary consisted of a single naos set upon a platform. Wall decorations on the back wall to the left of the naos depicted a mummiform god standing on a blue socle before a cortège.

The Chapels Within the Enclosure Wall of the Main Temple

These were designated *Chapelle* or *Chapelles des Confrèries*. These included a group of four contiguous chapels situated on the southern side of the main temple. In addition to these chapels, there was one (originally excavated by Baraize) in the interior of the northwest corner of the enclosure wall to the temple. The excavation of this was completed by Bruyère who labelled it *Chapelle E* (fig. 23.2).[25]

During the Coptic period, when the temple area was used as a monastery, the chapels south of the temple underwent numerous alterations, some of which affected the basic plan of the structures.

Chapelle 1 (fig. 21b)

The main axis of the chapel was aligned northwest-southeast.[26] Little of the plan of the hall, pronaos and sanctuary survives. The hall originally had benches and columns, all of which have vanished, and contained a rectangular stone trough. A ramp set off with pillars joining screen walls led to the pronaos, which originally abutted the southern wall of the main temple. Later, a door connecting with the temple was set into the north wall of the pronaos.

Originally, the sanctuary was tripartite with vaulted ceilings. Only two niches remain today. The southern niche contained a bench 57 cm. wide × 1.10 m. long and 72 cm. high. Vestiges of a dado on the southern wall, 89 cm. from the ground, consisted of alternating bands of yellow ochre, turquoise, yellow ochre, and black. The bench was no longer present in the central niche.

Chapelle 2 (fig. 21b)

On a north-north-west to south-south-east axis, this chapel consisted of outer and inner halls, pronaos and sanctuary, and enclosure.[27] The outer hall, no longer visible, had benches on the north and south walls and columns. A flight of steps led to the inner hall in which was a rectangular pit 2.37 × 1.03 m., containing a partition dividing it unequally. The pit, called a crypt by Bruyère, was cut into the rock, and was brick lined and plastered. Today it is filled with debris.

The pronaos was entered between two pillars abutting screen walls and was vaulted. The sanctuary underwent three phases, but appears to have always been tripartite. The wall decoration, which may have come from the central niche of the first phase, bore painted cartouches of Tuthmosis III between recumbent sphinxes superimposed on a wall painting of a round-topped stela. A winged solar disc was depicted on the summit of the stela. During the second phase, the colours were altered on the painting. In the third stage, the southern niche became less deep than the central and northern shrines. The back wall of the central shrine preserved the wall decoration from the second phase, and showed a king wearing the *nemes* headcloth offering two jars of wine to a seated god with blue flesh. Behind the god was another king and also a queen.

There were benches in the central and southern niches. The first was 63 cm. high. All the naoi were vaulted, and during the Coptic period the northern niche became a magazine.

An enclosure abutted the southern wall of the inner and outer halls. What appears to be a blocked door led from the enclosure into the inner hall; it was 78 cm. wide. Another blocked entrance, 97 cm. wide, was contained in the southern wall of the enclosure leading into *Chapelle 3*.

Chapelle 3 (fig. 21b)

Oriented northwest-southeast, the plan consisted of an inner hall, pronaos and sanctuary.[28] The building had two phases. Benches, of which little survive, were set against the north and south walls of the hall, which had two columns axially placed. Two pillars joining screen walls defined the pronaos. A platform lay before the sanctuary inside the pronaos. In its first stage, it contained only one naos, which was vaulted. In its second phase, the sanctuary became tripartite, and had a flat ceiling. It appears not to have had wall decorations, being only whitewashed. Benches were set against the back walls of each niche. These were 42 cm. high and between 42-50 cm. deep. Slots were visible in the mudbrick thresholds to each shrine, indicating the presence of architraves.

The sanctuary was cut into the rock behind at an oblique angle. Behind it was a narrow corridor, which continued from the rear to the north side of the sanctuary. To the south of the pronaos was a flight of stairs leading to the rock terrace above. A narrow annexe abutting the south wall of the chapel was entered by a doorway in the wall of the inner hall.

Chapelle 4 (fig. 21b)

The chapel had an outer and inner hall, pronaos and sanctuary, and was on a northwest-southeast axis.[29] Little remains of the outer hall, which had a bench against its southern wall. Two piers set off the entrance to the inner hall and pronaos. The pronaos, into which the shrine projected, was of the same dimensions as the inner hall: 5.92 m. wide × 2.31 m. long. It was marked off from the latter area by two column bases joining partition walls. A platform, 58 cm. high, projected from the shrine, which was set off by a whitewashed bench, now vanished.

The sanctuary consisted of a single naos faced with limestone. It had an arched door 1.08 m. high × 1.07 m. wide. It may have been surmounted by a cavetto cornice and torus moulding. The back wall of the niche was of gypsum-plastered brick. Traces of two squatting figures with upraised arms appeared on either side of the doorway. Dependencies, consisting of a series of enclosures called *silos* by the excavator, lay behind the sanctuary; abutting the north wall of the chapel was another annexe containing an oven.

Chapelle E (fig. 23.2)

The chapel is no longer visible. It lay on an east-west axis and was described as 'two chapels' by Baraize.[30] It was, in fact, a single chapel, the 'two chapels' composing part of the tripartite shrine. The chapel was damaged by the temple enclosure wall, which passed through it.[31] It consisted of a forecourt, inner hall, pronaos and sanctuary. Part of its northern wall was shared by chapels outside the northern enclosure wall. The forecourt was trapezoidal and entered by two steps. The inner hall was provided with a bench on its western and southern walls. Two steps led to the pronaos. The central shrine, which was the widest, was also entered by a short flight of stairs.

Chapelle E and Chapelle 2 have been dated to the Eighteenth Dynasty. Porter and Moss provided this date for the first chapel.[32] However, Baraize did not date this chapel in his report.[33] According to Plan I (*Rapport* 1935-1940, fasc. I), the chapel was dated to the Ramesside period, and was grouped with the chapels, also of that date, at the northwest angle of the enclosure wall. The earlier date was based upon the discovery by Baraize of a small limestone statue of Tuthmosis III kneeling with jars[34] near the west wall and northwest corner of the enclosure wall of the main temple. However, this is an unreliable method of dating, since such objects could have survived in use into a later period.

Similarly, Bruyère tentatively placed Chapelle 2 in the Eighteenth Dynasty because of wall paintings showing cartouches bearing the name of Tuthmosis III, *Men Kheper Re*. In addition, he suggested that the statue of Tuthmosis III may have come from this chapel because of the presence of the cartouches.[35] One of the functions of this chapel was the serving of the cult of this king, which more than likely was carried on long after his death, making an early date questionable. Bell also rejected an Eighteenth Dynasty date for this chapel.[36] Problems concerning the ancestor cult are reserved for Chapter 5.

The Chapels East of the Enclosure Wall of the Main Temple

The third group of cult structures to be discussed in this series are two buildings, one of which Bruyère called a temple and the other a chapel. These lay east of the enclosure wall of the main temple on the lower slopes of Qurnet Mura'i.

The Small Ramesside Chapel (fig. 22a)

The building was situated opposite the southeast corner of the enclosure wall and was on a southeast-northwest axis.[37] The chapel was later transformed into a Christian church. It was cut into the cliff behind, and consisted of a hall, pronaos and sanctuary. The hall, entered by a flight of steps, contained a bench along its southern wall, which was 1.90 m. long × 38 cm. deep and 25 cm. high. Another bench had once been set against the northern wall.

A staircase of four steps with a balustrade ascended to the pronaos, which was set off by two axially placed pillars. The tripartite sanctuary was provided with benches in each of its niches. The central shrine had partition walls ending in columns projecting beyond the side niches into the pronaos towards the west. Traces of wall decoration were preserved on the northern wall of the sanctuary.

The Temple of Amun of Ramesses II (fig. 22b)

The temple was on a southeast-northwest axis and consisted of a forecourt, outer and inner halls, pronaos and sanctuary.[38] Abutting its northern wall was an annexe that served as a chapel.[39] A series of steps led to the forecourt of the temple, which was faced with pylons. The floor of the court was paved. Beyond lay two limestone steps before the entrance to the outer hall. In its first stage, this chamber was the forecourt to the temple before it became enlarged. Later, it became an outer hall with benches on the north and south walls with five seats to the north and seven seats to the south. Two columns were axially placed in the centre of the hall. Neither the benches nor the columns are present today. Bruyère did not mention specifically that benches were present in this hall, but they were included in the plans. The hall was 6.40 m. wide and 5.20 m. long, and was paved.

Steps, in the form of tiers spanning the width of the outer hall, lay before the doorway into the inner hall. A limestone threshold, consisting of two unequally cut slabs, showed architrave grooves and a pivot hole to the right, suggesting a single panel door to the inner hall. The southern partition wall, dividing the inner hall from the outer, had a niche that may once have accommodated a stela. The hall was vaulted and had a paved floor.

A flight of six steps, running between balustrades with rounded coping and ending in returns, led to the pronaos. At the summit of the steps were columns axially placed on either side and disengaged. No screen walls were present. Two small brick buttresses projected from the north and south walls of the pronaos on the same axis as the columns. A surround in a *serekh* pattern had once been applied to the base of the walls.[40] Traces of a kneeling man were still visible on the southern wall.

The sanctuary was reported to have been badly destroyed. It was tripartite and may have had benches, although traces of them could not be found. The overall dimensions for the

The sanctuary was reported to have been badly destroyed. It was tripartite and may have had benches, although traces of them could not be found. The overall dimensions for the shrines were 2.00 m. deep by 1.90 m. wide. A small side chapel, which had at least two phases, abutted the north side of the temple and consisted of an outer and inner hall, and a sanctuary with a single naos. It, too, was in a ruinous state. At first, the entrance to the chapel was in the northern wall of the outer hall of the main building. Later, the wall became solid with the entrance to the chapel in the west. This consisted of a flight of stairs, which today number ten steps. A small step, beside which was a rectangular brick compartment, led to the inner hall or pronaos. Many fragments of painted wall plaster came from the chapel, as well as a statue of the Vizier Panehesi.[41]

The Chapels North of the Enclosure Wall of the Main Temple

The fourth and last group of chapels at Deir el Medina lay to the north of the enclosure wall of the main temple, and cover the rising escarpment to the cliffs behind. This group was called *Chapelle* and *Chapelle Religieuse*.

The Chapel of Hathor of Seti I (fig. 23.1)

The chapel lay on a north-north-west to south-south-east axis and consisted of a forecourt, outer and inner halls, pronaos and sanctuary, and a left annexe and dependencies.[42] The forecourt was entered from the southeast over a ramp with a central slide flanked on either side by ten steps. The plans are inconsistent here. One showed a centre slide with twelve steps to the south and thirteen to the north.[43] Another presented the ramp with a central slide and fourteen steps on either side,[44] and a further plan showed the centre slide with fourteen steps on the north and thirteen to the south.[45] Finally, another plan depicted the ramp without a slide, and fifteen steps, whereas Bruyère reported the presence of a slide.[46]

The forecourt was paved in limestone. It had two tomb shafts, one of which existed prior to the construction of the chapel and the other dated to the Ramesside period. They were numbered 1434b and 1435 respectively. A flight of five steps led from the forecourt into the outer hall. A bench with five seats was set against the southern wall. Bruyère suggested that another bench with seven seats was positioned against the northern wall. The dimensions of the existing bench is 3.45 m. long × 35 cm. wide and 49 cm. high. Two column bases were aligned on either side of the central axis. The floor was paved in limestone.

Two steps led from the outer hall into the inner, hypostyle hall. A rectangular limestone basin, no longer present, was sunk into the floor at an angle to the columns. There were originally two limestone altars near the staircase to the west of the hall. Fragments of wall painting also came from this part of the chapel. A flight of seven steps ascended to the pronaos between balustrades with rounded coping and ended in returns. Bruyère reported only five steps, which appear in a deteriorated state in photographs.[47] However, the same flight of stairs were shown in another photograph reconstructed with seven steps and in pristine condition.[48] The plans appear to show the area after restoration.[49] The seven steps are present today.

The pronaos was narrow and without architectural ornament, opening directly into the tripartite sanctuary. Originally, the shrines were symmetrical; during the Ptolemaic period, the central and northern shrines were altered. The southern shrine was 2.00 m. wide × 2.50 m. long. Abutting the southern wall of the chapel was an annexe divided into two sections. The first was entered by a door in the outer hall and down two steps. Two ovens were set against the southeast wall of the chamber with diameters averaging 37-40 cm. A small rectangular platform of limestone slabs ran against the southern wall. It is not clear whether this could be the remains of paving.

Adjacent and lying to the west of this chamber was another which was entered from the inner hall. The entrance consisted of a stair-well at a lower level than the inner hall floor. Unlike its neighbour, this chamber was a small side chapel consisting of an antechamber procession of six men and six women carrying offerings in the direction of the shrine. The figures were in yellow ochre and outlined in red lines on a gypsum background. The north side of the chapel abutted a series of at least three large enclosures.

Chapelle A (fig. 23.3)

Oriented on a northeast-southwest axis, the chapel consisted of a large hall with a single naos.[51] A wall, forming a right angle, joined the entrance of the chapel and the rear wall of the Chapel of Hathor. The hall was entered by a doorway in the northeast corner. At the opposite end of the hall were two columns placed before the naos, which was flanked by two small whitewashed niches. The columns were in the form of papyrus and carried the name of Khons, son of Sennedjem. Fragments of decorated wall plaster and a head of the goddess Taweret also came from the chapel.

Chapelle B (fig. 23.4)

Oriented west-north-west to east-south-east, it included a forecourt, outer and inner halls, sanctuary, and left annexe, and lay north and west of Chapelle A.[52] The forecourt was 3.29 m. wide × 3.60 m. long; at one time it accommodated three jars of different sizes. The outer hall beyond the court was 4.92 m. wide × 4.78 m. long, and had benches set against its southern, eastern and part of its northern walls. Against the northeastern wall was a low limestone platform. A doorway in the southwestern corner led to an annexe partitioned into two sections.

The inner hall was 2.81 m. wide × 2.65 m. long, and within it were small projecting piers set on either side of the doorway. These were 56 cm. wide and 54 cm. high. Tomb shaft 1436 was adjacent to the northern wall. Two steps led from the inner hall to the small sanctuary, which contained a single niche and a bench around all its walls. The bench averaged 38-42 cm. wide and 49 cm. high. A limestone threshold with a pivot hole indicated that the sanctuary once had a door. A stela once lined the back wall of the niche. This may have been the stela of the foreman Amennakht, who was shown seated holding two *w3dt* signs.[53]

Chapelle C (fig. 23.5)

The chapel was on an east-west axis and shared its southern wall with Chapelle D, both of which lay the furthest up the escarpment and north of the northwest angle of the main enclosure wall.[54] The building consisted of a forecourt or outer hall, an inner hall, pronaos and sanctuary. The building underwent numerous alterations. The outer hall was approached by two steps and was 4.44 m. wide × 3.80 m. long with a bench against its north wall. One step led into the inner hall, which was 4.00 m. long × 1.90 m. wide.

Two pillars, abutting walls a single course of brick thick, divided the pronaos from the inner hall. Projecting from the northern pillar was a wall that formed part of the asymmetrical sanctuary. It consisted of central and southern niches of nearly equal size, and an **L**-shaped niche or compartment to the north. Before the two former niches was a platform.

Chapelle D (fig. 23.6)

The chapel, whose location has been discussed above, was on the same axis as Chapelle C.[55] It was cut into the steep cliffs and was dedicated to Amenhotep I and Ahmose Nefertari. Little remains of the structure, which consisted of an outer and inner hall, pronaos and shrine.

The outer hall, or possibly forecourt, was entered from the east by a flight of stairs. A doorway in the northwestern corner of the court led into the inner hall, beyond which was the pronaos. This was delineated by pillars surmounted by columns abutting low walls. Two steps led into the pronaos which had been decorated with a wall-surround of red, white and black horizontal bands. Nothing remains of the royal couple, to whom the chapel is dedicated, who were shown seated on a throne decorated with the *sm3-t3wy*.[56]

Numerous statues came from this chapel:[57] a seated statue of Amenhotep I and a wooden statuette of Ahmose Nefertari found by Drovetti; a wooden statuette of Ahmose Nefertari and a seated double statue of Pendua and his wife Nefertari found by Schiaparelli; a wall fragment with the head of Mut and a stela fragment found by Bruyère. Also included in this group, as a result of Bruyère's report, is the kneeling statue of Tuthmosis III found by Baraize (see above, p. 47).

Chapelle F (fig. 23.7)

This chapel and Chapelle G were called *Chapelles Religieuses* by Bruyère. The chapel was on an east-west axis, and abutted the north wall of Chapelle B.[58] It consisted of an outer and inner hall and pronaos. At the time of excavation, the sanctuary was no longer surviving.

The chapel was approached from the southeast by a double staircase of three steps each. These led to two terraces. From the second terrace, two elongated steps, followed by a flight of stairs with four steps set between the usual balustrade, led to the outer hall. This area was 4.20 m. wide × 4.75 m. long and had pylons before its entrance. According to Bruyère, the pylons were 85 cm. thick. An engaged brick pillar abutted the centre of the southern wall and supported at one time a main beam of the roof. A limestone staircase leading into the inner halls seems to have had six steps originally,[59] but the plans and photograph (after reconstruction) show only five.[60]

A bench 3.25 m. long, 34 cm. wide and 35 cm. high abutted the south wall. This, in turn, was adjacent to a limestone platform in the southeast corner, which was 1.64 m. × 88 cm. × 26 cm. high. On the north wall the bench was 1.37 m. long × 38 cm. wide × 46 cm. high.[61]

A double stairway with three steps to the south and two to the north led to the pronaos. This part of the chapel was delineated by brick piers rather than walls. Two piers abutted the north and south walls of the pronaos and one pier marked the centre. The piers measured (from south to north) 1.23 m. × 1.01 m., 65 cm. × 50 cm., and 1.25 m. × 62 cm. There were troughs in the two outermost piers. Judging by the foregoing arrangement of the pronaos, it probably had two principal shrines, with a compartment to the south.

This chapel is the only instance where roofing material was mentioned in any detail by the excavator. The nature of the roofing material indicates that the roofs of the two halls were flat. Beams, poles and coarse grass were used together with mud mortar. The overall thickness of the roof was 25 cm. Lighting was provided by apertures in the ceiling.[62]

Chapelle G (fig. 23.8)

This chapel lay north of Chapelle F and was on a west-north-west to east-south-east axis.[63] It is dated to the Ramesside period, and consisted of an approach ramp, outer and inner halls, two side chambers contained within the structure, a pronaos and sanctuary. A ramp of undressed stone set between brick balustrades, and with overall measurements of 5.50 m. long × 2.75 m. wide, led to the outer hall or court. The court had pylons on either side of its entrance; the southern pylon was 73 cm. thick, the one to the north was 76 cm. thick. They were plastered and whitewashed. The court was 5.43 m. wide × 5.47 m. long and was built over an earlier tomb shaft.[64]

Pylons also framed the entrance to the inner hall. A limestone threshold in the entrance had two pivot holes and grooves for architraves, indicating that a double door served this part of the building. The inner hall had three phases of building. In the third phase it became hypostyle, with two columns and a flat roof. The column bases had a diameter of 70 cm. The floor of the inner hall was of packed earth. The walls were decorated. Part of the design consisted of a floral frieze, which circumscribed the wall in the style of the Ramesside period.

Two small enclosures on the interior of the eastern wall to the inner hall, and on either side of the entrance to it, had dimensions given by Bruyère of 1.85 m. long × 75 cm. wide.

These formed a corridor 1.75 m. long, which had a vaulted roof painted in yellow and red ochre to imitate wood.[65] No benches appeared either in this or the outer hall.

Four limestone steps in the west of the inner hall led to a limestone platform before the sanctuary. On either side of the flight of stairs was a small enclosure. The walls of the sanctuary abutted them from the rear. The sanctuary consisted of a single naos cut into the cliffs behind and measured 3.73 m. long × 2.50 m. wide. The interior rear wall of the niche had a retaining wall 57 cm. thick.

Discussion

Before comparison with the chapels at Amarna is attempted, some grouping of the chapels is needed.

Chapelles Votives

The chapels designated *Chapelle Votive* on the south and southwest side of the temple enclosure wall show distinctions within the group. The overall plans are variable and some chapels resemble small oratories, that is, a structure consisting of a shrine, antechamber and no benches. Others have no resemblance to the basic chapel layout of halls and sanctuaries. The following categorization is based on the presence/absence of benches and association, or lack of it, with a tomb:

1. **Chapels without benches and associated with a tomb, house or dependencies:**
   C.V., C.V. 1193, C.V. 1211 (house probably a dependency).
2. **Chapels without benches and not associated with a tomb:**
   C.V. 2, C.V. 1198, C.V. 1215, C.V. 1222 (association with tomb 215 not proved), C.V. 1223.
3. **Chapels with benches and not associated with a tomb:**
   C.V. 1 (association with the adjacent tomb shaft 1240 not proved), C.V. 1212, C.V. 1221, chapel northeast of village enclosure wall.
4. **Chapels with benches and associated with a tomb:**
   C.V. 1190 (dependencies 1217, 1218), C.V. 1213.

Two of these in my opinion do not fall within the definition of a private chapel (Chapter 2, 23; Chapter 3, 34) used in this text. The first is C.V. 1211. Despite the dependency attached to it, its situation among tomb chapels proper, its association with a tomb, and the iconography contained in the sanctuary, all serve to identify it as a tomb chapel. The second building is the chapel abutting the northeast wall of the village. This bears little resemblance to the usual chapel plan. The only common features are the sanctuary and benches. It seems more like a building for secular use, such as a meeting hall for the village *qnbt*. However, provision was made for a god, in this case probably Min (see above, p. 45; below, Chapter 5, 69).

C.V. 1193 and 1198 appear as small oratories, as does 1223. The chapels having at least one or two halls without benches, (see above, sections 1 and 2) presumably served a cult which did not require an assembled group of people such as in C.V. 1 and Chapel of Hathor of Seti I. The chapels with one or two halls and benches, with or without a tomb association, are those which most closely resemble the Amarna chapels. These are C.V. 1, 1190, 1212, 1213, 1216 and 1221.

The size and overall plan of C.V. 1 can be compared with Chapel 561 at Amarna. The similarities are found in the large forecourt and tripartite shrine with benches. However, the inner hall of C.V. 1 was provided with benches, rather than its outer hall, as in Chapel 561. Both chapels have a side annexe on the left, although no shrine is apparent in that of C.V. 1.

C.V. 1190 shares certain features common to many chapels at Amarna, especially those in the northern and several in the southern group. These consists of a bench in the inner hall like all the chapels in the northern group, a tripartite shrine as found in both areas, and steps leading directly to the sanctuary as in Chapels 552 and 553. The dependencies of C.V. 1190 (1217, 1218) are comparable to Buildings 528 and 534, the former containing a **T**-shaped Basin and oven, and the latter containing an oven. The stairs to the hypogeum in C.V. 1190 are similarly situated in Chapel 555.

The constituent parts of C.V. 1212 are no more than those of a side chapel, but they are placed to the front of C.V. 1213. C.V. 1212 is comparable to the side chapel of Chapel 561, although the arrangement of the shrine is different. However, the idea of an outer chamber to a sanctuary is present in both cases.

The arrangement of the benches, pronaos and sanctuary in C.V. 1213 is similar to Chapel 525. In addition, the pronaos and sanctuary of C.V. 1216 are characteristic of the same area in Chapel 525. The receptacles sunk into the bench and pronaos of C.V. 1216 can be compared with Chapel 551.

Chapels within the Enclosure Wall

The group of chapels within the temple enclosure wall all share similar features in plan and architectural details. The only exception is Chapelle 4, which has a single naos, instead of the usual three. Therefore, the purpose of these chapels must have been the same. They do share many aspects of the Amarna chapels. The arrangement and disposition of the benches is similar to many of the chapels in the southern group at Amarna, where the benches are often found in the outer hall. The pillars and screen walls in these chapels are also a familiar feature at Amarna, such as Chapels 561, 522, 529 and 532. The tripartite shrine has already been cited. Columns are used as a support in the outer hall of Chapelle 3, whereas pillars are used in Chapel 556 and in the inner hall of 554 at Amarna, but the principle is the same. Although the single naos is distinctive in Chapelle 4, with its limestone facing, a uni-cellular shrine is not an unusual feature at Amarna, as seen in Chapels 522, 530 and 570. Chapelle E can be compared with Chapels 532, 535 and 536, with steps into the forecourt, benches in the inner hall, and steps leading to the pronaos and shrine.

Chapels East of the Enclosure Wall

The small Ramesside Chapel and the Temple of Amun of Ramesses II to the east of the enclosure wall are dissimilar in plan, but both underwent various transformations during their period of use. The former is considerably smaller than the temple and has benches, whereas the latter once had benches, but in its final stage, when it became a temple, it dispensed with them. Both buildings are tripartite. The temple has a left annexe, whereas the small chapel has none. Both may, however, have served the same purpose, at least before the temple entered its last phase. The bench in the hall of the small Ramesside chapel is, as already noted, a common feature at Amarna. The stairs to the pronaos with the two columns set back and before the central shrine is similar to Chapel 525, except in the latter case, the columns are on either side of the stairs. The three shrines had benches, as in Amarna chapels.

Before the Temple of Amun of Ramesses II achieved its final phase, it was nearly a replica of Chapel 561. The latter had the same formal lines commencing from its outer hall through to the sanctuary. The forecourt of Chapel 561 was less symmetrical, and the pylons were placed before the outer hall instead of the court and outer hall, as in the temple. Steps led to the outer hall in both buildings, but in the temple the hall was hypostyle. The roof was flat at this point in both buildings. The halls in both had benches on the north and south walls with a doorway in the north wall leading to an annexe housing a side chapel. In the case of Chapel 561, the chapel was situated to the northwest, whereas in the temple it was in the northeast.

The inner hall in both buildings was without benches and had a flight of steps between a balustrade with returns leading to the pronaos. Columns, and not screen walls, delineated the pronaos in the temple, whereas pillars and screen walls appeared at this point in Chapel 561. The same *serekh* pattern appeared as a wall surround in the pronaoi of both buildings.

The sanctuaries were tripartite in each building, with benches presumably present in the three shrines of the temple. In the temple, the floors were paved and the roof was vaulted from the inner hall to the sanctuary, whereas in Chapel 561 the floors were hard-packed mud, and the roof was flat throughout.

In its last phase, the Temple of Amun of Ramesses II adopted the formal style of an Egyptian state temple in miniature. The benches disappeared and the door was blocked from its outer hall to the side chapel, which then received a separate entrance in the west.[66] No building of this nature existed in the Workmen's Village at Amarna.

Chapels North of the Enclosure Wall

The groups of chapels lying to the north of the enclosure wall are not all alike in plan. The Chapel of Hathor of Seti I is the largest among them, consisting of the usual number of halls, tripartite sanctuary, an annexe and dependencies.

Chapelle A, although it had a naos, does not conform to any accepted idea of a cult building, being no more than a hall with two column bases and a niche, and may have had a secular use. Chapelles B, C and D share similar architectural features, but vary in the treatment of the sanctuaries. They probably served the same purpose. Chapelle F still retains benches, but adopted the simplified lines of a small temple. It may have had a use additional to that of Chapelles B, C and D.

Chapelle G, with its symmetrically arranged divisions and clear-cut plan, appears as the connecting link between a chapel and small temple. It emphasized the simplicity of line already present in Chapelle F, but does not quite attain the stature of a small temple on the lines of the Temple of Amun of Ramesses II. Its use may have differed from the other chapels in the northern group.

Only some of these buildings are comparable to the chapels at Amarna. These are the Chapel of Hathor of Seti I, Chapelles B, C and D, and aspects of Chapelle F. The overall plan of the Chapel of Hathor had much in common with Chapel 561. Correspondences are the large unsymmetrical forecourt approached by steps or steps and slide in the Chapel of Hathor, outer halls with benches on the north and south walls, and none in the inner halls. The halls in the Chapel of Hathor were hypostyle. The same style of staircase led to the pronaoi of each chapel, although pillars and screen walls were absent in the Chapel of Hathor. Both buildings had a tripartite sanctuary and a left annexe. The annexe of the Chapel of Hathor was entered from both the outer and inner halls, whereas in Chapel 561, it was entered from the outer hall and from an outer corridor behind the main building. The annexe was divided in both chapels, and the side chapel contained within it was transposed in each building. In the Chapel of Hathor, it abutted the inner hall, and in Chapel 561 it abutted the outer hall and only part of the inner hall. In the former building, the outer hall had ovens, whereas the use of the corresponding section in Chapel 561 is unknown. Chapel 561 had ovens in its dependencies on the other side of the building. Dependencies, although unidentified as to use, were also attached to the other side of the Chapel of Hathor.

The irregularities of the features of Chapelles B, C and D correspond to those in certain chapels at Amarna. This consists in the siting of benches and the plan of the sanctuary. Chapels 521 and 529-532 are comparative examples. The naos of Chapelle B with its surrounding bench is unknown at Amarna, and is the only one of its kind at Deir el Medina. The benches in the inner hall of Chapelle F and the double flight of stairs to the sanctuary represent a simplified plan of the same feature in Chapel 554 at Amarna.

Many of the chapels at Deir el Medina have similar architectural features to those at Amarna. No two at either site are exact replicas. Difference in date may be important here. The Amarna chapels are all of the Eighteenth Dynasty, whereas the chapels at Deir el Medina have been dated to the Nineteenth and Twentieth Dynasties by Bruyère,[67] and the evidence for placing any in the Eighteenth Dynasty has been shown to be weak. As much as 250 years may thus separate the earliest from the latest, and building styles could have changed within that period. Deir el Medina was also occupied for a much longer period than Amarna and, with the progression of time, plans and architectural features used in the Eighteenth Dynasty could have been modified beyond recognition. The same essential building material of mud brick, stone, mortar and gypsum was used, as well as similar roofing constituents. As far as can be determined, the vaulted roof was more in use at Deir el Medina than at Amarna. Most sanctuaries and halls had wall decoration at both sites. Differences in terrain may also have been significant.

The foregoing observations suggest that these buildings probably shared similar purposes at both sites, but those at Deir el Medina, seemingly because of a longer period of time, appear to be more diversified than at Amarna. The next Chapter will attempt to investigate this problem.

Notes

1. Bruyère, *Rapport* (1931-1932), 57. Others who excavated at Deir el Medina are Möller (1913), Gauthier and Leconte Dunoüy (1917-1918), Kuentz (1921). See Bonnet and Valbelle *BIFAO* 75 (1975), 429-430.
2. Bruyère, *Rapport* (1929), 5-7; (1931-1932), 56-57; (1935-1940) fasc. I, 92-96; 99-106; 121-126; (1945-1947), 17-27.
3. Ibid. (1927), pl. I; (1929), 55, no. 16. B. Porter and R.L.B. Moss, *Topographical Bibliography of Ancient Egyptian Hieroglyphic Texts, Reliefs, and Paintings* I, Part II (Oxford, 1964), 689 (hereafter *PM*).
4. Bruyère, *Rapport* (1930), 20; pl. 1.
5. Bruyère, *Rapport* (1929), 37-38, pl. 1.
6. Bruyère, *Rapport* (1931-1932), 56-60.
7. Ibid., 60-61.
8. Bonnet and Valbelle, *BIFAO* 75 (1975), 435-446, pl. LXIII, LXIV; *BIFAO* 76 (1976), 317-328. D. Valbelle, *Les Ouvriers de la Tombe: Deir el Médineh à l'époque Ramesside* (Cairo, 1985), 10, 23-26, 114 (hereafter *Ouvriers*).
9. Bruyère, *Rapport* (1922-1923), 66-67; (1929), 17-18.
10. Ibid. (1929), 18.
11. Ibid.
12. This chapel is not discussed by Bruyère, but only indicated on the plan. Ibid. (1931-1932), pl. 1.
13. Ibid. (1922-1923), 58-59; (1929), 18-19.
14. Ibid. (1922-1923), 59-60; (1929), 19-23.
15. Ibid. (1929), 23-35.
16. Ibid., 35-36.
17. Ibid., 38-44.
18. Ibid. Kemp, *AR* III, 2, fig. 1.1.
19. Bruyère, *Rapport* (1929), 44-45.
20. Ibid. (1929), 45-50.
21. Ibid., 100.
22. Ibid. (1931-1932), 61-62.
23. Ibid., 62-63.
24. Ibid. (1934-1935), II, t. XVI, 36-39.
25. Ibid. (1935-1940), fasc. I, pl. 3; 40-41.
26. Ibid., 92.
27. Ibid., 92-95.
28. Ibid., 95-96.
29. Ibid., 96.
30. Baraize, *ASAE* 13 (1913), 35.
31. Bruyère, *Rapport* (1935-1940), fasc. I, pl. I.
32. PM I², 690.
33. Baraize, *ASAE* 13 (1913), 35. Bierbrier in a personal communication holds to an Eighteenth Dynasty dating for Chapelle E, owing to what is speculated as a foundation deposit, and whose provenance is uncertain. This consists of a bronze axehead inscribed with the cartouche of Tuthmosis III dug by Baraize and rediscovered by V. Davies in the Cairo Museum. An earlier date for this chapel is still questionable owing to the tenuous attribution of the above object.
34. Ibid., 37, pl. X.
35. Bruyère, *Rapport* (1935-1940), fasc. I, 93, fig. 48; fasc. II, 3, No. 43507. Spencer (*Brick Architecture in Ancient Egypt* 66) dates Chapelle D, dedicated to Amenhotep I and Ahmose Nefertari, just outside the northwest angle of the temple enclosure wall, to the Eighteenth Dynasty. This is probably because Bruyère has also suggested a provenance for the Tuthmosis III statue to this chapel (*Rapport* (1935-1940), fasc. I, 105). Spencer may have confused this chapel with Chapelle E found by Baraize, on the other side of the

northwest angle of the enclosure wall, which is dated to the Eighteenth Dynasty by Porter and Moss (see above n. 32). Bruyère has not given an Eighteenth Dynasty date to Chapelle D.

36. Personal communication. Valbelle (*Ouvriers*, 18) also notes the uncertainty of this dating.
37. Bruyère, *Rapport* (1935-1940), fasc. I, 120-121.
38. Ibid., 121-126, pl. 11.
39. This chapel has been listed separately from the temple in PM I², 691, 700, but in this survey it has been grouped with the temple, since it is the earlier phase that is important for comparative reasons.
40. Bruyère, *Rapport* (1935-1940), fasc. I, pl. XXIV.
41. Ibid., 125; 126, fig. 68.
42. Ibid., 99-104.
43. Ibid., pl. 1.
44. Ibid., pl. 3.
45. Ibid. (1948-1951), pl. 1.
46. Ibid. (1935-1940), fasc. I, pl. 10.
47. Ibid., 102-103, figs 54, 55.
48. Ibid., pl. XIV, XV.
49. Ibid., pls 1, 3, 10; (1948-1951), pl. 1.
50. Ibid. (1935-1940), fasc. I, 103.
51. Ibid., 104.
52. Ibid., 105.
53. PM I², 694.
54. Bruyère, *Rapport* (1935-1940), fasc. I, 105.
55. Ibid., 105-106.
56. Bruyère, *Rapport* (1935-1940), fasc. I, pl. XIX, XX.
57. PM I², 693-694.
58. Bruyère, *Rapport* (1945-1947), 17-21.
59. Ibid., 18.
60. Ibid., 19, fig. 7; (1948-1951), pl. 1.
61. Although Bruyère does not mention a bench against the north wall of the inner hall, it appears in a photograph and is still present today. Ibid., 1945-47, 20, fig. 8.
62. Ibid., 18.
63. Ibid., 21-27.
64. Ibid., 26.
65. Ibid., 25.
66. Ibid. (1935-1940), fasc. I, pls 1, 11. Plan 1 shows the later stage.
67. See pages cited from *Rapport* above.

Chapter 5

The Purpose of the Private Chapel

Suggestions as to the purpose of the private chapel have been made by Peet, Bruyère, and Kemp.[1] Their ideas have oscillated between a funerary or religious function, both of which will be argued to be correct. Bruyère has been the most explicit, but Deir el Medina evidence is voluminous compared with that from the chapels at Amarna, which, because of the lack of epigraphic evidence and unresolved architectural features, poses more difficult problems.

From the preceding discussion of the chapels from the point of view of architecture, plans and other details, it appears that the chapels at Amarna had a more limited use than those at Deir el Medina. The purposes of the chapels at Amarna appear to have been several: 1) a chapel dedicated to certain gods, 2) a tomb chapel, 3) a chapel for accommodating an ancestor cult, either royal or private. That some of the chapels may have served for oracular purposes, as in the case of Deir el Medina, cannot be proved. However, it is likely, especially if an ancestor cult was practiced.

The aspects to be examined within the context of each chapel in order to discover its use and function are the distribution of the benches, architectural elements in the sanctuary, annexes and dependencies, wall decoration, and the presence of certain objects. This will be clarified, where relevant, by comparison with Deir el Medina.

THE NEW CHAPELS

The Main Chapel 561

This chapel produced more surviving wall decoration than any other at Amarna.[2] Most of it came from the inner hall, the remainder from the sanctuary and side chapel (Chapter 2, 9-11). Heads of a man and a woman from the north wall of the inner hall originally faced towards the sanctuary. A sistrum may have been held by the lady. The top of the instrument shows no trace of fingers, which suggests that it was probably being shaken. It could also have been depicted as an object in isolation. From the same wall came a fragment of inscription reading *šmꜥ*. The association of the lady and the sistrum suggests a restoration *šmꜥyt*, 'chantress'.[3] If the lady were a chantress, she could have been depicted in the act of propitiating the gods in the sanctuary beyond, or a god who was once depicted before the couple on the north. From the opposite wall of the same hall came fragments of the name Sennufer,[4] which may have belonged to the man already mentioned. Also from this hall were the remnants of the phrase *n kꜣ*.[5]

The remains of two Nekhbet vultures with outstretched wings and a *šn* sign and fan clasped in either claw and a winged solar disc came from the sanctuary.[6] Kemp has sited them behind the windows and door of the pronaos, because of the available wall space.[7]

Although the Nekhbet vultures could have appeared on the inner face of the pronaos wall (Chapter 2, 10), as one does in an antechamber in the Temple at Luxor, it seems iconographically incorrect to have the solar disc placed out of sight on the rear side of a room. I know of no instance where this occurs. The solar disc symbolized Horus the Behdetite and was a protective device emanating power from the deity. It was placed on the right or facing side of a wall over entrances to temples and shrines throughout Egypt.[8] The extent of the solar disc at Amarna covered less width in wall space than the vultures and, in my opinion, should be set over the central shrine in the sanctuary. The vultures could have appeared either on the inside of the pronaos wall or over the two side shrines. The wall may have been higher than Kemp allows, which would permit more space above the shrine for the solar disc. The dimensions of the building materials vary within a structure and an allowance should be made for this by taking the optimal count.[9]

From the objects found in the halls and sanctuary of the chapel, it appears that certain ritual practices had taken place. This included the burning of incense on the portable offering stand in the outer hall and the partaking of food in the same chamber. The principle food consumed over a period of time were fish, duck, cereals, melon, nuts, possibly olives, goat and cattle.[10] Presumably, the participants were seated on the benches on either side of the room (see Chapters 2 and 3).

In the outer hall was a bronze spearhead and the pottery head of a dog (Chapter 2, 9). These items may be connected with the wooden military standard bearing the image of Wepwawet on a stand found before the northern partition wall to the central shrine. If these objects belong to guards, as suggested by Kemp,[11] they could have belonged to a regiment under the aegis of the god Wepwawet, who may have had a function in the chapel. Wepwawet was the tutelary deity of Assiut, which lies a few miles south of Amarna. He also had associations with the necropolis and was known as a saviour god.[12] The guards in question could have been employed to protect the necropolis in the nearby Royal Wadi. The scratch marks concentrated along the side of the niches in the sanctuary could have been made by the spears, as suggested by Kemp, to absorb the potency of the chapel, or alternatively, by the pushing of offering vessels or objects near the god or gods presumably once represented on the shrine walls.

In the inner hall, the 'hearth' on which the hieroglyph *wȝ*[13] is painted, and the gypsum coated paddle from a boat (Chapter 2, 10) (white had a ritual significance and gypsum also coated the pottery offering stands)[14] suggest religious practices associated with the dead or ancestors.

The lower strata of Chapel 561 sometimes contained naturally formed stones that could easily be mistaken for worked objects.[15] These were either perfect spheres, like a marble, or they contained small circular indentations. One was incised with the hieroglyph *wȝ*. Petrie,[16] Keimer[17] and Dreyer[18] have suggested that these stones are simple votive offerings. Petrie suggested that the ordinary man saw them lying in the desert and associated their shape with a particular deity, such as a baboon.[19] In Chapel 561, they may have been offerings to the deity or the ancestors. The question concerning the ancestor cult will be discussed in more detail later.

The side chapel (Chapter 2, 11) produced a wall fragment with glyphs representing *mn* which may have been part of the divine name *Ỉmn*.[20] The grape trellis probably covered the ceiling. The grape, besides being associated with Horus, Osiris and Renenutet, also symbolized resurrection.[21] It is not possible to identify positively the deities associated with this chapel, but it seems likely (since he figures in Chapels 525 and 529) that Amun was one and may have occupied the central shrine. Possibly the side chapel was dedicated to the ancestor cult in which Wepwawet also figures. At Deir el Medina in the Chapel of Hathor of Seti I, the side chapel (Chapter 4, 48) was dedicated by *Bw-qntw-f* to Amenhotep I and Ahmose Nefertari, as well as Amun and Hathor. On the bench was a seated statue of a jackal.[22]

The owners of Chapel 561 were presumably Sennufer and his family, who after death would have been remembered during festival occasions, and along with the deities represented symbolically partook of the ritual meals. The chapel may also have been visited when petitioning the gods or ancestors, at which time the simple little pebbles or pottery figurine of the dog head were offered.

No tomb was directly associated with this chapel, so it was not a tomb chapel *per se*, but if the suggested observance of an ancestor cult is correct, it had a funerary connotation. If a tomb were connected with this chapel, it may have been one of the shafts on the crest of the terrace east of the building.

Annexe 450

This dependency to Chapel 561 accommodated several activities. The **T**-shaped basin lying before it, which had ritual significance, will be discussed with **T**-shaped basins in general in Chapter 7. One of the activities was the keeping of animals in some of the enclosures. Although the organic material found here has not yet been analysed by a specialist, it appears to be a mixture of fodder and decayed coprolite. Some coprolite was distinguishable from the general mass of organic matter, and may have been a mixture of pig and goat. The tethering stone in the westernmost enclosure is more likely to have held a goat than a pig, but pigs were kept in area 400,[23] about a metre south of Annexe 450, and some could easily have been maintained in the latter area. The two gypsum coated chambers to the east appear to have been used for slaughtering. The rear room was probably where the animal was killed, and possibly the blood drained into the circular aperture in the northern wall of the room.[24] The outer room may have been where the animal was skinned and quartered, owing to the abundance of scratch marks in the floor. The animals sacrificed here may have been goat, since evidence of its ritual significance appears in the village. Apart from the goat phalange found in the outer hall of the chapel,[25] the hind limb of the goat found between the two walls in Chapels 570-571 had cut marks on the bone,[26] which implies that it had been killed, rather than had died, and may have been a sacrifice in connection with these chapels. Another instance was found near **T**-basin 3 before the southern wall of the village. This was the hind leg of a goat, still retaining some of its hide, which had been cut and sewn together with thread.[27] Another goat limb wrapped neatly in a cloth bandage came from the dump south of the basins before the village. In almost all cases the part of the goat singled out was the hind limb.

The small garden plots near the slaughter area had a symbolic use rather than a practical one, of which more will be said later (see below, p. 61). The oval receptacle abutting them may have once held water.

In the oven area in the southeast of the annexe, the semi-circular enclosure containing a platform of three bricks may have been a niche for a presiding deity, possibly Renenutet (fig. 8, area xi),[28] since she was the goddess of the harvest, and therefore particularly appropriate to an area where baking and wine-making was carried out. She was known as the snake who nourishes, and as mother of the grain god Nepri.[29] This goddess is often depicted as a serpent, and the Workmen's Village has produced cobra figurines and cobra bowls from the houses and dumps.[30] She is also known to have been provided with a shrine in granaries,[31] and although baking was carried out in this area, its association with nourishment and grain is obvious.

The chamber in the North Annexe, reached by the passage to the rear of Chapel 561 by passing through Annexe 450, may have served as a storage chamber for vessels and other items necessary to the chapel, or lodgings for a guardian, to be discussed later.

Chapels 570 and 571

In Chapter 2, it was suggested that Chapels 570 and 571 were probably associated with each other. This seems especially likely because of the presence of the goat limb lying on fill between two walls near the southwestern and northwestern corner of the respective chapels. It was noted above that this limb contained cut marks from a knife, suggesting it could be a foundation offering. However, this is not the customary Egyptian practice, which was to place the offering beneath the wall. Bietak has pointed out that the above anomaly is a Canaanite custom. In both secular and religious buildings in the Canaanite settlement at Tell el Dab'a, deposits of bones appeared near the corner of buildings in the palace area and in Temple V between the lower courses of bricks.[32] In a personal communication, Bietak informed me that he knew of no other instance where this occurred in Egypt.

The two offering stands before the niches in Chapel 571 (Chapter 2, 16) had attached bowls. This type of stand was more likely to be used for food offerings, whereas the stand incorporating a separate bowl was probably used for burning incense.[33] The two stands numbered 50177 and 50178 were coated in gypsum, sanctifying them for ritual use.[34] The former stand had a stick piercing the bowl (which was filled with gypsum) and running the total height of the stand. The small fragments of blue and turquoise faience in and around the bowl suggest that this stand was not used for food or incense. The tethering stone and fragment of rope nearby also suggest that goats were probably once sacrificed. It seems unlikely that this act would have been carried out in the hall. Since no animal enclosures were attached to this building, like those in Chapel 561, the killing of the animal probably took place somewhere outside the building.

Once again some form of meal seems to have been provided in the hall, and the burnt patches on the floor may have been caused by cooking activity (Chapter 2, 16). The benches surrounding part of the hall probably served the dual purpose of seating people and standing objects.

The offering stand in the second chamber from the east in the magazines (Chapter 2, 15) had a bowl in which the interior showed traces of burnt gypsum. The small cluster of lancet shaped leaves lying on the floor near it have not yet been identified by a specialist, but their shape appears identical to the olive.[35] Assuming that this is correct, it is known that the olive was associated with cult and funerary practices, certainly by the New Kingdom, when floral broad collars made with olive leaves, cornflowers and berries from the nightshade plant were worn by the guests at funeral banquets.[36] Olive leaves composed part of the 'Crown of Justification' worn by Tutankhamun[37] around the uraeus and Nekhbet vulture on the forehead of his first mummiform coffin. Another example, not associated with a funerary purpose, is a hand holding an olive branch under the rays of the Aten, from a limestone relief from Hermopolis.[38] The olive may, therefore, have had a solar association.

The foregoing observations offer only tentative ideas pertaining to the function and dedication of this chapel group. In addition to these, the alteration of the sanctuary from a tripartite to an essentially unicellular niche with an adjoining compartment indicates some change in dedication, (Chapter 2, 16). The first phase may have accommodated a triad of deities such as Amun, Hathor or even Shed (Chapel 525). Deities like Hathor or Re may have presided during the second phase. The deceased presumably was represented in some way during both phases. The small adjacent niche may have held anything from a small statue to a stela like that of Ptahmay in Chapel 525 (Chapter 3, 31) or only ritual paraphernalia. The blue and turquoise faience found before the sanctuary could have played some part in an offering to Hathor in her role as a funerary goddess. She granted rejuvenation and renewal,[39] symbolized by the colour turquoise or green. If olive leaves were used, Re may also have figured in some ritual.

The adjoining Chapel 570 could have been a tomb chapel in the 'true' sense (Chapter 2, 17), but may also have been a side chapel serving another deity, or some aspect of an ancestor cult. It is doubtful, owing to the lack of benches in the hall of this chapel, that ritual meals were eaten, but the burnt patches on the floor (Chapter 2, 16) could have come from ashes dropping after burning incense or some other ingredient, such as selected parts of plants. Renfrew suggests that the incense mixed with botanical remains found in the middens were swept from the chapel after a ceremony and thrown on the village dumps.[40] The whisk broom left in Chapel 561 may have been used for this (Chapter 2, 9).

THE REPLANNED CHAPELS

Chapel 522 and Annexe 523.

This chapel and its annexe are a modified version of Chapel 561 and its annexe. The limestone tank in the northern annexe would have provided for a means of purification before entering the chapel. All the chapels at Amarna were probably once supplied with a tank, since purification is an important part of ritual. However, apart from three T-shaped basins to be discussed in Chapter 7, only six rectangular types are recorded from the chapels. The presence of the benches in Annexe 523 suggests that ritual meals were consumed. The evidence of organic matter in some of the enclosures in the annexe support the idea of animals being kept, presumably for ritual use. The gypsum coated floor in the easternmost chamber (Chapter 2, 19) was probably where the animals were slaughtered. Its whitewashed floor would have been easier to keep clean.

The unicellular shrine may have been dedicated to the deceased and his protective deities. The wooden *s* bolt from this chapel could either have been an amulet or an actual bolt to a small wooden shrine or naos containing a statue (see below, p. 65). If so, this must have resided in the sanctuary.

Chapel Group 528, 529, 530, 531

Building 528

This area was designed as a funerary garden. The elements of masonry containing a series of receptacles, a T-shaped basin and an oven found in it presumably served the purpose of the regeneration of the deceased. In all probability the goddess Nut or Hathor played a major role in this drama, to be discussed with T-shaped basins in Chapter 7.

The arrangement of the receptacles in the masonry formed a balanced pattern. On either side of the central projection, and in it, the containers were symmetrical in number until the addition of the oven later (Chapter 2, 19). The projection acted as a central axis with seven receptacles sunk into the main body of the bench on either side. The balance was maintained with two compartments containing four receptacles and three more sunk into either side of the main body of the projection. The total on each side was fourteen. The gypsum lining of these containers may have served to reduce porosity or to make cleaning easier. No contents remained, but they could have held some liquid or solid, perhaps oil or wine and grain or fruit. Some of the grain and fruit identified at Amarna and appropriate to chapel use includes emmer wheat, hulled six-row barley, lentil, rye-grass spikelets, date, dom nut, persea, sycamore fig and acacia pod.[41]

If this hypothesis is correct, the arrangement and number of receptacles may have served in some ritual pertaining to the god Re or even Min.[42] Re had fourteen *kas*[43] representing the positive polarity and fourteen *hemusets* equalling the negative.[44] It was stated above that the goddess Nut or Hathor must have been represented in Building 528 because of the T-shaped basin. Nut was the mother of Re, who was regenerated when he was swallowed by her in the evening and reborn again at dawn.[45] In a similar way, the deceased would undergo his transformations in the underworld to be born a fully reconstituted being in the eastern horizon. The funerary garden and its contents provided a catalyst in the act of regenerating the deceased, and the plants represented in this type of garden were those valuable to the deceased.[46] For instance, the grape was associated with Horus, Osiris and Renenutet, and it also symbolized the resurrection of the deceased. The dom nut was associated with Thoth, Taweret and Min; the deceased, by identifying with Min, died and was regenerated again.[47]

The alluvial mud placed around the T-shaped basin in the rectangular plot (Chapter 2, 20) will have provided for the growth of some plants with a shallow root system, for there is no evidence of tree pits in this area. The soil from this area has not yet been examined for plant remains by a specialist. The presence of a token garden would have been to provide sustenance and pleasure to the deceased.

Southwest of the **T**-shaped basin, the small circular patch of alluvial mud may be the remains of a post hole (Chapter 2, 20) to hold a standard designating the presence of the god. These are known since the early dynastic period. Examples are known from the sanctuaries of Neit and the Ibis.[48] Given the funerary associations of Building 528, if a standard were present, it is more likely that it represented the *imywt*.[49] The pole could have been either with or without a pot.

The oven in the northwest corner would have supplied the bread eaten during rituals, possibly for all three chapels in this group.

Chapel 529

Benches were in both halls in this chapel. The ritual meal is more likely to have been eaten in the outer hall, and the benches in the inner hall would have taken the votive offerings.

The disk and horns (Chapter 2, 21) from this chapel are presumed to be from a statue of Hathor who may have resided in the sanctuary. The pedestal, also from here, appears to be the base to another object and the inscription *ir n sdm ʒš m st Nḥmmʒrtyw* inscribed on it was translated by Peet 'made by the servant in the kitchen, Nehemmaatiu'.[50] This is better read as, 'made by the worker (servant) in the place, *Nḥmmʒrtyw*'. At Deir el Medina the common appellation is *sdm rš m st mʒrt*, 'worker (servant) in the place of Truth', i.e., the Theban necropolis. *Nḥmmʒrtyw* must have been a worker in the necropolis, although here the *mʒrt* is not present.

The wall painting fragments of a vine and trellis and a human face found in the sanctuary (Chapter 2, 21) indicate that the deceased possessed a niche in this chapel, and Hathor must have been one of his protecting deities. The symbolism of the grape vine as instrumental in the resurrection of the deceased has been mentioned earlier.

Chapel 530

The surviving benches in this chapel suggest that they maintained the same arrangement as those in 529. Therefore, their use would have been the same, and the presence of burnt patches in both halls (Chapter 2, 21) suggests that this is so.

The limestone **L**-shaped object from this chapel (Chapter 2, 21) and also from Chapel 552 are likely to be architectural fragments.

The significance of the stone trough has been discussed when reviewing Chapel 522 (see above, p. 61).

The single naos was probably devoted to the cult of the deceased and his protective deities. He probably shared the benefits of Building 528, since no garden was directly connected with his chapel.

Chapel 531

This chapel was provided with its own garden plots and therefore probably did not share in some of the rituals performed in Building 528. The benches are arranged in the same way as the other two chapels and undoubtedly were used in a similar fashion. The circular slab of limestone (Chapter 2, 22) appears to have been a small dais for placing objects or offerings, perhaps a jar (Chapter 2, 10).

The pair of shrines of the same dimension in the sanctuary (Chapter 2, 22) may have been dedicated to two separate deities, or alternatively, one deity and the deceased. The third compartment could have been reserved for ritual paraphernalia or have contained a dedication. This half-screened compartment is similar to one in Chapelle F at Deir el Medina, which was believed to be dedicated to the cult of Ramesses II.[51] Equally, one of the naoi in C.V. 1213 at the same site was believed to be dedicated to the goddess Taweret because of the presence of a statue and stela to that deity. It is impossible to confirm the owners of the niches in Chapel 531, but the plan suggests that, apart from the deceased, other dedications existed.

Chapel 556

This chapel and Chapel 561 yielded the clearest evidence of the nature of the ritual meal and where it occurred in these cult buildings. It seems always to have been provided in the outer hall, if an inner hall was present or, in the case where there was no outer hall, in the one chamber. The four jar emplacements and part of a vessel used as a pot stand, as well as the presence of the hemispherical bread mould in the outer hall of 556, confirm this (Chapter 2, 22). The benches would have provided the seating, and the hearth probably served the dual purpose of heating in cold weather and cooking.

The contents of the **L**-shaped annexe supplement the information on the activities performed in this chapel. These consist of storage jars, a compartment filled with a quantity of bread moulds, garden plots and two ovens (Chapter 2, 23). It is evident that bread was cooked on the premises, as in several of the other chapels. The storage jars may have contained the dry ingredients for the bread. The presence of the 'goblet' type moulds (fig. 24a), however, are unique to this chapel. The example found in the outer hall is noteworthy, since it was the only one to bear decoration. Although this was identified as slurry which had shaped itself into a design, the pattern in my opinion was too defined and regular to be accidental. It consisted of a dark red chevron pattern applied towards the upper part of the body. Perhaps this mould was adapted for use as a lotus cup. The re-use of vessels for a purpose other than originally intended has already been observed in the outer hall, where a jar neck was adapted as a pot stand. The chevron pattern on the mould could be a schematic representation of the petals of a lotus. Lotus cups were found at Deir el Medina[52] and were also depicted on tomb reliefs and stelae (fig. 24b). The examples from Deir el Medina and on the reliefs shows goblets decorated with the calix of the lotus flower.

Nagel states that the smaller goblets were used for drinking, but in banquet scenes the wide rimmed cup was the one always represented. He cites only one example where the lotus cup is used for drinking. This is from Tomb 1 of Huya at El Amarna, where Akhenaten is shown sipping from it.[53] The larger lotus cup is shown singly set before a deity in its animal form. These include Hathor, Mertseger, Amun as a ram, the falcon, the goose, the antelope, the cat and Renenutet as a serpent. Often the contents shown in these cups are plants serving as food or offerings to the respective deity. Sometimes the lotus cup is seen on a table before the deceased surmounted with a floral decoration. Whether it was used for drinking in this instance is not certain.

Assuming that the mould in question was used as a lotus cup, it may have served as a container for small plants or for drinking. Since the base of the stem of most of the moulds was not level, this example, in order to keep it erect, could have been inserted into a hole in the floor or set on a small stand before a figure. Alternatively, its proximity to the jar emplacements in the outer hall of 556 suggests its use as a cup (fig. 15). The jars may have contained beer, wine or water, which could have been served from here during the meal. The idea of partaking of drink and bread conjures the image of the goddess Nut offering these commodities from the sycamore tree, and in this way, by sympathetic magic, the living communed with their ancestors or relatives in the other world.

The benches in the inner hall were probably used for placing votive objects or offerings, although no trace of anything of this kind was found.

It is likely that the centre niche was dedicated to the deceased and his protective deities. The two side compartments would have contained stelae or other objects devoted to lesser gods, such as Shed.

The Northern Group

The elements of this chapel group, discussed in Chapter 3, are fairly consistent. A ritual meal may have been eaten in all of them. However, with the exception of Chapel 553, which shared its outer hall with Chapel 556, the meal in the chapels in this group may have taken place in the hall nearest the sanctuary, which was the only area containing benches. Chapels 556 and 551 contained gardens, but there may have been others that were unrecognized and unrecorded. The sanctuary is the most variable in this group and will be central to the discussion below.

Chapel 551

The three rectangular pits in the bench of the sanctuary in this chapel were not described as plastered with mud or gypsum. This suggests that they may have been socles for stelae or statues. The arrangement of the two rectangular pits to the east could have caused one of the presumed stelae to be blocked either wholly or partially from view. This may be due to a second phase of construction, but it seems unlikely that the Egyptian sense of symmetry would permit this. However, this method of siting stelae is known in the Levant, and occurs in the Stelae Temple at Hazor.[54] Foreign interconnections will be discussed in Chapter 6.

A vine pattern covered the ceiling of the sanctuary (Chapter 3, 28) which presumably was dedicated to the deceased and the funerary gods.

Chapel 552

This chapel was provided with at least four ablution troughs. The two altars in the outer hall (Chapter 3, 28) were probably surmounted by offering tables. Behind, on the platform, may have been statues of the deceased or votive statues centred between the series of engaged columns.[55]

Found in both the inner and outer halls was an **L**-shaped angle, which, like the one from Chapel 530 (see above, p. 21), may have been a votive object.

The square pillar in the inner hall (Chapter 3, 29) may have been a pedestal to a statue or an offering table or may have been used for standing a vessel on. The gypsum lined trough nearby seems to have been an ablution receptacle.

The painted wall plaster from one of the three niches in the sanctuary, not recorded in detail by Woolley or Peet (Chapter 3, 29), depicted offerings of a loaf and a lotus, which could either have been presented to a god by the deceased, or to the deceased by a member of his family. The **L**-shaped chamber behind the westernmost niche was presumably a storage chamber or lodgings (see above, p. 59).

Chapel 553

The sanctuary of this chapel is the only one at Amarna to have had a niche equipped with a pedestal containing a square socle (Chapter 3, 29). It is clear that something was inserted into the depression; the object may have been one of any number of objects, for example, a small pillar-like stela, an obelisk or baetyl, a statue of a god or the deceased or an ancestor bust. That the niche was singled out from the other two in the sanctuary with a flight of stairs suggests that it was important in the cult. The size of the object could not have been much more than the base. A baetyl[56] (a cylindrical, round or square vertical stone object) was usually *c.* 30-40 cm. in height and often inserted into pedestals (see Chapter 6: Foreign influence in the Workmen's Village).

Alternatively, the pedestal may have held a stela to the Aten. Altars resembling pedestals are depicted in some Amarna tombs, and surmounting them is a rounded object resembling a round topped stela,[57] not unlike the one in the Great Aten temple. That the rounded outcrop symbolized offerings is unlikely, as no internal features are represented.

Another possibility is that a statue or ancestor bust resided in this niche. C.V. 1213 at

Deir el Medina contained a statue of Taweret and an ancestor bust nearby (see below, p. 69). A stela from the same chapel depicted the head of the same goddess surmounted on a baetyl.

The centre shrine contained the normal bench, and the back wall may have had paintings of an offering scene comparable to Chapel 552. The western shrine had no bench, suggesting that in it could have been a statue or a stela set against the wall.

Chapel 554

The prominence given to the shrines in this chapel suggests that both deities and deceased owned naoi (Chapter 3, 29). The easternmost naos may have had the same type of dedication as the similarly placed shrine in Chapel 553. No pedestal was found here, but this could have disappeared or, alternatively, a statue or stela may have been present. The central shrine with the bench was probably assigned to the deceased or a deity. The other possibility is that the deceased occupied the westernmost niche.

Chapel 555

The unfinished tomb shaft in this chapel suggests that, apart from other dedications, it was also intended to serve as a tomb chapel, assuming that the shaft was meant to lead to a burial chamber (Chapter 3, 30). The single naos may have served for deceased relatives to which later was to be added the crypt for a related family or person in the village.

The limestone slab with two bars on its underside from this chapel (Chapter 3, 30) is a table. One similar was found in the house in Gate Street No. 8.[58] Fragments of others have appeared in areas outside the Walled Village. These barely skim the floor and it seems impractical that one should appear in a chapel, where the benches are much higher than the dais in a village house (Chapter 6, 89). To eat, a man would have to forego the bench and squat on the floor.

The Southern Group

The essence of the cult performed in the northern chapels was continued in the southern group, namely the ritual meal. Once again, in some of the buildings this would have taken place in the hall nearest the sanctuary, since no benches appeared elsewhere. These also presumably served as podiums for votive objects. In chapels where the benches were considerably abbreviated (chapels 526 and 527), these presumably acted only as stands. That some of these chapels had funerary gardens that were not recognized as such by the excavators is possible (Chapter 3, 18). The following discussion will be concerned mainly with the sanctuaries and the significance of some of the objects.

Chapel 521

This chapel may have served the cult of a deity as well as the deceased. The presence of a slate with remains of powdered malachite and a wooden doll suggest that Hathor may have occupied one of the niches in the sanctuary (Chapter 3, 30). Malachite was associated with this goddess and was ground on palettes for the purpose of applying the paint to the eyes of her statue.[59] One of her many aspects, that of a goddess of fertility,[60] may have prompted the presumably votive offering of a wooden doll.

The two fragments of wood (Chapter 3, 30), one with three painted panels and the other with a rounded end, suggest the remains of a shrine in the style of the *pr wr*. The first fragment was probably a side of the shrine and the second the back, indicating that it had a vaulted roof. Perhaps this contained a statue of Hathor. At Deir el Bahari the sanctuary in the Chapel of Hathor resembled the *pr wr* and had a vaulted ceiling.[61]

It is impossible to confirm that a triad of deities resided in the tripartite unit of the sanctuary and that the side niche to the south was reserved for the deceased. Amun is mentioned in fragments of text from walls of other chapels (525, 529, 561) and he may have been included in the dedications.

Chapel 524

This chapel provides some interesting suppositions, albeit based on tenuous and fragmentary evidence, which suggest that, apart from a dedication to the deceased, it may have also included a dedication to the Aten, or the cult of the king, as represented in house or garden shrines in the Main City.[62]

Firstly, Peet reported that the brick pedestal in the central niche (Chapter 3, 31) was like the one in Chapel 553, but did not specify that it contained a square depression in its top surface. If it did, it could have supported an object similar to the possibilities discussed under Chapel 553.

Secondly, the fragment of wall painting on the brick found in Peet's dump in square T18 probably came from this chapel (Chapter 3, 36). It could not have come from 523, for dependencies of this nature did not have wall paintings. Nor did it come from Chapel 561 or Annexe 450, because the dump existed before these were excavated. The only possibility left is Chapel 524, the nearest to the dump. Since the features depicted on the brick were unlike any portrayed in the Main Chapel and conformed clearly to the Amarna style, they may have been a representation of Akhenaten or a member of the royal family. The shrines connected with many of the houses in the Main City usually showed Akhenaten and Nefertiti bathed in the rays of the Aten on a stela set against the back wall.[63] This same theme may have been painted on the back wall of the central niche in 524.

Lastly, the fragment of papyrus mentioning the Aten found in the narrow passage between 524 and 523 (Chapter 3, 31) could have blown from anywhere on the site, but it may have belonged to 524.

Chapel 525

Chapel 525 is one of the few to provide the identity of the deity housed in one of its naoi. The two stelae, which stood on the floor and were set against the back wall of the westernmost niche, were dedicated to Shed (Chapter 3, 31). The first depicted the god facing right, with a staff in his right hand and a bow in his left. Before him was a scorpion surmounted by two arrows with the points downwards. The remains of an inscription read 'Shed, great god, lord of heaven, lord of the Two Lands, Ruler ...'

The other stela represented Shed, again facing right, with a sidelock of youth and a *wsḫ* collar, carrying a staff, bow and quiver. Facing him on the right was Isis holding an *ankh* before his nose and carrying another in her other hand. Between them was a scorpion with the same arrangement of two arrows as in the first example. Near it was a whitewashed portable offering stand surmounted with a jug and offerings.

Below this scene a man, Ptahmay, knelt before two offering stands. The inscription read 'Giving adoration to Shed, kissing the earth to the great god; praise to the Lord of Love in peace, beholding thy beauty every day'. The remaining inscriptions on this side include the usual offering formulas to Shed and Isis.

Two scenes were shown on the left side of the stela. One showed Ptahmay seated holding a bowl, while a female standing figure, called lady of the house Thefy, poured liquid from a vase into it. Below a lady played a harp, while another danced. These were named as his daughters. The right side, also divided into two registers, had the same arrangement, except a small boy was added. These represented a lady of the house, Ptahmay's daughters and a son. On both sides the Aten was named.

The god Shed first appears in the Eighteenth Dynasty and was originally an Asiatic god.[64] He was connected with Re, Shu and Horus, and was predominantly a saviour god.[65] The votive stela on behalf of Ptahmay suggests that this deity may have figured prominently in the funerary cult at the Workmen's Village.

Besides the naming of Shed and the Aten, Amun is cited in an offering formula on the entablature over the sanctuary (Chapter 3, 31). He may have occupied the more prominent eastern niche, since it is known that Shed and the deceased claimed the western one.

Lastly, the large, round boulder aligned along the central axis of the chapel before the flight of stairs leading to the sanctuary may have served several purposes (fig. 61b; Chapter 3, 31). Peet suggested that it may have acted as a pedestal, arguing that because of its weight and size it could not have arrived in its position accidentally. Its alignment certainly favours this idea, but the low pedestals in all the chapels were constructed of brick or limestone and were whitewashed. Alternatively, it may have represented a baetyl or fetish stone — a type of primeval mound. The fetish stone was known in Egypt and composed part of the fetish *Tȝ-wr* on the standard of the Thinite nome.[66] Another instance is its appearance with two kites on either side from the Book of the Netherworld.[67] If foreign influence permeated some of the village culture (Chapter 6, 96-97), it could be an intrusive idea from outside Egypt. In Palestine, baetyls were known from earliest times and first served both as an idol and an altar.[68] Renfrew recognized a baetyl in the temple of Phylakopi[69] (fig. 55). It was a similar large, round boulder to the one in 525, and was also aligned on the central longitudinal axis.

Finally, Chapel 525 may have been intended to serve as a tomb chapel to a tomb shaft on the summit of the terrace above.[70] This was on a direct alignment to the longitudinal axis of the chapel.

Chapel 526

The sanctuary had one broad niche (Chapter 3, 32), presumably devoted to the deceased. The adjoining eastern chamber could not have been a niche because of its shape, and was more likely a magazine, or possibly a chamber belonging to a guardian. This will be discussed further under Chapel 527.

Chapel 527

The sanctuary contained one large niche, again probably devoted to the cult of the deceased. The **L**-shaped compartment behind, similar to that in Chapel 552 (Chapter 3, 29), contained some painted wall plaster. It is unlikely that it served as a niche, more probably as a treasury or lodgings for a guardian. Its irregularity is suggestive of a similar compartment in the area of the sanctuary in C.V. 1190 at Deir el Medina, which Bruyère identified as quarters for a chapel guardian.[71] However, the enclosure abutting the western side of Chapel 527 in the shape of the hieroglyph ⌑ may also have served as lodgings. A parallel at Deir el Medina is C.V. 1193/1220, to be discussed below.

Chapel 532

The sanctuary was unicellular; no evidence exists to indicate its dedication. It can only be assumed that it was dedicated to the deceased.

Chapel 533

The three or four niches in the sanctuary suggest that deities, as well as the deceased, had a cult in this building. Only assumptions can be made as to the identity of the possessor of each niche. The northernmost (Chapter 3, 33) may have been provided with a stela, if we can use 525 as a comparison. The deceased may have occupied the next niche with the bench, and other deities the main shrine.

Chapel 535 and Building 534

The presence of the oven in connection with this chapel confirms that meals were certainly provided or offered in the main hall (Chapter 3, 33). Presumably the denuded sanctuary possessed at least two niches, if not more. The presence of the female figurine in Building 534 suggests that one of the niches may have been devoted to Hathor (see above, p. 30, Chapel 521).

Chapel 536

There is no reason to believe that this chapel differed radically in its dedication from the others, although the sanctuary is heavily denuded.

The unusual position of the benches in the hall (Chapter 3, 33) has no parallel earlier than the Roman triclinium used in funerary banquets and the rites of Mithras centuries later, as seen in the Bab Kalabsha Chapels of the Roman period.[72]

Discussion

From the foregoing assessment, it can be concluded that the chapels at Amarna were used for a funerary and religious purpose.

The funerary evidence was established by various epigraphic fragments from wall plaster, objects such as the paddle from Chapel 561, the stela of Ptahmay and some pottery vessels. Added to this is the presence of tomb shafts in the surrounding area. However, only twelve shafts have so far been discovered in the Workmen's Village, five of which[73] were unfinished. Only one of this number had been occupied and this may have been after the village had ceased to exist as an organized unit.

Twelve shafts can hardly accommodate the twenty-two chapels so far discovered. Furthermore, only about three of that number can be attributed with any certainty to a particular chapel. This being the case, what are the funerary connections with the chapels, if they were not just tomb chapels? A possible answer is that the chapels originally served an ancestor cult for various members of the Workmen's Village. These may have been relatives or ancestors, perhaps passed away a generation or more before, and buried elsewhere. The tomb shafts were probably constructed after the chapels were built, i.e., each shaft after the chapel to which they presumably belonged.

The village appears to have had a short occupancy, perhaps even less than the twelve or more years of the Main City (Chapter 2, 7). During that span of time people in the village must have died, but not enough to have built up a necropolis on the scale of Deir el Medina, where tomb chapels and private chapels are clearly distinguishable. If the inhabitants of the Workmen's Village of Amarna were moved from elsewhere, for instance Deir el Medina, they would have had to leave their ancestral ground and tombs of their relatives. This would necessitate the construction of new shrines in their memory.

The ancestor cult was an important function in the life of the ordinary man and may be implicit in the 'Letters to the Dead' from at least the end of the Old Kingdom.[74] Deceased relatives were believed to have supernatural powers and were appealed to by the living in times of need. They were also feared as evil entities who might harm the living if they were antagonized in any way, for instance, negligence in providing for their needs in the afterlife.[75] Therefore, it was necessary to remember them in festival times and perform rites in their memory. These rites could be observed in a domestic shrine, tomb chapel or the private chapel.[76] By the Nineteenth Dynasty, their cult was well established at Deir el Medina, aspects of which are seen in the *ȝḫ iqr n Rꜥ* stelae and the ancestor busts.[77] Admittedly, there are no examples of either of these at Amarna. If stelae or busts were present at Amarna, they may have been carried off when life in the village ceased. Another possibility is that the ancestor cult during the Eighteenth Dynasty at Deir el Medina may have taken a different form, since the stelae and busts begin to occur mainly in the Nineteenth Dynasty. However, the small pebbles from the Main Chapel, one of which was inscribed, have already been suggested as votive objects connected with some form of ancestor worship.

The presence of a royal ancestor cult existing in the Workmen's Village cannot be proved, but owing to the religious schism during this period, it may have existed in the simple worship of the Aten through the medium of the king, Akhenaten.

The gods mentioned in textual evidence from the chapels are the Aten, Amun, Isis and Shed. Those who may have been worshipped on the evidence of artifacts and architectural features such as the T-shaped basin are Hathor (Isis), Nut, Re-Harakhty, Min, Wepwawet and Renenutet. Some of these deities may have figured in the ancestor or funerary cult. However, others such as Hathor and Shed appear to have been sought for different reasons.

A Comparative Analysis of the Function of the Amarna Chapels with similar types at Deir el Medina.

Earlier it was noted that the chapels at Amarna were not as diversified in their function as those at Deir el Medina (see above, p. 57). Added to the uses listed for Amarna, the Theban examples included provisions for an oracle and for an assembly hall, presumably for the *qnbt* (Chapter 4, 51). Valbelle saw the chapel constructed against the northern side of the village enclosure wall (figs 21a, 25 no. 6) as serving the cult of Opet, because of the file of force-fed bulls,[78] which are similar to those in the Opet procession on the western inner face of the Colonnade usurped by Horemheb in the Luxor temple.

The royal ancestor cult was active in the village and among those honoured were Amenhotep I, Ahmose Nefertari, Tuthmosis III, Amenhotep II, Tuthmosis IV, Ramesses II and Seti I. A private ancestor cult also flourished. Bruyère identified the existence of brotherhoods, which he called *confrèries*, composed of the *sḏm ꜥš m st mꜣꜥt*, 'servants in the Place of Truth', who were present at or performed rites in the chapels. The coterie which formed these groups usually consisted of twelve or possibly more members. Bruyère believed that these groups evolved out of, and were based upon, ancestor worship of deceased *sḏm ꜥš*. The cult was served by a priesthood derived from the ranks of the *sḏm ꜥš*. Women also served in the cult. Apparently, most of the chapels were provided with guardians. Few of them were associated with certainty with a tomb.

The intention here is to discover how closely the purposes of the Amarna chapels can be identified with those of Deir el Medina. The chapels whose function have little bearing on those at Amarna will not be referred to in this survey. These are 1) Chapelle A and the chapel abutting the northeastern wall of the village, which may have served as meeting halls for secular purposes, 2) C.V. 1211, which is classed as a tomb chapel, 3) Chapelle G and the Temple of Amun of Ramesses II (second phase), which fill the category of a small temple.

The chapels to be discussed below are those which offer the most complete evidence. These are C.V. 1213, C.V. 1190, C.V. 1, the chapel of Hathor of Seti I, and Chapelle D. The remaining chapels listed in Chapter 4 will be referred to where appropriate.

C.V. 1213

This chapel may have been dedicated to the goddess Taweret, since fragments of a statue and stela depicting her were found in it (Chapter 4, 42). On the stela her head was portrayed surmounted by the Abydian fetish *Tꜣ-wr*.[79] Fragments of purification basins inscribed with her name were also found in C.V. 1213. Part of one inscription reads *ḥtp di nsw Tꜣ-wrt pꜣ mw wꜥb di st ꜥnḫ wḏꜣ snb n kꜣ n ꜥnꜥ m st mꜣꜥt ...*.[80] 'A boon which the king gives to Taweret, the purifier, may she grant Life, Prosperity and Health to the ka of *ꜥnꜥ*[81] in the Place of Truth ...' These objects were presented by a sculptor and various *sḏm ꜥš* as *ex votos* to the goddess.

Many basins found at Deir el Medina were dedicated to this goddess, who presided over the rites of purification in the village. In the Moscow museum is part of a wooden door to a naos from Deir el Medina dedicated to this deity.[82] Whether its origin is from C.V. 1213 is unknown, but no doubt a similar naos housed the statue of the goddess found in this chapel. Her cult was one of those popular at Deir el Medina.

Just east of the chapel an ancestor bust was discovered which may once have stood in the sanctuary of the building.[83] Keith-Bennett, contrary to Bruyère, believed that these busts may have been used outside the domestic context.[84] Six were found near or in the huge well north of the main temple and not far from the chapel of Hathor of Seti I.[85] Friedman suggested that the bust could be transported from the house to the tomb or chapel,[86] although she did not stipulate which type of chapel-tomb of those under discussion. The bust was used as a medium of contact between the world of the living and the deceased or gods.

Referring back to C.V. 1213, on the assumption that a bust did occupy a place in the chapel, it could have served the needs of the women in the village, who were left alone during the week while most of the men were cutting out the tombs in the Valley of the Kings. Taweret, as one of several female deities of the village, acted as protector against child mortality and sickness.

The hypogeum on the same axis behind C.V. 1213 (Chapter 4, 42) contained only some sherds and straw, and no evidence of a burial. It may, therefore, have served as quarters for a guardian to the chapel below. Bruyère suggested that a small dwelling or enclosure just west of the chapel may have accommodated a guardian because of the presence of a quantity of ash, presumably from cooking.

C.V. 1190

The gods and kings depicted in this chapel were Ptah, Amun criocephalus, a king (probably Seti II, since his cartouches were present), a goddess or queen and a hippopotamus (perhaps Taweret). These representations came from the central niche. Depicted on the door frame was a goddess with a green face, oriented south. The deity to whom the central niche belonged cannot be determined with any certainty, nor can the owner of the southern niche be identified.[87]

The northern compartment bore the name of *Mry-Shmt* on its door frame.[88] He was described as a draughtsman of Amun and a guardian (*p3y iry*), and consequently the northern compartment may, according to Bruyère, have been his lodgings.

The door jambs to the staircase before the northern niche that led to the crypt below were inscribed with the text 'to the ka of the draughtsman of Amun in the Place of Truth, Merysekhmet'. The gypsum plastered, but undecorated, hypogeum contained several fragments of stelae and part of an offering table. The stelae belonged to the cult of Amenhotep I and Ahmose Nefertari. The crypt may have originally served this royal cult, and then later become the tomb of the guardian of the chapel, *Mry-Shmt*. A similar instance to this is C.V. 1193 and the neighbouring hypogeum no. 1194 (Chapter 4, 43). The chapel was dedicated to the cult of Amenhotep I, and served by a priest who may have lived in the crypt that later became his tomb. Alternatively, he may have occupied the nearby house (1220). Referring back to *Mry-Shmt*, he too may have occupied the crypt in his lifetime and the stelae belonging to the cult of Amenhotep I may have been lodged in the southern niche, later removed to the hypogeum.

One of the stelae showed, in the top register, a queen with two sistrums before Amenhotep I in an Atef crown and Ahmose Nefertari in the vulture headdress with two straight plumes. Men and women appeared in the bottom register carrying offerings. Among the uneffaced names were: Nakhtuf, justified; brother ... his son Baki, justified; his son Merysekhmet, justified; his son Pashed, justified; his son, *Iwwn Imn*, justified; his daughter, Mutnefert, justified. These persons were members of the family of *Mry-Shmt*, and were enlisting the protection of the deified king and queen.[89]

Fragments of the other stela showed that it was a dedication to Amenhotep I by the *sdm ꜥš*, Hay.

Ex votos given as a prayer or petition also occurred in C.V. 1190. In the forecourt was a wooden stela to *St Nbw* inscribed with, *St Nbw ꜥ3 phty nb pt ... n H3w*, 'Seth, the Ombite, great of strength, lord of heaven ... by *H3w*'.[90]

The dependency to C.V. 1190 numbered 1218 (Chapter 4, 43) containing a bench, an oven and another enclosure could also have been lodgings for the guardian *Mry-Shmt*. The duties of a guardian entitled *iry* or *s3wty* consisted of looking after the chapel and the magazine. The following examples, taken from Bruyère,[91] show the frequent use of this title:

1.   Amenmopet, *s3wty m st m3ꜥt*, T.356, Deir el Medina, on canopic jar and coffin.
2.   *s3wty m st m3ꜥt*, Penbwy, T.10, Turin, Statue No. 173.

Other titles connected with the cult of gods and kings in the chapels were: *hm ntr*, *hry hbt*, *b3k*, *wꜥb*, *hsy*, *sdm ꜥš n nb t3wy*.

These titles were found in the following:

1. Tomb 359, Inherkhawy: *ḥm nṯr n nb t3wy*
2. Shabti No. 2684, Louvre: *ḥm nṯr tpy n nb t3wy*
3. Stela No. 3447, Louvre: *ḥry ḥbt (Ḏsr k3 Rꜥ)*

The *b3k* were in charge of chapel belongings. Tomb 3 referred to *b3k n šnꜥ n Ỉmn m nỉwt rsy P3šd*. The *wꜥb* were numerous, serving different cults: the *wꜥb* of Ptah of Tasetneferw, the *wꜥb* of *Ḏsr k3 Rꜥ*, and the *wꜥb* of Amun-Re of the diadems, of the two lands.

A priest or an attendant was not confined to one chapel, but could serve in several cults. Merysekhmet also served in the cult of Mertseger of the Theban mountain, in his role as a workman of the necropolis.

C.V. 1

To which deity or king this chapel was dedicated is not known, since no textual or pictorial evidence survives. Its main importance to this study is the information it provides concerning the *confrèries*. This evidence is disclosed in the series of limestone seats found inserted into the benches in the inner hall, already referred to in Chapter 4, 40. Sixteen of these seats are now in the Turin museum, but not all of them appear to have come from C.V. 1. Unfortunately, Schiaparelli, who found them, did not record the provenance of each, but from the four uninscribed seats that remained when Bruyère re-excavated this chapel, it is clear that others had been present.

The seats in the Turin museum are all inscribed with the name of the owner and his occupation. Some are prefixed with *n k3 n*.[92] Since many of the others are fragmentary, the missing pieces may have borne the same description. Bruyère posited that these seats were inscribed at the death of a member in his memory, and those still unmarked were used by the living members. Therefore, by the name still persisting the deceased could continue to participate in the cultic rites involving the ancestors. Whether these inscribed seats were used by new living members of the *confrèries* or left vacant cannot be proved, and additional names inscribed on any one seat do not appear. If the analogy of the modern practice of labelling park benches in memory of someone can be used, then the seats of the original owners probably were occupied by a new member.

Some confusion arises as to the number of members comprising a *confrèrie* in some chapels. Bruyère suggested fourteen for C.V. 1, although there were twelve seats in the chapel (Chapter 4, 40). If the plans for this chapel, the Chapel of Hathor of Seti I and the Temple of Amun of Ramesses II (phase I) are to be believed, then there were spaces for twelve seats. Twelve could be correct, if the six men and six women represented on the walls of the side chapel in the Chapel of Hathor were members of a *confrèrie* (Chapter 4, 49). There may have been significance in the limitation of the number to twelve, but the reasons for it are obscure and cannot be pursued here.

Lastly, Bruyère posited that an oracle was probably consulted in this chapel, because of the unusual side door leading into the south side of the sanctuary.[93] Therefore, the southern naos may have been dedicated to the cult of a king. Nearby, to the south of the chapel, hypogeum no. 1240 may have belonged to the guardian of C.V. 1 and the group of enclosures abutting the annexe to the chapel could have served as living quarters.

The Chapel of Hathor of Seti I

The dedication of this chapel was to Hathor and Amun. The main evidence was provided by two altars at the foot of the pronaos that may once have stood in the sanctuary. Each was inscribed with the name of one of the deities quoted above. Presumably Amun occupied the central shrine. Whether Seti I was honoured as a 'living' king in one of the niches is not known, but the texts on the two altars already mentioned contain this king's cartouches, indicating that this chapel was dedicated by him to these deities.

The side chapel or shrine to *Bw-qntw-f* contained fragments of wall paintings depicting Amun, Hathor, Amenhotep I and Ahmose Nefertari, who were the dedicatees of the shrine. The name of *Bw-qntw-f* appeared in a text on the door jambs to the shrine. One of the inscriptions reads, *dỉ·f ꜥnḫ wḏꜣ snb n kꜣ n sḏm ꜥš m st mꜣꜥt Bw-qntw·f mꜣꜥ-ḫrw*, 'May he give life, prosperity, health to the ka of the servant in the Place of Truth, *Bw-qntw·f*, justified'. *Bw-qntw·f* was undoubtedly a member of the *confrèrie* of this chapel and the men and women represented on the walls of his side chapel must have been his *confrères*.[94]

In his observations, Bruyère pointed out that side chapels were always constructed to the left of the main chapel, and that the founder may be the same for both the principal and minor sanctuary or, alternatively, that the former could be someone of high rank and the latter a subordinate of the first. The dedication of the side chapel could have been to a lesser deity or complementary triad, or the same as in the main sanctuary. Finally, the side chapel was always built contemporaneously with the main building and not added at a later time.[95]

Among the votive objects from this chapel was a fragment of a statue base of Mertseger from the forecourt, dedicated by Hay, and an offering table of Didi and son Amennakht, servants, to Amenhotep I and Ahmose Nefertari.

Noteworthy from this chapel is a stela fragment from the group called *ꜣḫ ỉqr n Rꜥ*. It is attributed to *Ḥꜥpy-ꜥꜣ*, dating from the end of the Eighteenth to the Nineteenth Dynasty. Demarée translated the text as follows '(offering?) all good and pure (things?) for the *ka* of ... beer, oxen, fowl, cool water. Offering ... things, ... (*ḥtp?*) to the *ka* of the able spirit of Re, Hapy'o, justified, in peace'.[96]

This class of stela dates from the end of the Eighteenth Dynasty to principally the Nineteenth and Twentieth Dynasties. Its main provenance is Deir el Medina with others appearing in the Theban area and Abydos. Their loci in the village were in houses, niches, the eastern cemetery and four chapels, including the one under discussion.[97] The other chapels were C.V. 1215 (fig. 26), C.V. 1216 and C.V. 2. In the last named chapel, the stela was found on the southern bench,[98] together with other votive offerings.

Those portrayed on the stelae were usually from the more elite ranks of the village society.[99] The *ꜣḫ ỉqr n Rꜥ* or the 'able/perfect spirit of Re' was one who had achieved the privilege of sitting in the solar boat of Re and of being admitted into the sun-god's company. He could act as a judge of the deceased and an intermediary between the gods and the living on earth, to whom petitions could be made by relatives when in need. Their cult was propitiated with offerings in which the stela acted as the focal point of contact.[100] These stelae, together with the ancestor busts (see above, p. 69) were objects of an ancestor cult which was a primary form of worship at Deir el Medina and observed at sites other than this locality.

Chapelle D

This chapel may have been one of the major buildings devoted to the cult of the deified royal couple, Amenhotep I and Ahmose Nefertari, since it produced more statuary of this pair than any other in the necropolis (Chapter 4, 50, for a list). The fragment of wall painting depicting the goddess Mut suggests that the Theban triad may have also occupied a position in the sanctuary.[101]

Among the first royal burials of the Eighteenth Dynasty at Thebes, and the possible founders of the community of Deir el Medina,[102] Amenhotep I and Ahmose Nefertari were one of the most popular of the royal ancestor cults. Their representation figures in numerous tombs in the necropolis and in private chapels.

The consultation of an oracle was one of the functions of the royal ancestor cult. The deified king could be consulted in his chapel. Ostracon BM 5625[103] tells of the workman Kenna, who appealed to the oracle Amenhotep I, about being unjustly prevented by the workman, Merysekhmet, from living in the ruined *ḫnw* of Pekhaw, which he, Kenna, had rebuilt (see Appendix, 120). The oracle could also be sought when the statue of the king was taken in procession during one of his festivals. At Deir el Medina the image would be taken from its naos and transported across the necropolis, where it was set down before Tomb 360 of Kaha.[104] The festivals in honour of this deified monarch, whose clergy were the most numerous and diversified in the village, have been identified by Valbelle as occurring during *ȝḥt* I, days 29 and 30, *prt* II, day 20, *prt* III, day 15 ff.; *šmw* I, day 27, and *šmw* III, day 11 ff.[105] Chapelle 1 (Chapter 4, 45) contained a fragment of a carrying-shrine with the cartouche of Amenhotep I.[106] Besides consulting a deified king, the god Amun was also sought.[107]

In the chapels dedicated to a deified king or Amun, the oracular function was performed. C.V. 1222 may provide an example of one way in which this was executed. Tomb 1244 ran directly under the inner hall of the chapel (Chapter 4, 44). A rectangular aperture was cut through the roof of the tomb, which at the same time formed the floor of the hall. This was covered over by a stone slab. Bruyère suggested that this was a device used for giving the oracles of the god.[108] It is clear from my own observations that the rectangular cut in the ceiling is intentional, and it is difficult to conceive of any other reason for placing an opening here.

Discussion

The evidence given above has established that the chapels at Deir el Medina were centred mainly on a royal and private ancestor cult. Additionally, cults existed for major and minor deities, and finally an oracle could be consulted. Among the cults flourishing at Deir el Medina were those of Ptah, Hathor, Amun criocephalus, Osiris and special cults comprising animal forms of the goose, swallow, cat and the serpent as Renenutet. Dedicatees on some of the stelae offered by the *sḏm ꜥš* were Min, the Asiatic gods Reshef, Qadesh and Anat, and the three cataract gods: Anukis, Satis and Khnum.[109]

Evidence shows that the benches fulfilled a dual function: for standing votive objects and for seating people. In some chapels, twelve persons may have made up the *confrèrie* when assembling, but whether this was held to rigidly in all the chapels provided with benches cannot be proved. The chapels with benches aligned against opposite walls, and not those surrounding three walls, may have been those devoted to the strict number of twelve, especially ones equipped with limestone seats. The other chapels, such as Chapelle B, C, D, C.V. 1213 and C.V. 1216, may have been used for both purposes, the numbers of participants being variable. Presumably, food offerings were given to all the dedicatees of the chapels and the *confrèrie* participated in this as a form of reversal of offerings. Unfortunately, environmental remains were not carefully tabulated by Bruyère and consequently there is no way to prove this in the same way as has been done at Amarna. However, the presence of cooking facilities in C.V. 1190 and the Chapel of Hathor confirm that this activity was carried out to some extent in at least two chapels.

Whether garden plots were attached to some of the chapels is again uncertain, a consequence of the same lack of attention to organic remains. None of what Bruyère called *silos*, which could at first glance be thought to be the remains of garden plots, forms a grid pattern in the same way as the plots at Amarna. Exceptions to this are small grids connected to or near tombs: P.1281, P.1276 and Tomb Chapel 215.[110] The *silos* or pits in the area of the chapels are irregular in plan, some are gypsum- or mud-plastered and reach a depth of up to 1.40 m., quite unlike a plot. In the late (Saite) period, a sycamore grove of five trees was planted near the Chapel of Hathor of Seti I, about a metre above the Ramesside level.[111]

How similar in function are the chapels from the two workmen's villages? The issues to be discussed are 1) types of cult, 2) the use of the chapel, 3) the personnel.

Types of Cult

It is clear that both settlements included the worship of major and minor deities. Among these are principally Amun and Hathor. It is impossible to tell if Amun was criocephalus at Amarna. Among the minor deities, some were favoured more than others at the respective sites. For instance, Shed and Renenutet appear at El Amarna, whereas Mertseger, Renenutet and Taweret were favoured at Deir el Medina. The difference in choice was influenced by regional and topographical variations. For instance, the mountain peak, El Qurn, overlooking the King's Valley and close to the Theban necropolis where the workmen from Deir el Medina worked, became sacred to Mertseger, whose cult was popular in the village. No such feature appeared at Amarna. Asiatic gods were worshipped at the Theban village and possibly the cult of some foreign god was observed at Amarna, if the theory concerning the baetyl is correct. The point here, however, is not so much which deities were being worshipped, but that facilities existed for their cult in both settlements. This emphasizes that the ordinary man was carrying on his own religion quite independently of the state, at least during the New Kingdom. Furthermore, a developed private ancestor cult existed in both villages. At Deir el Medina it is more graphically disclosed in the shape of *ꜣḥ iqr n Rꜥ* stelae, ancestor busts, and limestone seats from the chapels. At Amarna, it is more of an understatement in the form of small stones (*jeu de nature*, some inscribed) and the preponderance of the number of chapels to that of tombs. The outward expression of this cult did not reach its final achievement, in the form of the stelae and other refinements, until the Nineteenth Dynasty and is therefore not apparent at Amarna.

A royal ancestor cult flourished in the Theban settlement and may have been present at Amarna, but this may have been centred only on Akhenaten and as Aten worship. That other kings of the Eighteenth Dynasty were worshipped in the village cannot be proved. The possibility exists, however, suggested by a roughly fashioned limestone figurine of the falcon god Horus found lodged near the southern gate of the Walled Village in 1981.[112] The figurine suggests mainly the cult of Horus, but may have included some connection with ancestors for the following reason. The ancestor cult harked back to Horus and his followers, the *šmsw Ḥr*.[113] Bruyère posited that this cult continued to survive under the *manes* or *ꜣḥw* invoked in this form at Hierakonpolis and Buto, of which the *sḏm ꜥš* were a survival of Horian origins.[114] The naming of a *sḏm ꜥš* in Chapel 529 implies that others also occupied the village.

To conclude, both villages had a developed and independent religious structure, in which ancestor worship figured prominently.

The Use of the Chapel

The use of the chapel at both sites was in essence the same, and the layout of the buildings followed mostly the same pattern. Water troughs for lustral purposes were present, and ovens were used with some of the chapels. The performance of the ritual in the Amarna chapels appears to have been less elaborate than the Theban counterpart, although equally as defined. There is no way of knowing if *confrèries* existed at Amarna, but if some of the occupants were from Thebes, it is possible, and likely if *sḏm ꜥš* were present. Presumably the insertion of limestone seats into the benches was a later refinement, and that the number composing a *confrèrie* had always been fixed.

At Amarna, ceremonial meals presumably were held in all the chapels except 570, on festival and other auspicious occasions. This same function seems to have occurred in most of the chapels at Thebes, except perhaps C.V. 1193, 1198, 1215, 1222, 1223 and C.V., where no benches were reported in the halls.[115] Simple votive offerings may have been given here.

Some of the dependencies attached to the chapels at Deir el Medina may have included facilities for keeping animals, but this is conjecture without the proof of organic remains.[116] The dependencies at this site were more developed than those at Amarna, for they include living quarters, e.g., C.V. 1193/1220, Chapel of Hathor, and possibly Chapelle 2. The chapels dated to the latter part of the relative chronology at Amarna began to develop more elaborate dependencies, which could have included provisional living quarters, i.e., Annexe 523, the north annexe of Chapel 561 and Annexe 450, and possibly the southern annexe of 536.

In summary, the function of the chapel at both sites was essentially the same, except that ceremonial meals may not have been provided in all of those at Thebes.

The Personnel

The evidence is abundant concerning the servicing of the chapels at Deir el Medina. They were provided with a priesthood ranging from *ḥm nṯr* to different categories of *wꜥb* (see above, p. 70). Besides the priesthood, most chapels, if not all, had a guardian whose lodgings were either within the chapel or in a small domestic building attached to or near the chapel (C.V. 1, C.V. 1190).

Amarna provides no information in this quarter. This must be obtained by searching for parallels in the Theban counterpart. From the evidence provided by some of the chapels at Deir el Medina, it is more than probable that guardians were associated with at least some of the Amarna buildings. These living quarters may have been the L-shaped compartments running behind the sanctuary (see above, pp. 59; 67), or may have been one of the chambers in the larger dependencies. There must have been at least a part-time priesthood, since no chapel could be run without one and, as at Deir el Medina, it was undoubtedly chosen from elite members of the village. Unfortunately, no epigraphical evidence exists to support this statement, leaving only rational deduction.

The Difference between the Tomb Chapel and the Private Chapel

Before concluding this Chapter, some discussion is needed to make clear the difference between the tomb chapel and the private chapel.

In a sense, both types of chapels can be classed as votive, since offerings and prayers are made in each. However, it is the intention behind the petition and oblation that distinguishes the two, and that is realized in the architecture, decoration and offerings. The main distinction is that the tomb chapel is devoted to providing for the welfare of the *ka* of the deceased in the next world, as well as acting for its contact with the material world. The private chapel, as already pointed out, goes beyond this and includes various religious cults and an oracle.

The tomb complex at Deir el Medina could vary from a simplified structure of a courtyard, a single chamber and niche to an elaborate plan of a ramp leading to a forecourt, followed by successive halls and a sanctuary. It was almost invariably, with but a few exceptions, connected to a tomb, and benches were absent from all its halls or chambers. Tomb no. 8 of Kha,[117] chief in the Great Place, who lived during the reigns of Amenhotep II, Tuthmosis IV and Amenhotep III, had a courtyard before a single-chambered tomb chapel surmounted by a pyramid. The scenes represented the deceased with his wife, daughter and son before offerings. A banquet scene with female musicians and dancers together with guests was also depicted. The burial chamber to this chapel was one of the rare instances where tomb and chapel were separated, the former being cut into the northern cliffs opposite.

Tomb no. 250 of Ramose[118] (who had two other tomb chapels: nos 7 and 212) consisted of a court with a shaft. West of the court were three contiguous chapels. The central one portrayed two funeral processions of men and women in the company of other people before the Hathor Cow emerging from the western mountain. Another scene showed a man with a jar of corn before seated people and another group of people before six seated women.[119] A stela was painted on the west wall of the central chapel, showing the deceased adoring Osiris and his wife worshipping Amenhotep I. On the same stela, people were depicted worshipping Anubis and Ahmose Nefertari. Below this were funerary scenes of a libation priest, the Opening of the Mouth implement and a lector priest with five women before five female mummies.[120]

Tomb no. 7 consisted of a court and one chapel, and tomb no. 212 of a simple corridor and shaft cut into the lower slopes of the northern cliffs.[121] Tomb no. 216 of Neferhotep,[122] a foreman from the time of Ramesses II until Seti II, had the largest tomb in the necropolis. A ramp led to a forecourt, followed by outer and inner halls with an inner chamber or shrine containing a tomb shaft.

Many of the tombs at Deir el Medina showed Amenhotep I and Ahmose Nefertari. Amenhotep I, Ahmose Nefertari, Horemheb and Tuthmosis IV were shown in Tomb no. 7. Tomb no. 359 of Inherkhau included twenty royal ancestors, amongst whom were Amenhotep I and Ahmose Nefertari. The deceased is censing before them while his wife is worshipping.[123] The role of the royal ancestor here differs from that in the private chapel. In the tomb they were called upon for protection in the Netherworld, while in the world of the living they granted prayers or answered problems by means of oracle.

Lastly, some of the tomb chapels could be connected to a domestic enclosure in the same sense as the private chapel. These may have housed guardians. Some of the enclosures contained querns. These areas may have been used simply for preparing food offerings for the deceased and not necessarily have provided for living quarters.

Bruyère identified several of these types of tomb complexes: 1450, 1452, 1453 and 1454.[124] Tomb chapel no. 1453 (fig. 27) consisted of a courtyard and two contiguous vaulted chambers, the westernmost containing a flight of stairs sunk into the hall leading to an inner room. Abutting the southern side of the complex was a single enclosure, its entrance to the east. In the courtyard was a kneading trough constructed of bricks and four grinding stones situated near a mortar of sandstone. Nearby were grains of wheat and esparto grass.

In conclusion, it has been demonstrated that the tomb chapel was concerned exclusively with the cult of the deceased and providing for the welfare of its *ka* in the other world. In architectural terms this could range from a simple chamber to a complex of several halls. Food offerings were provided regularly for the needs of the deceased, and some tombs may have had the further advantage of a guardian.

The essence of these points are likewise included in the purpose of the private chapel, but, whereas the former was limited in its intention, the latter extended beyond these boundaries and includes a religious structure served by a priesthood. A priesthood served at the burial of the deceased, but this would be a single event as opposed to a recurring ritual. The ritual continuing in connection with the tomb would be carried out by members of the deceased's family, who would provide for him on festival days and other occasions in an informal manner.

Conclusion

It has been shown that the private chapels at Amarna and those similar at Deir el Medina were united in purpose. Minor variations within each over choice of deity or the elaboration of a cult, i.e., ancestor worship, was due to regional variations and evolution over time. Evidence from the chapels shows that by the New Kingdom the lower ranks of society had an active and well-structured cultic life, some of which was derived from the state religion in the form of the major deities and the royal ancestors. The other aspect grew from the 'soil' of the common man in the form of cults pertaining to minor deities and private ancestor worship. In addition, the private citizen had access to his own oracle at any time and was not limited to consultations with the god during festivals, such as Opet or the Valley Festival.

Finally, the evidence provided in the foregoing material demonstrates that the nature of the cult or cults performed in the chapels was both funerary and religious.

Notes

1.   Peet and Woolley, *COA* I, 99. Bruyère, *Rapport* (1929), 5-9. Kemp, *AR* I, 31.
2.   Kemp, *AR* II, 18-28.
3.   Robins in ibid., 120.
4.   Ibid., 111.
5.   Ibid., 113.
6.   Kemp, ibid., 26-27, fig. 2.6.
7.   Ibid., 28. This was calculated at seventeen courses of brick totalling 1.87 m., which, added to the wall stump of 70 cm., brings the total height to 2.57 m., plus the thickness of the roof.

8. H.F. Fairman, 'Worship and Festivals in an Egyptian Temple', *Bulletin of the John Rylands Library* 37, 1 (1954), 195. Horus the Behdetite, who was dominant in Upper and Lower Egypt protected the King, the living and the dead. His symbol was also depicted on naoi, kiosks of kings, and surmounting stelae. S. Cauville, *BIFAO* 83 (1983), 65, pls III, IV, V.
9. The average depth of a brick is from 9-10 cm. and the average layer of mortar is from 1-2 cm. The calculation follows: $17 \times 10 = 1.70$ m. plus $17 \times 2 = 0.34$ m. 1.70 m. + 0.34 m = 2.04 m. + 0.70 m. = 2.74 m. for the total height. The difference between the two given heights is 0.17 m.; halved, this is 8.5 cm. This, added to 2.57 m., would give a total height in rounded numbers of 2.66 m. for the wall, allowing for discrepancies in building materials.
10. Hecker in Kemp, *AR* III, 82, 85-87.
11. Ibid. I, 28, fig. 2.11; 33.
12. E. Hornung, *Conceptions of God in Ancient Egypt* (Great Britain, 1983), 226, 234 n. 66, 284. J. Gwyn Griffiths, *The Origins of Osiris and His Cult* (Leiden, 1980), 143-147, 233.
13. Rose in Kemp, *AR* III, 105, No. 57281.
14. Ibid., 111.
15. The workmen often used to single out these 'pebbles' as something significant.
16. W.M.F. Petrie, *Abydos* II (London, 1903), 27.
17. L. Keimer, *Études d'Égyptologie*, Fascicule II (Cairo, 1940), 'Jeux de la Nature', 1-21. Keimer writes at length about these natural flint objects used as ex-votos and amulets. He cites many coming from Deir el Medina, some of which the artist has drawn figures on the shape to emphasize the features, see pl. V 1a and b, pl. 8 1a and b; 11, fig. 8. Bruyère, *Rapport* (1934-35) II, t. XVI, (1939), 144; ex-votos found in *laraires* or tombs in the necropolis were formed from natural flint: hippopotamus, crocodile, Mertseger or Renenutet, scarab, solar disc incorporated in a little votive stela from a house. The purpose of these objects is religious and magical. Human busts were completed with sketches. These resemble miniature ancestor busts. See J.L. Keith-Bennett, *BES* 3 (1981), 64, figs 1, 2.
18. G. Dreyer in W. Kaiser, G. Dreyer, G. Grimm, G. Haeny, H. Jaritz, C. Müller, *MDAIK* 31 (1975), 51-58, Tafel 26a. The Satis Temple at Elephantine contained in its foundation deposit a collection of small stones, some of which resemble those found in Chapel 561. Thus a special cultic significance may be attached to them. Dreyer, in a personal communication, said that they appear in all periods of Egyptian history.
19. Petrie, *Abydos* II, pl. IX, natural flint (194) resembling the head of a baboon found with baboons artificially worked. Baboon figurines were found in the dumps and animal pens at Amarna.
20. Robins in Kemp, *AR* II, 127.
21. M.F. Moens, *OLP* 15 (1984) 28, 44.
22. Bruyère, *Rapport* (1935-1940), fasc. I, 103.
23. Kemp, *AR* I, 40-59.
24. Alternatively, this depression may have held a vessel.
25. Hecker in Kemp, *AR* III, 86. Dr Hecker, in a personal communication, said the phalange is from a hind leg. The two other examples from Chapels 570-571 and T-shaped basin 3 are also hind limbs. Dr Hecker suggests that this part of the animal may have had some ritual significance. The animal was always a young goat.
26. Kemp, *AR* I, 38. Dr Hecker informed me personally of the cut marks on the goat limb from this chapel.
27. This was found by me in 1981, and I have since discussed it with Dr Hecker, who has examined the foot.
28. Sir J.G. Wilkinson, *The Manners and Customs of Ancient Egypt* I (London 1878), 385, fig. 11. The figure shows the goddess Renenutet in a small shrine presiding over the activities in wine-making. A. Badawy, *A History of Egyptian Architecture* (Berkeley, 1986), 132, fig. 86. Renenutet presides over the magazines.
29. Hornung, op. cit., 281.
30. Kemp, *JEA* 67 (1981), 14-16, fig. 6.
31. A. Erman, *Life in Ancient Egypt* (New York, 1971), 273.
32. M. Bietak, *Eine Palastanlage aus der Zeit des späten Mittleren Reichs und andere Forschungsergebnisse aus dem östlichen Nildelta (Tell el-Dab'a 1979-1984)* (Wien, 1985), 330-331.
33. L. Carless Hulin in Kemp, *AR* I, 175.
34. Ibid., 166, fig. 12.1; 170, fig. 12.5.
35. Renfrew in Kemp, *AR* II, 176. Renfrew had identified olives in the village dumps.
36. W.C. Hayes, *The Scepter of Egypt* II (Metropolitan Museum of Art, 1978), 303, fig. 188.
37. C. Desroches Noblecourt, *Tutankhamen* (London, 1969), 241, fig. 146.
38. C. Aldred, *Egyptian Art* (London, 1986), 177, fig. 142.
39. C.J. Bleeker, *Hathor and Thoth* (Leiden, 1973), 52.
40. Renfrew in Kemp, *AR* II, 175.
41. Ibid., 176.
42. Bleeker, op. cit., 29. Min and Hathor were associated since early times. Min was known as god of vegetation.
43. H. Frankfort, *Kingship and the Gods* (University of Chicago, 1979), 75.

44. Ibid., 74-75.
45. Hornung, op. cit., 146-147. Nut, 'she who bore the gods'. Nut bore the sun according to the Pyramid Texts. See: R. O. Faulkner, *The Ancient Egyptian Pyramid Texts* (Oxford, 1969), line 1688. See: A. Piankoff, *The Tomb of Ramesses VI* I, (New York, 1954), 385-387, 'The Book of Day and the Book of Night'.
46. Moens, op. cit., 43-52.
47. Ibid., 28, 32, 56.
48. E.A.E. Reymond, *The Mythical Origin of the Egyptian Temple* (Cambridge, 1969), 330, fig. III.
49. U. Köhler, *'Das Imiut'* (Wiesbaden, 1975), Teil A. Abb. 1; see other illustrations. Bruyère, *Rapport* (1935-1940), fasc. I, pl. 11. The plan shows a standard within the temple of Amun called the *wsr-ḥȝt*. Symbol of power and superiority. *Rapport* (1935-40), fasc. III, 39.
50. Peet and Woolley, *COA* I, 101.
51. Bruyère, *Rapport* (1945-1947), 21.
52. G. Nagel, *La Céramique du Nouvel Empire à Deir el Médineh* (Cairo, 1938), 199-206.
53. Ibid., 203, fig. 172.
54. Y. Yadin, *Hazor, The Schweich Lectures* (1970) (London, 1972), pl. XIVa.
55. Bruyère, *Rapport* (1935-1940), fasc. I, pl. 11. See reconstruction of the Temple of Amun of Ramesses II.
56. L.B. Paton, *AASOR* (1920), 51. G. Goyon, *ASAE* 49 (1949), 359, fig. 7. A small cube-like stone with rounded summit resembling a baetyl was found by Goyon in the chapel called 'Amun of the Pure Mountain' used by the miners near the Wadi Hammamat.
57. Badawy, op. cit., 34, fig. 19.
58. Kemp, op. cit., III, 6, fig. 1.4.
59. A. Lucas and J.R. Harris, *Ancient Egyptian Materials and Industries* (London, 1962), 80-84.
60. Bleeker, op. cit., 39.
61. Vandier, *Manuel* II, 571-572.
62. Badawy, op. cit., 103, pl. 6.
63. W.S. Smith, *The Art and Architecture of Ancient Egypt* (Harmondsworth 1981), 310-311, figs 301, 302.
64. G. Loukianoff, *BIE* 13 (1931), 67-83.
65. Ibid.
66. Frankfort, op. cit., fig. 31.
67. Piankoff, op. cit. I, fig. 78.
68. C. Renfrew, *The Archaeology of Cult* (London 1985) 430, Plan: fig. 4.1.
69. Paton, op. cit., 51.
70. Peet and Woolley, *COA* I, 94.
71. Bruyère, *Rapport* (1929), 43.
72. Strabo, *The Geography of Strabo* VII (London and New York 1930), XVI, 4, 26. Strabo mentions the Nabataeans, who adopted the triclinium, as having banquets consisting of thirteen people. Significance in the number assisting a banquet or ritual gathering seems apparent when comparing the number twelve as a group in some of the chapels at Deir el Medina (see p. 71). H. Ricke, *'Ausgrabungen von Khor-Dehmitt bis Beit el Wali'* OINE II (Chicago, 1967).
73. Four shafts were unfinished on the terrace summit (Peet and Woolley, *COA* I, 94) and the fifth was in Chapel 555.
74. R.J. Demarée, *The ȝḫ iḳr n Rꜥ-Stelae* (Leiden, 1983), 217.
75. Ibid., 277-278.
76. Ibid., 182, 183, fig. 1; 283.
77. Keith-Bennett, op. cit., 43-71.
78. Valbelle, *Ouvriers*, 326.
79. Bruyère, *Rapport* (1929), 20, fig. 1.
80. Ibid., 21.
81. Bruyère, *Rapport* (1933-1934), 49. Men with the title ꜥȝnꜥ, possibly Chief of Works.
82. Bruyère, *Rapport* (1929), 22.
83. Keith-Bennett, op. cit., 47.
84. Ibid., 47-48.
85. Ibid., 47.
86. F. Friedman, *JEA* 71 (1985), 97.
87. Bruyère, *Rapport* (1929), 43.
88. Ibid.
89. Ibid., 40.
90. Ibid., 44.
91. Ibid., 10-15.
92. Bruyère, *Rapport* (1931-1932), 59.
93. Ibid., 60.
94. Bruyère, *Rapport* (1935-1940), fasc. I, 103.

95. Ibid., 104.

96. Demarée, op. cit., 84, pl. VIII, A 30.

97. Ibid., 182, 183, fig. 1.

98. Demarée does not state whether a bench in the sanctuary or the inner hall is the place of provenance. Today no benches appear in this chapel, which presumably was equipped with them in both chambers and the plans do not record them. Possibly Demarée assumes a bench in the southern niche.

99. Ibid., 282, n. 10.

100. Ibid., 279-290.

101. Bruyère, *Rapport* (1935-1940), fasc. I, 106. PM I², 694.

102. Tuthmosis I is considered the founder of the actual village of Deir el Medina (leaving Amenhotep I as founder of the community), owing to stamped bricks bearing his name. Bonnet and Valbelle, *BIFAO* 75 (1975), 432, n. 2.

103. A.M. Blackman, *JEA* 12 (1926); 181-183. S. Allam, *Hieratische Ostraka und Papyri aus der Ramessidenzeit* (Tübingen, 1973), 46-7, no. 21. R.J. Demarée and J.J. Janssen, *Gleanings from Deir el Medina* (Leiden, 1982), 118-119.

104. Bruyère, op. cit. (1930), 72; pl. XXIV.

105. Valbelle, *Ouvriers*, 332-335.

106. PM I², 690.

107. J. Černý in R.A. Parker, *A Saite Oracle Papyrus from Thebes* (Providence, R.I., 1962), 35-48.

108. Bruyère, *Rapport* (1931-1932), 62.

109. Bruyère, *Rapport* (1924-1925), 195-196.

110. Bruyère, *Rapport* (1931-1932), pl. 1.

111. Bruyère, *Rapport* (1935-1940), fasc. I, 99.

112. Kemp, *JEA* 69 (1983), 15, pl. III, 2.

113. Frankfurt, op. cit., 89-91.

114. Bruyère, *Rapport* (1934-1935) II, t. XVI, 151-167.

115. It is quite possible that chapels in this group may have had benches once, which had deteriorated during the course of time before excavation. One such example is C.V. 2 (see n. 98).

116. Bonnet and Valbelle, *BIFAO* (1976), 318, 320, fig. 1.1. A quarter was reserved for animals within the village compound during the Eighteenth Dynasty.

117. PM I¹, 16-18.

118. Ibid., 336.

119. Bruyère, *Rapport* (1926), 62-63, pls vii, viii.

120. Ibid., pl. VI.

121. PM I¹, 15-16. Bruyère, *Rapport* (1926), pl. I.

122. PM I¹, 312-315.

123. Bruyère, *Rapport* (1930), pl. ix.

124. Bruyère, *Rapport* (1948-1951), 92-126.

Chapter 6

The Architectural Origins and Development of the Private Chapel

The architectural singularity of the private chapel at Amarna and Deir el Medina demands an investigation into its origins and development. Despite the variability of the plan and the component elements of the chapels, two common features can be identified. Firstly, the chapels mainly adopt the tripartite plan of forecourt, hall (one or two) and sanctuary. The sanctuary is often tripartite and sometimes the hall is hypostyle. The axis is mostly longitudinal. All this conforms to the general pattern of the Egyptian state and smaller temples. In addition, the plan can contain some irregular internal features, also not totally uncommon in the Egyptian temple.

Secondly, the private chapel is almost always provided with benches, which are one of its distinguishing features. These are never found, as far as is known, in any Egyptian temple. Benches associated with structures other than the private chapel will be discussed below. The task of tracing the architectural origins and development of the private chapel is generally straightforward for the first group of elements. The second category presents problems more difficult to resolve. This arises from the paucity of examples of cult buildings containing benches pre-dating the New Kingdom. The possibility that private chapels with benches still await discovery is not excluded, but to date excavations have produced little that can be compared with this type of cult building. Clearly, more excavations of urban and small settlement sites, including other workmen's villages, are needed so that some sequence of development can be distinguished in the private chapel. This, of course, assumes that such chapels exist. Sites such as Kahun, Memphis and Thebes, where such features might be expected, have produced nothing so far. The only sites that can offer some information concerning this feature are Tell el Dab'a and Bab Kalabsha (Chapter 5, 68). The first site in this study is more important, since it pre-dates Amarna. The last dates to the Roman period and may reflect a quite different cultural influence (Mithraic?).

The noticeable absence in Egypt of the private chapel with benches before the Amarna period leads one to look beyond its borders to some of the neighbouring countries. In the Levant and the Aegean, examples of cult buildings with benches exist from the Early Bronze Age into the Iron Age. This being the case, the next question follows. To what extent are the private chapels of the New Kingdom the result of foreign influence? Do the architectural similarities of the Levantine and Aegean cult temples to many of the private chapels of the New Kingdom imply that foreigners or descendants of foreigners make up some of the inhabitants of the workmen's villages, introducing architectural elements indigenous to their country into the structure of the private chapel? Alternatively, did the Egyptians, having been exposed to some of these ideas, absorb them into their own culture?

It may be that the greater freedom allowed by the somewhat isolated location of the two workmen's villages and the growing democratization of religion since the Middle Kingdom led the inhabitants to provide for their own religious and cultic needs and that this, combined with exposure to foreign ideas, resulted in the creation of the private chapel during the New Kingdom. In examining these points, the Egyptian precursors to the plan of the chapel will be studied first, followed by an investigation into possible foreign interconnections.

ELEMENTS OF THE EARLY EGYPTIAN CULT TEMPLE REPRODUCED IN THE PRIVATE CHAPEL

The Egyptian temples to be discussed under this heading are those which have parallels with the private chapel, from the Archaic period to the New Kingdom. The example from Tell el Dab'a, because of its uniqueness, will be examined separately. The two earliest known cult temples are the Satis Temple on the Island of Elephantine in Upper Egypt and the temple of Khentamenti at Abydos. The former will be reviewed first.

The most ancient structure belonging to the Temple of Satis[1] dates to the First Dynasty and consisted of a sanctuary and antechamber measuring *c.* 1.60 × 2.20 m. (fig. 28). During the Third Dynasty, a larger outer court was added, in which appeared, later in the Fourth Dynasty, a brick altar (fig. 29). In the late Sixth Dynasty and until sometime during the Eleventh Dynasty, the court acquired the additional features of an oven and fireplace along the eastern wall (fig. 30). Against the western wall, before the altar, was a broad brick bench *c.* 1 m. wide × 3 m. long, which may have been used as a depository for cult objects. To the left of the bench was a narrow passage leading to the sanctuary, which occupied a niche in the granite. In the Sixth Dynasty, another brick feature appeared, which abutted the eastern wall of the court. This has been identified by the excavators as a bench. The plan, however, showed a loose and decayed articulation (fig. 29). The bricks lay on their side instead of their face, suggesting a collapsed wall and not a bench.

The Satis Temple increased in size during the Old Kingdom from its former dimensions, given above, to *c.* 7 m. wide × 9 m. long, inclusive of court and sanctuary. The temple had features not unlike some of those in the private chapels of the New Kingdom. Some of these were the oven and fireplace in the court, which also appeared in Building 528 at Amarna, although in different phases. The square brick altar or plinth in the Satis temple was no more than 20 cm. high, and its position before the brick bench in the temple dating from the Sixth Dynasty was not unlike the position of the plinths in Chapel 561. The presence of the bench echoes those in the niches of the sanctuaries in the New Kingdom chapels. In embryo, the early Satis temple encapsulates some of the main features of the private chapel: facilities for cooking and a small altar or plinth for placing objects or food before the shrine (fig. 30).

Turning to the other early temple at Abydos, the First Dynasty structure already had a basic temple plan of an outer court, which was used for sacrifices, a hall divided subsequently into three compartments and a tripartite sanctuary (fig. 31).[2] On the left side of the inner hall was a long narrow chamber. This plan persisted until the Eleventh Dynasty, when the layout of the sanctuary becomes unclear. By the Sixth Dynasty, the processional aspect of the little temple was emphasized by the addition of two gates in the enclosure wall, with a colonnade of *c.* six pillars running at a right angle to the temple (fig. 32). The tripartite plan and sanctuary were well established in many of the private chapels. Of particular interest is the appearance of a chamber on the left side of the main body of the temple at Abydos, seen in some private chapels, notably Chapel 561, the Chapel of Hathor of Seti I, and C.V. 1. However, the annexe in the Abydos temple was narrower than the later examples.

The Middle Kingdom examples, such as Qasr el Sagha with its seven niches[3] and the peripteral style temples at Tod[4] and Medamud[5] have little bearing on the plan of the private chapel. However, one temple from this period does have features which can be compared with those in the chapels. This is Medinet Ma'adi[6] in the Fayum, which had a small hall with two columns set before a tripartite sanctuary. The central niche was dedicated to Renenutet and the others to Sobek and Amenemhat III (fig. 33). The two columns before the sanctuary in the temple of Medinet Ma'adi are seen again with the presence of square column bases in the hall before the sanctuary in chapels 530 and 554 at Amarna and in the two halls of the Chapel of Hathor of Seti I, Chapelle 3, C.V. 1213, the Temple of Amun of Ramesses II in its earlier phase and Chapelle G at Deir el Medina. The tripartite shrine was, of course, a normal feature.

By the New Kingdom, the prototype of the private chapel is more easily recognizable. This is especially so in the mortuary chapel of Wadjmose[7] on the west bank at Thebes, south of the Ramesseum (fig. 34). Since Wadjmose was the son of Tuthmosis I, the main elements of this building are dated to the early Eighteenth Dynasty. It was repaired during the reigns of Amenhotep II and III and during the reign of an unidentified pharaoh of the Twentieth Dynasty. Unfortunately, Grébaut, who excavated this chapel in 1887, did not describe the Eighteenth Dynasty building in detail, so it is difficult to determine some areas of its original plan. However, it is doubtful that the building was radically altered when under repair.

The chapel was built over an earlier building. Its dimensions were 30 m. long × 28 m. wide. It was fronted by a pylon that led to an outer and inner hall. A ramp with a centre slide and two flights of steps on either side rose from the inner hall to the pronaos and tripartite shrine. A doorway led from the left side of the inner hall to an annexe, which flanked the chapel on its southern and western sides. Within the annexe was a complex of whitewashed rooms acting as storehouses and lodgings for temple personnel with a kitchen and hearth. Originally the floor of the chapel was simply of beaten earth, except in places where it had been painted red. During the Twentieth Dynasty, stones stolen from tombs, together with stelae, were laid as flagstones. Although this chapel was dedicated to a member of the royal family, it appeared to be a place of pilgrimage for the populace. Found within its precincts were votive stelae dedicated to Amun, Montu, Hathor, Taweret and Renenutet. One of the stelae was donated by the chief workman of Deir el Medina, Pashed.

At Amarna, Chapels 561 and 524 have similar parallels with the Chapel of Wadjmose, especially the arrangement of the annexe or dependencies and the flight of stairs leading to the pronaos. At Deir el Medina, the Chapel of Hathor of Seti I, the Temple of Amun of Ramesses II, and C.V.1 can especially be compared, as well as other private chapels whose tripartite sanctuaries were approached by stairs.

The small Nineteenth Dynasty cult temple to Tuthmosis III at Gurob[8] in the Fayum had a plan typical of many of the private chapels (fig. 35). This chapel, with its sanctuary lying to the southwest, was fronted by a pylon leading to an outer hypostyle hall. In the northwest of this hall were two steps, which probably served as a tiered bench for the placing of jars or other objects. Beyond was an inner hypostyle hall with a flight of six steps leading to a pronaos and tripartite sanctuary. Two columns stood before the stairs ascending to the pronaos. Before the steps were four stones set in a square, which may have formed an altar base or plinth such as that in Chapel 561 at Amarna. The majority of stelae fragments lay before the easternmost shrine, to the left of the central naos. Possibly this was the niche in which the cult of Tuthmosis III was practiced. No other evidence exists to identify the use or dedication of the remaining shrines, but Loat suggested that they may have been used as treasuries. The floor of the temple was of packed mud.

A left annexe spanned the whole of the eastern side of the chapel with an entrance at each end. Within the annexe were three alcoves and a flight of six steps. Loat suggested that it was an area for stabling animals for the people coming to worship in the temple and the alcoves were used for fodder. Alternatively, they could have been subsidiary cult niches to the main chapel. No information is available on objects or details of construction, such as whitewashing, or whether the stairs led to a roof or a side door into the sanctuary, which could indicate its use. The presence of a left annexe in a number of the chapels from the two villages has already been discussed.

The recent excavations at Deir el Ballas in 1983-1985 under the directorship of P. Lacovara may have exposed another workmen's village and chapels (fig. 36).[9] Remnants of a building built in marl brick to the east of the South Hill was labelled Chapel 1 (fig. 37). Its dimensions were approximately 10 m. wide × 18 m. long. Two unequally divided compartments lay to the west, and before them was another rectangular enclosure, centrally divided. No vestiges of benches were reported, either in the rectangular enclosure, which, if this building were a chapel, could have served as both outer and inner halls, or in the compartments to the west, which could have been the sanctuary. Unfortunately, when I was able to visit this site, the sand had covered most of the foundations, leaving little visible. Continued excavation of this area is needed to allow a proper comparison with the known private chapels. Until such time, it must remain uncertain whether this building is a chapel. Although no firm architectural comparisons can be made here, this site is potentially important as it dates to the early Eighteenth Dynasty and would pre-date Amarna and the surviving buildings of Deir el Medina. Also, its hypothetical chapel is strategically placed on the slopes of a hill, not unlike the position of the chapels in the two other settlements.

Of interest is the small sanctuary or temple dedicated by Seti I to several deities (see Appendix, 120) at Kanais in the Wadi Mia/Wadi Abbad east of Edfu (fig. 38a).[10] This was a rock-cut temple used by the goldminers, consisting of a simple plan of an outer hypostyle hall of four columns (two pillars were added in the Ptolemaic period) and an inner hall of four pillars, off which were three naoi, each fronted by a flight of stairs. The presence of columns and pillars in the halls of some of the chapels in both settlements has already been noted. Two flights of stairs ascended directly to the sanctuary in Chapelle F at Deir el Medina and two symmetrical flights and a smaller flight to three shrines in Chapel 554 at Amarna.

Last in this discussion of comparative material are several small temples in Nubia. These are Buhen, Sesebi, Amara West and Kumma, which date to the Eighteenth and Nineteenth Dynasties. The temple of Amenhotep II at Buhen (fig. 39)[11] followed the essential tripartite division with a tripartite sanctuary, two of the naoi being slightly oblique. A pylon fronted the entrance to the temple leading directly into the forecourt, which had niches by the entrance for accommodating stelae. This hall had a row of six pillars forming a portico in the west and a row of two pillars on either side of the entrance forming a right angle to those in the west. Screen walls, possibly of a later date, spanned the intercolumnar space, except for the two end piers on each side of the western row. This area may have been roofed. Beyond the court or outer hall was another hall, equally divided by partition walls, the westernmost division acting as the pronaos to the sanctuary. Steps led from the outer hall on the south side to a series of enclosures abutting the wall of the temple. It has been suggested that these were probably living quarters for the priests. In the fourth enclosure was a rectangular brick hearth and jars buried in the floor to serve as containers.

Living quarters in close association with the temple are paralleled at Deir el Medina, with C.V. 1193 and dependency 1220 and C.V. 1190 and dependency 1218. A possible parallel at Amarna could be Chapel 561 and Annexe 450, but this is tenuous. Apart from the elaborate arrangements of the pillars, the plan of the temple was basic to many of the private chapels.

The three temples at Sesebi (fig. 38b),[12] dating to the early part of Akhenaten's reign and sharing the same courtyard, are noted here because of the contiguity of their plan. This is a characteristic of most of the private chapels at Amarna and some at Deir el Medina, namely C.V. 1215 and 1216 and Chapelles C and D. The large courtyard common to the three temples is essentially comparable to the inter-connected forecourt before Chapel Group 529-531 at Amarna.

The temple at Amara West (fig. 40a),[13] dated to Ramesses II, adopted the tripartite plan usual to the chapels, but of significance are the bent axis approach to the outer court or hall, access to magazines or dependencies off the outer hall on both the eastern and western sides, and the flight of stairs to the roof on the western side of the sanctuary. The bent axis approach appeared in C.V. 1223, except through the outer hall instead of the outer court as at Amara West. However, a straight axis approach was also present in the former building. The same feature appeared in Chapel 561, which had a straight and bent axis approach, the latter of which was through Annexe 450. The same was true for Chapel 522 and its left annexe. A flight of stairs on the east side of the sanctuary of Chapel 524 and the southern side of the sanctuary of Chapelle 3 apparently led to the cliffs behind, whereas it led to the roof at Amarna. However, the location of the stairs in all three cases was the same.

The asymmetrical features of the temple at Kumma (fig. 40b),[14] built by Hatshepsut and Tuthmosis III and enlarged by Amenhotep II, displayed an originality not unlike some of the chapels. The oblique back wall to the sanctuary of the Kumma example and Chapelle 3 at Deir el Medina were both constrained by the outline of features of fortress wall and cliff respectively. The approach to this temple was on a bent axis, already discussed above. Although there was no sanctuary at Amarna or Deir el Medina exactly parallel to that at Kumma, it had its own individuality, like many of the sanctuaries at Amarna, and an asymmetry of plan seemingly characteristic of the Eighteenth Dynasty.

Mortuary Temple I at Tell el Dab'a

There are two reasons for examining Mortuary Temple I separately from the other temples. Firstly, this temple falls in the Second Intermediate Period, when Tell el Dab'a was essentially a Canaanite settlement.[15] In Syro-Palestinian chronology, as determined by Bietak's latest dating, this would correspond to MB II B 2-3, *c.* ±1670-1650 BC.[16] Secondly, the temple is the only one known so far to possess benches before the advent of the chapels at Amarna. A temple to Hathor of the Eighteenth Dynasty[17] existed near the site of the Ptolemaic one at Deir el Medina, the vestiges of a possible Eighteenth Dynasty chapel lie under Chapelle G,[18] and Valbelle referred to other earlier ones in the Theban village (see Chapter 4, 41; 54, n. 8); however, nothing substantial remains to be examined. Thus Mortuary Temple I, although some three hundred years earlier than the New Kingdom private chapel, plays an important role in the effort to understand the development of this type of cult building.

Mortuary Temple I lay in the sacred precinct northwest of the large Canaanite Temples III and V (fig. 41b). Immediately south of it was a cemetery. The plan of the temple was nearly square and consisted of a transverse antechamber or pronaos before a sanctuary containing three shrines. Benches were set against the outside wall of the antechamber and against the internal southwestern partition wall before the sanctuary. On the inner face of the northern wall of the pronaos, on either side of the entrance, were two short parallel projections. Two benches appeared on the inner northern face of the sanctuary wall on either side of the entrance, and shorter ones were placed on either side of the partition walls to the sanctuary. The eastern wall of the pronaos projected beyond the outer wall of the sanctuary, causing an angle on this side of the temple, where a flight of stairs may once have been.

Bietak has convincingly pointed out that although this temple contained Egyptian architectural elements, it was essentially Canaanite.[19] This he has shown by comparing Temple I with the temple from area H at Hazor, which dates to MB II C and LB I (fig. 41b and c). The plan is nearly square with an antechamber and pronaos and single niche. The presence of benches and short internal projections on either side of the main entrance to the Hazor temple are typical Canaanite features found in many temples in the Levant. Levantine temples will be discussed more fully later. The major difference between the Hazor temple and Temple I was that the former had one niche, the latter had three. The angle on the east side of Temple I and its three niches or shrines comprise the Egyptianized aspects of this building. Bietak referred to the small cult temple of Amenemhat I at Ezbet

Rushdi, not more than a kilometre from the sacred precinct of Tell el Dab'a, as a probable Egyptianizing influence on the small mortuary temple.

The temple at Ezbet Rushdi (fig. 41a) was 41.5 m. long × 31 m. wide.[20] Its plan, too, was nearly square and consisted of a transverse hypostyle hall with six columns on square bases. This was followed by a tripartite sanctuary, the entrance to which contained an offering table. The central shrine was wider than the two lateral shrines. A narrow corridor, 1.10 m. wide, led off from the forecourt along the western side of the temple, around the rear of the sanctuary and as far as the length of its eastern outside wall; it was filled with sand and Shehata Adam suggested that it may have given solidity to the internal sanctuary walls. This temple had no benches or internal parallel projections on either side of the main entrance. The elements which correspond to Temple I are the tripartite sanctuary and the angle formed on the outside longitudinal wall.

The amalgamation of architectural features from two different cultures found in Temple I suggests the possibility of the same occurrence in the New Kingdom private chapels. Among the architectural features cited by Bietak as Levantine, the two that are relevant to the chapels are the bench and double wall with filling.[21] The former item is common to the chapels whereas the latter is not, but the one specific case of use is of especial significance (Chapter 2, 16).

Before continuing with a discussion and comparison of Syro-Palestinian temples relevant to the chapels in Egypt, a clarification is needed of types of benches or stone tables found in rare cases in other structures outside the domain of private chapels, which might appear to contradict the above theories.

The first example was found in the Sixth Dynasty mastaba of Prince Mena at Dendera, excavated by Petrie. Abutting the north side was a court with a continuous bench 66 cm. wide × 85 cm. high, set against the north and east walls. Petrie remarked on the unusual occurrence of a court and benches appearing with a mastaba (fig. 42a),[22] and as far as is known this feature does not appear in any other mastaba from this or other periods. Clearly, the bench was much larger than any found in the New Kingdom private chapels and would not have been used for seating people, but more likely for accommodating objects or offerings (cf., Chapter 5, 72). The use of the bench in connection with funerary purposes shows a parallel with the intention of some of the benches in the private chapel. Its siting in an open court can only be compared with Building 528 at Amarna. In the latter example the receptacles were sunk into the bench,[23] whereas in the former, if they were used, they would have been placed on the surface. However, this one isolated case of a court with a continuous bench on two sides cannot be termed a characteristic feature of Egyptian architecture, since no other examples are available.

The next example appeared in the same dynasty, during the reign of Pepi II. Abutting the east face of the Pyramid of Queen Neit, one of the royal wives, was a small chapel containing a stone altar approached by three steps.[24] Against the north wall of the chamber was a limestone bench, or according to Jéquier, its excavator, a block with a projecting cornice, which 'servait de dressoir dans les cérémonies d'offrandes'. The south side of the chapel was destroyed, but Jéquier did not record or mention any traces of a bench on this side. The projecting cornice, although not a cavetto, classes this as the 'altar' type bench found in the naoi of chapels and not in the halls.

The last example appeared in some monuments of the New Kingdom. These structures were more like stone tables and appeared in some royal tombs and a temple. In the outer hall of the tomb of Queen Nefertari, wife of Ramesses II, in the Valley of the Queens on the west bank at Thebes, was one of these table-type benches.[25] It was provided with a cavetto cornice with a series of cubicles sunk into the masonry of the bench below. A similar arrangement appeared in the room with two pillars branching off the sarcophagus chamber in the tomb of Seti I[26] and in the second sanctuary of Osiris behind the seven chapels in the Temple of Seti I at Abydos.[27] These tables also probably provided a place for putting funerary objects and offerings in the case of a royal burial, and votive offerings in the instance of the latter example during the celebration of the mysteries of Osiris. These types of benches or tables with their cavetto cornice and niches are comparable to the architecture of the benches found in the shrines in the sanctuaries of the private chapels and bear no relationship to those found in the halls of the chapels. The benches in the Bab Kalabsha chapels have already been discussed and need not detain us here (Chapter 5, 68).

THE ARCHITECTURE OF SYRO-PALESTINIAN TEMPLES RELEVANT TO THE PRIVATE CHAPEL

The idea of Canaanite influence on the architecture of the private chapel has also been supported by Giveon, when discussing the Bethshan temples and the Amarna chapels. He said 'Only some small chapels at Tell el Amarna were built in that style [ie., the Bethshan temples]. Perhaps the position should be inverted: in this view the Amarna chapels are an imitation of Canaanite prototypes'.[28]

Syria-Palestine during the course of the Bronze and Iron Ages appeared as a melting-pot for many ethnic groups, such as Canaanites, Amorites, Moabites, Edomites, Philistines and Phoenicians to name only a few. As tribal groups formed small rural communities and later, in the Middle Bronze Age, large urban settlements like Megiddo, Shechem and Hazor, the intermixture of cultures produced no particular style that could be attributed definitely to any one ethnic group. Thus, unlike Egypt, a diversity in the style of the religious or cult building appears in Syria-Palestine. Out of this, however, can be recognized temples serving an official use and those accommodating the religious and cultic needs of the people.[29] The second group is important in attempting to understand the nature and origin of the private chapel, which hypothetically may relate to aspects of the non-official Levantine temple. The Late Bronze and Iron Age temples of Bethshan are central to this investigation. However, before examining these buildings, a brief background explanation, with some examples from earlier periods, is needed. From the embryonic structures of the Chalcolithic and Early Bronze Age to the more complex forms of the Middle Bronze Age, certain characteristic features in the buildings can be linked to the temples at Bethshan and by indirect association with the private chapels.

After presenting the relevant details of the early temples, points from these will be provided in an effort to understand the development of the chapels. This will be followed by a separate discussion on Bethshan.

Of the first structures in Palestine that can properly be called a temple or cult building were the *Breitbau*, with its axis on the long wall and the *Knickasche*, which originally, apart from its domestic purpose, served as the religious focal point for family religion (fig. 42b).[30] The *Breitbau* continued as the typical temple plan until it was superseded by the more imposing official axial temple, the *Langbau*. Unlike the *Breitbau*, this temple in its true form (the *Langbau* appears in composite forms) precluded the direct participation of the populace. Although the *Langbau* as a *megaron* was known from Pre-Pottery Neolithic B at Jericho, its monumental form appeared with the upsurge of the big city states of the Middle Bronze Age at Megiddo, Shechem and Hazor. At the first two sites it appeared as the 'fortress' or *migdol* temple. Another temple type from the Middle Bronze Age onwards was the *square* temple. It is, however, the *Breitbau/Knickasche* and *Langbau* in its humble aspect that are of principal concern here.

With the appearance of the official, urban *Langbau*, the *Breitbau* and *Knickasche* did not vanish, but continued as parochial types into the later periods. One of the distinctive features of these temples and the informal *Langbau* with a *Breitraum* cella is the presence of benches, which suggests a use different from those temples not equipped with this installation. It should be noted at this point that the *Breitbau* in the early periods could also appear without benches, as in the Ai Acropolis Temple of Early Bronze Age II-III and the Megiddo Porch Temples of EB III-EB-MB.[31]

The bench averaged about 50 cm. wide × 50 cm. high and was ranged against one, two or all the walls. Wright, Amiran and others see their derivation from the simple village house, of which the houses at Early Bronze Age Arad (fig. 43) are the 'classic' example.[32] Benches were set against at least two or all the walls of a broad room and a central column supported the roof. The temples at Arad followed in nearly all details the same construction (fig. 44).[33] Wright and Andrae, the excavator of the Archaic Ishtar Temple at Assur, see the benches as placed for standing terracotta figurines, found in these temples, as votive offerings and not for seating people (fig. 45).[34]

Other early examples of temples of this kind are the Ghassulian Shrine at En-Gedi,[35] dating to the Chalcolithic period (fig. 46) and corresponding to Pre-Dynastic to First Dynasty Egypt, and the *Knickasche* sanctuary from Jericho, Level VII,[36] dating to Early Bronze Age Ia, *c.* 3000 B.C. (fig. 47). In the *Breitraum* cella of the main shrine at En-Gedi, benches were lined against the north and south walls on either side of the entrance and shrine. The latter building at Jericho had a continuous bench around all the walls, with the 'niche' area broadening into a dais.

An example of an unofficial cult building from Middle Bronze Age Syria is Sanctuary B2 at Tell Mardikh (fig. 48)[37] dating to MB II, *c.* 1800-1600 B.C. This consisted of a complex of chambers separated by an open area from the *Langbau* Temple B1. On the north side of the courtyard to the sanctuary was a lateral room containing a small bench, into which were sunk two large basalt mortars. To the east of the courtyard was a large hall with a bent axis and low benches set against three of its walls. A rectangular brick dais was situated near the southern wall. Other chambers, some of which appear to have served ritualistic purposes from the presence of polished offering tables used for blood sacrifices, flanked the central hall on the north, south and east. Matthiae suggested that the sanctuary, together with Temple B1, may have served a funerary purpose, because the nearby rock face contained cavities, some of which have been identified as tombs.[38]

What is the relevance of these Levantine cult buildings, dating centuries before the Amarna period, to the private chapels? It has been stated already that the irregular plan and installations of these buildings were inspired by the domestic prototype. As the ordinary man's religious and cultic life developed, he provided it with an architectural form which was an extension of his house and the former centre of religious observance.[39] This was continuous throughout the Bronze Ages. Apparently, in Egypt the lower echelon of society did not share the same privilege until the New Kingdom. Baines has pointed out that the religion of the populace is 'poorly known in most of its periods and aspects', and except funerary aspects, practical religion is unknown before the New Kingdom.[40]

The Old Kingdom pyramid cities provide no clue, and the Middle Kingdom workers' settlement at Kahun had no private chapels.[41] The highly structured society of Egypt did not cater for the *rhyt* ('the populace') from the religious point of view, although it was their labour upon which the country depended. It could be said that since part of the state or the domains in which they worked were ultimately under the control of the pharaoh and his close administration, they were absorbed, unindividualized, into the outer perimeters of the pharaoh's divine orbit. The fragmenting of this single 'unit' had begun before the Middle Kingdom, and man could now 'speak to his *ba*'.[42] By the Second Intermediate Period, a thriving community of Canaanites from Syria-Palestine had settled in the northeast Delta and the rule of the Hyksos extended at least as far as Cusae. With them they brought their religious customs and methods of constructing cultic enclosures. An example of this is the sacred enclosure at Tell el Dab'a, with its two monumental *Langbau* temples and nearby mortuary temple (fig. 49; see above, p. 85), not reserved exclusively for royalty and its entourage but, judging from the proximity of the 'family' cemetery, including the people.[43] These evolving religious ideas, manifested in architecture in the Levant since earliest times, are visible in a similar flowering in the consciousness of the lower strata of Egyptian society, only much later than that of their Asiatic neighbours. It could be said that in the sphere of religion and cult, the Egyptian was beginning to be liberated. In the two settlements of Amarna and Deir el Medina, where foreign elements may have been present, the Egyptian expressed his religious ideas outwardly in terms of architecture that may have combined or metamorphosed certain Asiatic structural forms which had been in existence centuries before the appearance of the private chapels.

To reiterate, in most of the chapels at Amarna the benches ran along at least three or sometimes even four sides of the wall. At Deir el Medina, a noteworthy example is Chapelle B, where this not only occurred in the halls, but also in the shrine, which included a bench around all walls. This feature is well documented in the early cult buildings of the Levant, already cited above. Another point of comparison is the possibility of funerary or ancestral practices connected with Sanctuary B2 at Tell Mardikh, which might be similar to those occurring in some of the chapels at Deir el Medina and probably in all of the chapels at Amarna. It could be argued that the 'benches' in the central room in most of the houses in the Workmen's Village at Amarna were the prototype for those in the chapels. However, these are not benches, but a dais, and in the case of the house at Gate Street No. 8[44] only 7 cm. above floor level and with a greater depth than the benches in the chapels. Furthermore, they were L-shaped and against only two walls. This arrangement of the bench occurred in only some chapels (526, 561 — Side Chapel). The houses at Deir el Medina had no benches like those in the chapels, nor did they have daises like those in the workers' houses at Amarna. The benches appearing in some of the surviving houses at Medinet Habu, dating to Amenhotep III, are just less than a metre wide and span only part of one wall.[45]

In the Levant from the Early Bronze Age onwards, benches appeared sporadically in the domestic dwelling, but their presence in certain cult temples, notably the unofficial type, was a continuous feature until at least Iron Age II. The positions in which these benches were sited in the temple, and in many cases their size, compare most closely with those in the chapels.

The Late Bronze and Iron Age Temples at Bethshan

The similarity of the Bethshan temples of Levels VII and VI to the Amarna chapels has been recognized by scholars since their excavation by Rowe in 1921-1934. The view has always been that they are essentially Egyptian, a transposition, so to speak, of the Amarna chapels to Bethshan. The reverse supposition, already mentioned, was mooted by Giveon. Rowe also believed the Amarna chapels were influenced by the Bethshan temples.[46] The problem here is to try to discover whether in fact the plan of the Bethshan temples could have influenced the layout of the Egyptian private chapel or vice versa. Before this can be done, some discussion of the date of these temples is required.

Unfortunately, the date of the Bethshan temples has been a subject of much controversy, owing to speculation concerning the interpretation of stratigraphy, particularly of Levels VII and VI. The site has eighteen levels, but in Rowe's final report levels were listed only from one to nine. Level I was the latest, corresponding to the Arabic and Crusader period, and Level IX the earliest, dated to Tuthmosis III. The dates given for Levels VII and VI, which are the main concern here, are either high or low, causing the attribution of the temples to vacillate between the reigns of Amenhotep III and Ramesses III. The dates provided by various scholars and relevant to this discussion are as follows:

Rowe:[47]

Levels	Dates	Context
V	1292-1225 BC	Ramesses II; southern and northern Canaanite temples of Dagon and Anit; Late Canaanite.
VI	1313-1292 BC	Seti I; two levels: Late Seti, Early Seti Canaanite temple.
VII	1411-1314 BC	Amenhotep III; small upper stratum in part of this

		level; Canaanite Temple and traces of small shrine on west side of temple.
VIII	1447-1412 BC	Pre-Amenhotep III.
IX	1501-1447 BC	Tuthmosis III; Canaanite Mekal Temple.

Rowe's dates are disregarded by most scholars today. However, his attribution for the Level VII temple was thought to be possibly correct by Aharoni.[48]

Aharoni:

Levels	Context
V	Belongs to the Israelite period; second half of the twelfth to eleventh century BC. The two new southern and northern temples were built.
VI	Ramesses I; the lintel of Ramesses-Weser-Khepesh bearing the name of Ramesses III (found in Stratum V and in secondary use) came from commander's house (1500) of upper Stratum VI, which has two phases.
VII	Assigned to Amenhotep III, IV.

The reasons for Aharoni's dating of Levels VII and VI is the remarkable continuity and consistency of the scarabs found in the foundation offerings of the various temples from IX to VI. He was aware, however, of the unreliability of dating with scarabs, which could either be heirlooms or manufactured years after a king's reign. According to Rowe, and accepted by Aharoni, the foundation offerings of the Level VII temple consisted of a scarab, signet ring and an amulet all bearing the name of Amenhotep III, found beneath the altar steps. Aharoni's other reasons for the dating of Level VII were this temple's likeness to two chapels at Amarna (the numbers were not provided) and a papyrus capital similar to one found at Megiddo in the palace from Stratum VIII, dated to the Amarna period.[49]

James:

James dealt only with Iron Age Bethshan, thus only dates for Levels IV-VI are provided.[50]

Levels	Context
IV	destroyed c. 723 BC
Upper V	destroyed c. 800 BC
Lower V	destroyed c. 918 BC
Upper VI	destroyed c. 1100-1075 BC, end of Twentieth Dynasty.
Lower VI	constructed in the reign of Ramesses III, and was immediate reconstruction of VII.

James stated that the end of Level VI was affected by the stelae of Seti I and Ramesses II that were found in Lower Level V and not in VI, as well as a statue of Ramesses III in the same stratum. She said that upon the destruction of Level VI, these were moved and reused in Level V. In addition, James noted that the pottery forms corresponded to the dates given for the end of Level VI, i.e., they were early Iron Age types. She observed that Level VI pottery was completely different from Level VII, which contained typical LB II examples.

Owing to her demise, she was unable to finish her work on Level VII, which subsequently was completed by McGovern. In his observations on the pottery from this level, he concluded that the Egyptian, as well as the Palestinian material, appeared to belong to the Nineteenth Dynasty, i.e., to LB IIB, with the exception of some earlier LB I-IIA Palestinian examples, believed to have come from areas where the excavators dug into Level IX.[51]

Although a complete study of the Level IX stratum is yet to be done, McGovern has observed that it contains scarabs of the Eighteenth Dynasty, exclusively predating Ramesses I. He added that the Canaanite Middle Bronze architectural style continued in this level, changing with Levels VIII-VII from the complexities of the Mekal temple to the abbreviated plan of those under discussion.

Lastly, Dothan largely agreed with James's dating, suggesting that Level VI represented the pinnacle of the Egyptianization of Bethshan during the Twentieth Dynasty. She also stated that Level VII indicates an extensive Nineteenth Dynasty Egyptian occupation. This she attributed mainly to the extensive coffin burials in the Northern Cemetery corresponding to Level VII and VI, of which the later examples she assigned to the Sea Peoples, or possibly to the Philistines.[52]

Before discussing the dating and relevance of the Bethshan temples and private chapels on the basis of the data provided above, the plans and features of these two temples need to be examined.[53]

Level VII: (fig. 50)

The temple was oriented north-north-east to south-south-west. The plan consisted of a small vestibule entered from the southwest, with a door on a north to south axis leading to a central hall. Adjacent to the vestibule was a compartment whose eastern wall was formed by the street wall, on the other side of which were houses.[54] In the central hall, on either side of the long axis, were two column bases formed of stones. A bench, into which was set a semi-circular receptacle in the southwest corner and a rectangular receptacle in the northwest corner, was laid against the west, north and east walls. A lower altar abutting a secondary bench before a flight of steps cut into the sanctuary floor led to a *Breitraum* cella. This had an altar aligned on the same axis as the steps, lower altar, eastern column base and entrance to the secondary compartment adjacent to the vestibule. This was the main axis of the temple and was off-centre, lying in the eastern section of the temple. In the cella was a projection west of the altar, in the angle of which was a rectangular receptacle. A papyrus capital and foundation offerings, now questionable, came from this temple. From the sanctuary came a stela with a representation of the goddess Astarte wearing the Syrian conical crown with a streamer and two horns. Before the goddess was a woman with a lotus on her head offering flowers and surmounting the top of the stela was an indistinct hieroglyphic inscription.[55]

Level VI: (fig. 51)

This temple had the same orientation and nearly the same plan as Level VII, except for some alterations to the exterior and interior. An outer court was added to the vestibule, which then had entrances in its western and eastern walls. The compartment to the east disappeared. The entrance to the main hall remained the same. Two circular column bases replaced the stone foundations. The receptacles in the north and southwest corner disappeared and the bench was reduced in the north. The lower altar was then a separate unit, followed by a broad flight of stairs adjoining the sanctuary. The floor of the sanctuary now projected on a level with the inside face of the hall wall. The sanctuary was *Breitraum*, but had a solid partition wall further to the west and another in the east forming a compartment with an internal division. The upper altar, stairs and lower altar were aligned on the axis of the temple, which was now centred and passed between the two column bases. The entrance to the temple, however, lay to the left of the main axis. The overall plan of the Level VI temple was slightly reduced from that of Level VII, and its western wall became minimally concave. The foundation deposits (also questionable) of this temple were under the walls and floor, consisting of cartouches of Ramesses I.[56]

Discussion

How, then, do these temples compare with the private chapels? The plan of the temple in Level VII is generally un-Egyptian, except for the presence of two columns and steps rising to the sanctuary. Even so, columns were not unusual in a Canaanite temple, and in the earlier Mekal temple steps led to the sacrificial altar (fig. 52). Unlike an Egyptian temple, the Level VII temple had no symmetrical features and was aligned to an off-centre axis, also not an Egyptian practice. The only definitely Egyptian features were some external embellishments, already mentioned. However, aspects of this temple can be seen in some of the chapels at Amarna. The two chapels referred to without identification by Aharoni which can compare with the Level VII temple could be 551 and 552, to which could be added 554 and 553, together with some points from certain chapels in the southern group (figs 4 and 5). In the proposed relative chronology for the Amarna chapels, it was suggested that the northern group was among the first constructed (Chapter 3, 35). Comparable points between these chapels and Level VII were the broad inner hall and siting of benches and two piers in 554; the receptacles in 551, especially the sanctuary; the off-centre alignment of 552 and 553; and, in general, benches against the walls of nearly all inner halls before the sanctuaries in most chapels.

The Egyptianization of the Level VI temple is more evident: its main features on a central axis, the separation of the lower altar from the stairs and the tripartite division of the sanctuary, although still containing only one shrine. Although this temple was still a modified version of that in Level VII, it was similar to some of the chapels at Amarna and Deir el Medina (cf. figs 4, 5 and figs for Deir el Medina).

Having examined various scholars' dating, together with details and modifications of the architecture of these two temples and their comparison with the private chapels, how should the proposed relationship between the Bethshan and Egyptian cult buildings be regarded?

If one were to accept Aharoni's view, Upper Level VII would be attributed to Amenhotep III-Akhenaten and, after the complete destruction of this level, its rebuilding as Lower VI to Seti I. Upper VI would be assigned to Ramesses III.

Considering Aharoni's remarks on the foundations of these buildings, the reign of the previous monarch could be commemorated in these offerings, e.g., Amenhotep III by Akhenaten or at some point through to Horemheb and Ramesses I by Seti I. There is no need to assume several generations in between. That the life of a temple could continue throughout several reigns should be considered, since there is much evidence to support this. A building, of course, can undergo additions and internal restructuring during the passing of time, which may have been the case with Level VI temple, which apparently saw two phases. With these points in mind, together with the chronology given for the private chapels of Amarna and Deir el Medina, it is possible to recognize a development of this type of cult building. From a relatively unsymmetrical and irregular type of building in its early stages, the chapel progressively absorbed and metamorphosed certain foreign elements during the course of time into its essentially Egyptian structure.[57]

Alternatively, taking the evidence provided by James and McGovern, which appears the most reliable, Level VII would be equivalent to the Nineteenth Dynasty and Level VI to the Twentieth. As a result, the Amarna chapels would predate by approximately some fifty years the Level VII temple, whilst the Deir el Medina chapels would be contemporary with both Levels VII and VI.

How would this affect the interchange of architectural influences and subsequent development of the private chapel, especially at Amarna? Based on the series of examples of Levantine cult architecture given above, and upon foreign influence to be discussed below (94-97), it is reasonable to argue that some degree of extrinsic elements may have been absorbed and refined already into the chapel architecture. Therefore, if the Amarna chapels influenced the architecture of Level VII temple, one would expect a building on a more central axis and not as many asymmetrical features. However, despite the fifty years following the Amarna Period, the Level VII temple appears to have maintained, instead of to have lost, many Canaanite characteristics that previously the Amarna chapels seem to have mirrored in a more Egyptianized form. Nevertheless, the later dating of the Bethshan temples does not affect the suggested development of the Egyptian chapels, since both evolved along parallel lines.

Furthermore, why would the Egyptians, when building Level VII temple, have planned their building after some chapels from a remote workmen's village such as Amarna, which incidentally, by the reign of Seti I had become uninhabited? It would be more reasonable to pursue the layout of the typical Egyptian cult temple. Considering these points, it seems apparent that the Egyptians adapted the Bethshan temple plan to Canaanite traditions, and that, despite the later date of this temple, the Amarna chapels had earlier undergone a similar process for reverse reasons. Following on from this is the next consideration: the inhabitants of Bethshan.

Bethshan came under Egyptian influence in the reign of Tuthmosis III after the battle of Megiddo, and a small Egyptian command was maintained there. A *migdol* fort was situated not far from the Level VII temple,[58] where a garrison probably found its quarters (fig. 53). This disappeared in Level VI and was replaced by houses. In Upper Level VI, house 1500 produced the lintel of Ramesses-Weser-Khepesh, the commander of the garrison during the reign of Ramesses III.[59] With the destruction of the earlier Mekal temple, Seti I established a sizable garrison at Bethshan upon the expulsion of the invaders, all of which he commemorated in a stela.[60]

The main body of mercenaries in the employ of the Egyptians were probably forerunners of the Sea Peoples and have been associated with the anthropoid coffin burials in the Great Northern Cemetery.[61] As already mentioned, these appeared in both levels (the main corpus in Level VI) and have been dated and attributed variously to different Sea Peoples by Dothan and Oren.[62] The former dated the coffins from the thirteenth to the eleventh century B.C. and stated that they were first introduced by Egyptian officials or mercenaries and adopted later by the Philistines. Oren, however, suggested that the mercenaries were Denyen, identified as the Danuna of the Amarna tablets. These people, and the Sherden, invaded the eastern Mediterranean during the late Eighteenth, and especially the Nineteenth Dynasty. They were subsequently employed as mercenaries in the Egyptian army and were probably among those buried in the coffins. Owing to the presence of some of these coffins in Level VII, along with associated vessels, both Dothan and Oren attributed Level VII to Seti I.

Returning to the question of the inhabitants of the garrison city, the foreign mercenaries, together with Canaanites and Egyptians, may have used the temples. It seems reasonable that inhabitants of the vassal states of Syria-Palestine and such towns as Bethshan would be permitted to carry on their cultic practices and traditions unimpeded, adopting what appealed to them of the Egyptian culture. This, inevitably, would be impressed upon the final outcome of the temple architecture.

To conclude the discussion about the cult buildings of Bethshan and Amarna, it was suggested that both included features extraneous to their traditions, but integrated into the structure. The significance is not that the chapels of Amarna or the Level VII temple of Bethshan had an exclusive or mutual impact on either one or the other, but that, because of their similarities, both exhibit an architectural form developed from the integration of religious ideas from two different countries, which in both cases may have begun independently of each other.

Before returning to Egypt and the hypothesis of foreigners or their descendants in the workmen's villages, a brief investigation of one or two cult buildings in the Aegean will help to round out the picture concerning suggested influences within the fabric of the private chapel, and will be useful in the light of the possible Aegean connections of some of the Sea Peoples.

THE AEGEAN TEMPLE

In this survey of foreign cult buildings, those from the Aegean cannot be excluded, since they too used benches extensively. Here, as in the Levant, the people participated in visible religious activities, not bound by a structured society, like that of Egypt. Egypt had contact with the Minoan civilization certainly by the Middle Kingdom, since Minoan pottery has been found at Kahun, Lisht, Haragah and Aswan.[63] Minoans were depicted in Theban tombs of the New Kingdom, for instance, tomb no. 71 of Senmut,[64] and they may have exercised some stylistic influence on Egyptian art.[65]

The convening for cultic purposes in the Aegean occurred in diverse places: on the summit of mountain peaks, in caves, in sacred enclosures and in specially constructed crypts, in domestic and palace sanctuaries and in temples.[66] Benches, either of natural rock or constructed of stones and mortar, were found in some degree in all these sanctuaries throughout the Bronze Age and onwards. Rutkowski stated that the bench was probably present from Neolithic times and its function in the sanctuaries was the same as in the private house: for sitting and storing vessels and other objects.[67] He felt that its main purpose in the sanctuary was for standing objects on.

Two temples have been selected for examination here: those of Ayia Irini in Keos and Phylakopi in Melos. The temple in Keos (fig. 54) was a small sanctuary during the Middle Helladic period.[68] By Late Helladic IB the sanctuary was enlarged and rooms were added, and by about 1400 BC (Late Helladic IIIA) it was destroyed by an earthquake. It was rebuilt around 1200 BC. The overall plan was an extended rectangle consisting of several rooms and in its final phase it reached dimensions of 23 m. × 7 m. Benches were present throughout all the Bronze Age, the earliest dating to the Middle Bronze Age. These were in the rooms labelled IV and V (fig. 54).[69]

The temple of Phylakopi was erected near a defensive wall in LM IIIA and underwent several phases of development (fig. 55). The original temple was about 11 m. long × 7 m. wide. By Late Helladic IIIA, the temple had acquired its main features of two roofed rooms containing small benches or altars and a courtyard with a bench, near which was a baetyl (Chapter 5, 67).[70] The distribution of the benches in these two temples could be either in the courtyard or interior of the temple. In the private chapels, they were found in the halls and not always in the courtyard. If, however, Chapel 525 was correctly reconstructed by Newton (fig. 16) with an open court before the pronaos, the baetyl and bench in the Phylakopi example were in essence similar.

FOREIGN INFLUENCE AMONG THE LOWER RANKS OF SOCIETY IN NEW KINGDOM EGYPT

Centuries before the workmen's villages of the New Kingdom, Asiatics were filtering into the Delta for trade reasons and in search of grazing land for their flocks. Khety, a king of the Akhtoy family of the Ninth and Tenth Dynasty at Heracleopolis, instructed his son Merikare to set up frontier defenses in the Eastern Delta as a deterrent against the Bedouin.[71] These same people are believed to have introduced the copper-headed arrow into Egypt and to have served as mercenaries in Middle Egypt.[72] Amenemhat I also built defenses in the eastern part of the Wadi Tummilat. Other sources of foreign presence in Egypt before the New Kingdom were prisoners from small scale military campaigns and skirmishes. These became royal property, or sometimes were entrusted to a private owner. The slave trade, carried on by the Asiatics themselves, was a source of additional labour in Egypt.[73]

The Brooklyn Papyrus of the Late Middle Kingdom mentions the names of forty-five Asiatic men, women and children who worked in the household of an Upper Egyptian official. Hayes pointed out that if this were the case in many upper class households, the numbers of Asiatics in Egypt would have been considerable.[74] He added that this situation could have been instrumental in reducing Egypt's ability to prevent the Hyksos hegemony. Many of these foreigners, who worked alongside Egyptian labourers and servants, were subject to the corvée, which required them to work in the fields, harvest the crops and tend to the irrigation system. The Asiatics mentioned in the lists in the same papyrus retained their own names, but had been given Egyptian names to help their overlords to identify them. Their names are prefixed with *ꜥꝫm* or *ꜥꝫmt* (Asiatic and female Asiatic), indicating that they came from Syria-Palestine.[75]

Another point of contact between Egypt and the Asiatics was the mining expeditions in the Sinai.[76] Foreign groups of six to ten men were listed and depicted on stelae of the Middle Kingdom. Near the temple of Serabit el Khadim, the Proto-Sinaitic inscriptions, which adapted Egyptian hieroglyphs to Semitic words and were instrumental in the development of Canaanite, were discovered.[77] Goedicke referred to one of the earliest representations of an Asiatic — Abi Shai in the tomb of Khnumhotep at Beni Hasan.[78] He convincingly argued that Abi Shai was not part of a caravan, but was employed under the auspices of Senwosret II in mining galena in the Eastern Desert. In addition, the Hatnub graffiti mentioned Asiatic mercenaries from the beginning of the Twelfth Dynasty.[79]

The Minoan pottery found at the sites mentioned earlier (see above, p. 93) dates to Middle Minoan I-II. Helck correlated this to the Second Intermediate Period,[80] Kemp and Merrillees to the Middle Kingdom.[81] These may be trade goods or evidence of Aegean presence in Egypt. Petrie suggested that foreigners were the chief component of the work force in the settlement at Kahun, noting three types of measure there, none of which was the usual Egyptian cubit. One, a measure divided into two parts of about 13.2 inch units, he identified as Near Eastern in origin.[82]

Overwhelming evidence for foreigners in the Eastern Delta, especially Tell el Dab'a during the Second Intermediate Period, has already been discussed. The autobiography of 'Ahmose, son of Abana'[83] tells of the expulsion of the Hyksos from Egypt, but this is unlikely to have been total, and Ahmose was himself of foreign extract.

Weinstein and Redford have both pointed out that the initial penetration into Syria-Palestine was in pursuit of the Hyksos, and in the following years there were campaigns to prevent further invasions.[84] These punitive operations may have been completed by the reign of Tuthmosis I, when Shechem was once again destroyed, along with Beth Zur and some western and southern cities, and areas in inland Palestine.[85] From these campaigns came some booty and captives, but at this time no permanently organized Egyptian occupation was established.

It was after the taking of Megiddo by Tuthmosis III in *c.* 1482 BC that Egypt began to build its empire in earnest. The list of toponyms in the Annals of Tuthmosis give up to 350 names. By capturing Megiddo, the king gained control of all these towns, which show little evidence of a total destruction. Such an act would not have been in the economic interests of Egypt. Military strongholds were established and Palestine and southern Syria were organized into three administrative districts, with headquarters at Gaza, Sumur and Kumidi.[86] With this network, Egypt was able to exercise political and economic control over the Levant to its own advantage. Great wealth began to flood into Egypt in the form of goods and a human work force. From the Asiatic campaign of Tuthmosis, Amun received 1,588 Syrian prisoners. Amenhotep II claimed to have brought 89,600 Asiatic prisoners into Egypt to work on the temple estates, and the mortuary temple of Tuthmosis IV was provided with the citizens of Gezer.[87] A settlement near the mortuary temple of Amenhotep III was filled with Syrian slaves, male, female and children of unknown number.[88] Helck mentioned that in the larger cities, such as Memphis, quarters were set aside for Asiatics.[89] With them came their gods, including Reshef, Anat, Ba'al, Astarte, Ishtar, Qadesh and Hauron.[90]

Besides the wealth derived from the campaigns, active commercial relations were established with the Levant and many Syrian merchants and traders began to pour into Egypt to carry on business.

Of the pharaohs of the Eighteenth Dynasty, Akhenaten is the one depicted in scenes accompanied by the greatest number of military personnel, with regiments of Nubians, Libyans and Syrians. Reliefs depicted on talatat blocks from Karnak and the tomb of Ahmose (no. 3) at Amarna are among some examples.[91] Redford stated that Syrian spearmen served in the army and that many rose to higher status in government and religious offices.[92]

It is clear, therefore, that foreigners were present in considerable numbers in Egypt during the New Kingdom, and that they permeated all ranks of society and types of occupation. The implications for the workmen's villages, especially Amarna, remain to be considered.

At this point, it is worth glancing at the town of Medinet Gurob, north of Kahun. It flourished during the New Kingdom, from the end of the Eighteenth Dynasty until the early part of the Nineteenth Dynasty.[93] Before the town was built, Tuthmosis III constructed a temple in this area, which was demolished during the reign of Akhenaten. Houses were built over the site of this temple, which Petrie believed may have housed the masons or workmen. Rings of Akhenaten and one of Amenhotep III were discovered in the houses.[94] Petrie stated that Gurob was continuously occupied from the reign of Akhenaten until Ramesses II, and that it was inhabited mainly by foreigners. His evidence is taken from names, foreign weights, the use of the Cypriot alphabet and the presence of a quantity of Greek and Cypriot wares. He also pointed out that foreigners were largely employed at the end of the Eighteenth Dynasty and the beginning of the Nineteenth Dynasty.

It has already been noted (Chapter 5, 73) that Asiatic gods were worshipped at Deir el Medina. Although by now foreign deities were part of the Egyptian repertoire, this does not exclude the possibility that descendants of foreigners were present in the Theban village. Bierbrier has claimed that there is no evidence for this, since no foreign names were recorded, but non-Egyptians are known to have adopted Egyptian names.[95]

In the case of the Workmen's Village of Amarna, another possibility should be considered. The Stone Village,[96] still unexcavated, lying northeast of the Workmen's Village on the slopes of a neighbouring terrace facing the entrance to the Royal Wadi, could have been the village housing for the artisans who cut the Royal tomb and presumably the nobles' tombs. This village may date to the earlier part of Akhenaten's reign, whereas the evidence from the Workmen's Village seems to commence with the later years of the king's reign. The latter village may have housed some artisans, since there is epigraphic evidence from Chapel 529 of a *sdm ꜥš* or servant (Chapter 5, 62), i.e., a workman, but it may have also accommodated people employed in other occupations. Kemp has already suggested soldiers or guards, owing to the presence of a bronze spearhead and wooden military standard in Chapel 561.[97] This is possible, and if the Main Chapel is one which they used, it would fit in with the later dating, since the Royal Tomb would have been cut by then. The other possibility, based upon the evidence of the abundance of animal pens, is that animal husbandry may have been one of the main occupations of the village.[98] That the occupants of the village may have been employed differently from those at Gurob or Deir el Medina does not alter the possibility that foreigners or their descendants or foreign influence of some degree could have penetrated the village. If some of the population of the Stone Village were non-Egyptian labourers or artisans, as at Gurob, or possibly Deir el Medina, they could have easily had interrelations with the inhabitants of the Workmen's Village.

Unfortunately, the Workmen's Village is not blessed with an abundance of inscriptional evidence, like Deir el Medina, which leaves only tenuous areas for enquiry. These include objects and ceramics. The question of a probable baetyl in one or two of the chapels from the northern and southern group, and the instance of the goat limb, have been covered in Chapter 5. The field of ceramics is an unsatisfactory basis for argument, but some significant points can be raised nevertheless. A vessel in a foreign shape, and in Egyptian ware, could be made by an Egyptian and not a foreigner, but the significance is that the Egyptian has adopted a foreign form. One or two foreign-style vessels do not prove the presence of foreigners, but the infiltration of another culture at some stage; vessels in a foreign ware are more likely to be imports, but they could have been brought in by foreigners. Inside the Walled Village and associated with a house in Gate Street was a Palestinian type of vessel in Egyptian fabric.[99] Of the pottery offering stands from the chapels, no two are exactly alike.[100] Stand No. 51973 is unusual because of the two holes in the flared base. It is similar to Stand No. 51873 from the Main Chapel. The holes in the lower part of the stands follow a Syro-Palestinian tradition.[101] Carless Hulin stated that these are Egyptian vessels,[102] but noted that they are similar to the one found to the left of the altar in Fosse Temple, Phase III, at Lachish. Yeivin, on the contrary, asserted that this type of vessel is definitely Canaanite.[103] From the chapel dumps came a fenestrated incense lid with trapezoidal holes, instead of the usual circular apertures found on Egyptian examples of this type.[104] A lid of this kind has not been noted so far in Egypt, nor for that matter is it so far known in Palestine.

The views on foreign architectural influences in some of the private chapels discussed in this Chapter are not expected to be readily accepted. This is mainly because Egypt is generally viewed as being relatively isolated until it acquired an Empire, and even then the main channel of influence is seen as flowing in one direction: from Egypt to the Levant and elsewhere. However, no nation at any time, whether it be the conqueror or the conquered, can resist absorbing some of the cultural influences to which it is exposed. A salient example is the era of the British Empire and its rule in India, whose influences in the British Isles are self-evident. An unavoidable mutual exchange of ideas is the result.

Notes

1. G. Dreyer in W. Kaiser, G. Dreyer, R. Gempeler, P. Grossman, G. Haeny, H. Jaritz, F. Junge, *MDAIK* 32 (1976), 75-87. G. Dreyer and W. Kaiser in W. Kaiser, G. Dreyer, R. Gempeler, P. Grossman, H. Jaritz, *MDAIK* 33 (1977), 68-83.
2. Petrie, *Abydos* II, 7-14.
3. D. Arnold, *Der Tempel Qasr el-Sagha* (Mainz, 1979), Tafel 22.
4. Vandier, *Manuel* II (1955), 635-640.
5. Ibid., 628-634.
6. Ibid., 619-620.
7. E. Grébaut, *Le Musée Égyptien* I (Cairo, 1890-1900), 6-7.
8. L. Loat, *Gurob*, part volume with M.A. Murray, *Saqqara Mastabas* I (London, 1905), 1-2.
9. P. Lacovara, *Deir el Ballas* (Boston, 1985), Preliminary report issued to the Visiting Committee of the Department of Egyptian and Ancient Near Eastern Art, Boston, 1985.
10. B. Gunn and A.H. Gardiner, *JEA* 4 (1917), 242-245.
11. D. Randall-Maciver and C. L. Woolley, *Buhen* I (Philadelphia, 1911), 83-94, 105-106; *Buhen* II, Plans C, D.
12. A.M. Blackman, *JEA* 23 (1937), 145-151.
13. H.A. Fairman, *JEA* 25 (1939), 139-144.
14. D. Dunham, *Semna, Kumma* (Boston, 1960), 116-122. R. Caminos, *Kush*, 13 (1965), 74-77.
15. M. Bietak, *Avaris and Piramesse*, *Proceedings of the British Academy* 65 (1979), 232-238; 256-260.
16. Bietak, ibid., 237; *AJA* 88 (Oct. 1984), 471-485.
17. Bruyère, *Rapport* (1935-1940), fasc. I, 84-85, Pl. 2.
18. Bruyère, ibid., (1945-1947), 21.
19. Bietak, *Avaris and Piramesse*, 256.
20. S. Adam, *ASAE* 56 (1959), 207-226.
21. Bietak, ibid., 284, 1.4; 285, 1.14.
22. W.M.F. Petrie, *Dendereh* (London, 1900), 6.
23. The First Dynasty mastaba (Tomb 3038) at Saqqara has a room adjacent to its burial chamber with a large bench against three walls into which are sunk nine granary jars. W. Emery, *Great Tombs of the First Dynasty* I (London, 1949), Plans 22-26.
24. G. Jéquier, *Les Pyramides des Reines Neit et Apouit* (Cairo, 1933), 45, pls II, VI.
25. G. Thausing, H. Goedicke, *Nofretari* (Graz 1971), Chamber I, pls 16, 21, 23, 25, 26.
26. G. Steindorff and W. Wolf, *Die Thebanische Gräberwelt* (Hamburg, 1936), 85, Abb. 32.
27. A.M. Calverley, M.F. Broome and A.H. Gardiner, *The Temple of King Sethos I at Abydos* III (London and Chicago, 1938), vii.
28. R.Giveon, *The Impact of Egypt on Canaan: iconographical and related studies.* (Fribourg Switzerland/Göttingen 1978) (Orbis biblicus et orientalis, vol. 20), 25.
29. G.R.H. Wright, *Ancient Building in South Syria and Palestine* I (Leiden-Köln, 1985), 226-229; 245-247.
30. Ibid., 227-247.
31. Ibid., 217, 218.
32. R. Amiran, *Early Arad: the Chalcolithic Settlement and Early Bronze City* I (Jerusalem 1978), 14-15.

33. Ibid., 38-41.
34. Wright, op. cit., 242; W. Andrae, *Die archäischen Ischtar-Tempel in Assur* (Berlin, 1922), 32-38.
35. D. Ussishkin, *Tel Aviv* 7 (1980), 1-44.
36. J. Garstang, 'Jericho: City and Necropolis' *LAAA* 23 (1936), 73-74, pl. XLIa.
37. P. Matthiae, *Ebla, An Empire Rediscovered* (London, 1980), 55, 128-130.
38. Ibid., 130.
39. Wright, op. cit., 246.
40. J. Baines, *IAE* Fourth International Congress of Egyptology, abstract of papers (1985), 4-7; 'Practical Religion and Piety', *JEA* 73 (1987), 79-98.
41. W.M.F. Petrie, *Kahun, Gurob, and Hawara* (London, 1890), pl. XV.
42. M. Lichtheim, *Ancient Egyptian Literature* I (1973), 163-169.
43. Bietak, op. cit., 248, fig. 8.
44. Kemp, *AR* III, 6, fig. 1.4. The hearth near the dais, however, has a similar arrangement in the outer hall of Chapel 556.
45. Badawy, *A History of Egyptian Architecture* 69, fig. 39.
46. A. Rowe, *Bethshan, Topography and History* (Philadelphia, 1930), 19.
47. Ibid., 7-8.
48. Y. Aharoni, *The Archaeology of the Land of Israel* (London, 1982), 121-124.
49. Ibid., 121.
50. F. James, *The Iron Age at Beth Shan* (Philadelphia, 1966), 149-154.
51. I am indebted to P.E. McGovern for permitting me to quote his work on the Bethshan material before his publication of it. This has helped me considerably in attempting to provide a more complete picture on the discussions about this site.
52. T. Dothan, *Philistines and Their Material Culture* (Jerusalem, 1982), 81-82. The new chronology being adopted by Bietak for the Hyksos in Egypt and their eventual expulsion, at the lower date of *c.* 1540 B.C., if widely accepted, would alter completely Palestinian dating. Bietak's dates are based on the views of Helck, Beckerath and Hornung, who all favour the lower dating. R. Krauss, *Sothis und Monddaten* (Hildesheim, 1985): Krauss favours a further reduction of dates based on the heliacal rising of Sothis at Aswan instead of Thebes. Bietak, see above, n. 16, *AJA*.
53. A. Rowe, *The Four Canaanite Temples of Bethshan* II, Part I (Philadelphia, 1940).
54. P.E. McGovern, *Late Bronze Palestinian Pendants* (Sheffield, 1985), 10, Map 2.
55. Rowe, *Bethshan, Topography and History*, 19-23. Aharoni, op. cit., 121.
56. Rowe, op. cit., 23-30. James, op. cit., 149-150. Aharoni, op. cit., 121.
57. Wright significantly points out that the Egyptian methods of construction follow an evolved and coherent system which cannot be satisfactorily segmented and added on to an alien building process. He adds that the 'invisible' influences of measurement, building procedure and fabrics should be sought, rather than outer visible forms. Wright, op. cit., 475-476.
58. Rowe, op. cit., 21. McGovern, op. cit.
59. James, op. cit., 149.
60. Rowe, op. cit., 26-29.
61. James, op. cit., 150.
62. T. Dothan, *Qedem* (1979), 100-104. E.D. Oren, *The Northern Cemetery of Bethshan* (Leiden, 1973), 148-150. R.D. Barnett, 'The Sea Peoples'; *CAH II, Pt. 2, The Middle East and the Aegean Region c. 1380-1000 B.C.* (Cambridge, 1975), 359-378.
63. B. J. Kemp and R.S. Merrillees, *Minoan Pottery in Second Millennium Egypt* (Mainz am Rhein, 1980), 1-249.
64. PM I¹, 139-142.
65. W.S. Smith, *The Art and Architecture of Ancient Egypt* (Harmondsworth, 1981), 245.
66. B. Rutkowski, *The Cult Places of the Aegean* (New Haven and London, 1986), 20-149.
67. Ibid., 141.
68. Ibid., 169-174.
69. Ibid., 174.
70. Ibid., 182-185. Renfrew, *The Archaeology of Cult*, 430-431; 435-436.
71. R.O. Faulkner, E.F. Wente, W.R. Simpson, *The Literature of Ancient Egypt* (New Haven and London, 1973), 186-189, (lines 80-105).
72. G. Posener, J. Bottero, K.H. Kenyon, 'Syria and Palestine *c.* 2160-1780 B.C.', fascicle 29, *CAH* II, Part 2 (Cambridge, 1965), 4.
73. W.C. Hayes, *A Papyrus of the Late Middle Kingdom* (reprinted, Metropolitan Museum of Art, 1972), 99, 133.
74. Hayes, op. cit., 148-149.
75. Ibid., 92.
76. Giveon, op. cit., 56.

77.   Ibid.
78.   H. Goedicke, *JARCE* (1984), 203-210.
79.   R. Anthes *Die Felseninschriften von Hatnub* (Leipzig, 1928) (reprinted Hildesheim, 1964), 36-37; Gr. 16, 6.
80.   W. Helck, *Die Beziehungen Ägyptens und Vorderasiens zur Ägais bis ins 7. Jahrhundert v. Chr.* (Darmstadt 1979), 45 ff.
81.   Kemp and Merrillees, op. cit., 250-267.
82.   Petrie, *Kahun, Gurob, and Hawara*, 27. Dr R. David is currently continuing research on Kahun, paying specific attention to the presence of foreigners.
83.   *URK*.IV: 3-5. (3. Vertreibung der Hyksos.)
84.   J.M. Weinstein, *BASOR* 241 (Winter, 1981), 6-7. Redford, *JAOS* 99 (1979), 274.
85.   Weinstein, op. cit., 10.
86.   Ibid., 12.
87.   J.J. Janssen, *JEOL* 17 (1963), 141-147.
88.   J.H. Breasted, *Ancient Records* II (Chicago, 1906), 354-357 (paragraphs 880, 881, 884).
89.   W. Helck, *Oriens Antiquus* 5 (1966), 1-14.
90.   W. Helck, *Die Beziehungen Ägyptens zu Vorderasien im 3. und 2. Jahrtausend v. Chr* (Wiesbaden 1971), 446-473. R. Giveon, *JEA* 60 (1980), 144-145.
91.   N. de G. Davies, *The Rock Tombs of El Amarna* III (London, 1905), 27-29, pl. XXXI; D.B. Redford, *Akhenaten, The Heretic King* (Princeton, 1984), 29, 2.1.
92.   Redford, *Akhenaten, The Heretic King*, 28.
93.   Petrie, op. cit., 32-44.
94.   A bronze ring depicting Akhenaten seated on a throne was found in the house in Gate Street No. 8 of the Workmen's Village at Amarna during the season of 1985.
95.   Personal communication. See Hayes, op. cit., 99-101.
96.   Kemp, *JEA* 64 (1978), 26.
97.   Kemp, *AR* I, 33. These could have been the necropolis guards.
98.   Kemp, *AR* I, 40-59; *AR* III, 34-79.
99.   P. Rose, personal communication.
100. Carless Hulin in Kemp, *AR* I, 172.
101. Ibid., 171.
102. Ibid.
103. Sh. Yeivin, *JEA* 62 (1976), 114, pl. XV 2.
104. Carless Hulin in Kemp, *AR* I, 171.

Chapter 7

The T-Shaped Basin: its Use and its Religious Significance.

During the course of excavations at the Workmen's Village at El Amarna, a series of cultic features called T-shaped basins were revealed. Their prevalence, strategic position and association with the private chapels indicates their special significance. The T-shaped basin sometimes occurred in connection with the private chapel and seems to suggest a ritual or cultic significance within the context of the main intention of this type of religious building. This Chapter will investigate the reasons for its use and its religious and historical significance at Amarna and elsewhere in Egypt.

This type of basin draws its name from its shape, which was in the form of the letter T, and which had several symbolic associations with other Egyptian emblems or signs to be discussed later in this Chapter. Basically, the T is a form of the cross, which can be traced back at least to the Old Kingdom. If what appear as pot marks on vessels from the Tomb of Hemaka[1] from the First Dynasty (fig. 56a) can be read as the T, and not the shortened version for the vertical shaft in the glyph for *sbꜣ*, then we have an even earlier form of the ancient Egyptian cross.

During the Old Kingdom, the T was not used in the basin. However, it appeared in some of the architectural plans of funerary monuments (figs 77, 79, 81) and in embryonic form during the Sixth Dynasty in the simple offering table. From the available evidence, the emergence of the cross form appears to be associated with the funerary cult only (see below, p. 111-112) at this period. The funerary ideas which it embraced were concerned with primordial, solar and Osirian beliefs. In connection with the royal mortuary cult, the T-shape served the *Ka* and the *Ba*, but with the private person in the early Old Kingdom it was concerned only with the *Ka*.[2] Later, when the dimensions of the afterlife of the private person expanded to include the *Ba*, the T-shape began to serve primarily this aspect in the funerary cult.

It was during the New Kingdom that the T-shaped basin appeared as a fully developed form, having evolved into a formula synthesizing the ideas that had already existed for at least two millennia. The use of the basin during this period included not only a funerary function, but also a religious purpose in the world of the living. In addition to its cultic associations, the T-shaped basin, with its symbolic connotations, was incorporated into the gardens of domestic buildings and served a practical as well as a ritual use on a greatly extended scale, as a harbour to both cult and mortuary temples, as well as the royal palace.

This investigation will commence with an examination of the T-shaped basins at the Workmen's Village and then those connected with Amarna as a whole. Following this, the historical development and religious significance of the T-shaped basin will be discussed.

The T-shaped Basins at the Workmen's Village at El Amarna.

Eight T-shaped basins were associated with the Workmen's Village. Seven of these were cut into the ground and were either plastered with mud or lined with brick. The eighth basin was cut out of a limestone block. Five of these basins lay before the southern wall of the village enclosure and the sixth before Annexe 450 (fig. 3). The seventh basin was part of the composition of the forecourt to Chapel 529, that is, it was situated in Building 528. The eighth basin was located in the inner hall of Chapel 525.[3]

The group of six lying before the southern wall of the village and the Main Chapel are numbered T1-T6 and will form the first part of the analysis (figs 3, 61a). The basins numbered 1 to 5 were sunk into a hard-packed mud deposit which abutted the southern wall of the village. This series was situated between the southern gateway to the village, just west of T1, and the southeast corner of the village, just east of T5. These five basins were all oriented with their cross-bar to the north.

The angles of Basin T1 were rounded (fig. 57).[4] It was dug into the packed surface and roughly lined with marl plaster with rough stones lining part of its sides. Some of these had detached themselves and were lying on the pitted interior of the basin. The approximate interior measurements of this basin were 1.12 m. for the cross-bar and 1.05 m. for the vertical bar. The marl plaster which had lined the basin spread in some places about 30 cm. from the sides over the packed surface of the platform.

Basin T2 (fig. 58) showed at least three phases of renewal or superimposition of one basin on top of another, as well as a repositioning of a basin. The first basin followed the true T-shape and employed marl brick in its structure. When this basin, which was at a lower level than the others, outlived its use or needed repair, another basin (no. 2 on the plan) was superimposed upon it. This represented either a new basin or the filling up of the first basin for the cutting out of the basin (no. 2a) lying to the left of number 1. Numbers 2 and 2a were roughly constructed along the same lines as basin T1. The final basin from this group, basin T2, was constructed in the same manner as T1. It was plastered with marl and rounded at its angles. A marl brick was found lying in the bottom of the vertical shaft. The interior measurements of this basin were approximately 1.35 m. for the cross-bar and 1.12 m. for the vertical bar.

Basin T3 (fig. 59) formed the true shape of the T, except that its vertical shaft was slightly at an angle. This basin was constructed of marl brick and plastered. Remains of the plaster spread beyond the sides of the basin. The approximate outer measurements of this basin were 1.40 m. for the cross-bar and 1.38 m. for the vertical arm.

Basin T4 (fig. 60) formed a perfect T and was the best preserved of this group. It was constructed of marl brick and then plastered, with the plaster extending beyond the sides. Vestiges of an earlier basin remained after the superimposition of T4. In the plan, a gap at the top of the cross-bar shows a missing brick. In the interior of the basin, the line of eroded marl forming the angle to the base showed the height of the water line in the trough. The outer measurements of this basin were *c.* 1.38 m. for the cross-bar and 1.45 m. for the vertical shaft.

Basin T5, when excavated, was found in a ruinous condition, with nothing substantial to record.[5]

Basin T6[6] lay before the Annexe 450, its cross-bar oriented to the east. This basin, like those above, was dug into the ground and was lined with marl plaster, brick and some stone. In the centre of the cross-bar, axially placed to the vertical bar, was a miniature quay with a flight of gypsum plastered stairs on either side. Beyond the quay were a series of stones forming a narrow path that abutted the entrance to Annexe 450. The approximate inner dimensions of the basin were 1.31 m. for the cross-bar and 1.55 m. for the vertical shaft.

One can only guess which of these basins was the first to be built. However, I believe that those to the east were probably the first.[7] These maintain the true T-shape and, as has been observed in the group forming T2, a rectangular shaped basin was the first to be built. Later, the roughed-out basins were added. These showed no care in construction and this was probably caused by the fact that the villagers knew that life there was soon to draw to a close. When the basins were no longer in use, they were filled with earth or mortar, probably to neutralize their potency as a cult object.[8] If it had been done for a practical reason, for example, so the villagers would not to trip over them, the filling would have been level with the packed surface into which the basin was sunk, and the basin would not have been left as an obstacle.

The group of six basins lying before the southern wall of the village and the Main Chapel forms a significant assemblage, which by virtue of their orientation and strategic position appears to set off the importance of Chapel 561. In addition, this group seems to act as a link between the daily life carried out in the adjacent village and the other-worldliness which the private chapels served. The first five in this group marked out or formed a border to a passage-way leading to the Main Chapel and its annexe. The passage was irregularly marked out, since the basins do not lie in a straight line. Number T3 lies further north and T5 lies more to the south. Kemp has already pointed out that the natural path would be situated between the wall and the basins, as the packed surface formed a smoother walkway.[9] The area to the south of the basins was rougher terrain, consisting of rubbish-filled pits. Following the footpath, the pedestrian would be facing the cross-bar of the basins that lay before the village. There appears to be no fast rule as to which end of the tank the god or mortal should stand. Rather, the purpose of the basin in the cult would determine where the person should be positioned.

In the case of these six basins, their purpose could be interpreted in several ways, by analogy with the basins found at the Maru Aten (fig. 62) and at Deir el Bahari (fig. 70). Although a fuller description of these two sites will be given in the following pages, it is important to refer briefly to them here in order to make clear points of resemblance between them and the layout of this group of six basins. At Deir el Bahari and the Maru Aten, the basins were oriented north to south, like those before the village wall. In the case of the Maru Aten, the cross and vertical bars alternated from north to south, but the basins as a whole were oriented in the stated direction.

The six village basins could have formed part of a composition devoted to the solar cult, like those at the Maru Aten (but not on its formal lines), or in connection with their possible association with the monthly festivals of the *Mswt-Ìtn*.[10] The basins before the village wall may have symbolized the collective gardens of the villagers, which they could not, of course, have attached to their houses, as in the case of a nobleman's estate. The orientation to the north was the same used for the Sunshade temples of which the kiosk at the Maru Aten is believed to have been an example. This type of temple, which was associated with the queen, queen mother and Meritaten, intimates its feminine attribute.[11] In addition, a northern orientation was associated with the primordial ocean of Nun, from which the sun arose.[12] With these ideas in mind, it is logical to see the sun rising in the east, and during its journey across the sky passing successively over the basins before the village wall. This idea of exposing the life-giving waters to the energizing rays of the sun symbolized the notion of creativity and continuing life. The same idea was contained in the rite of exposing the temple statues on the roof to the rays of the sun during the time of inundation, as was done at Dendera.[13] Basin T6, with its miniature stairway oriented to the east and the rising sun seems to act as a pivot in the composition of these basins and suggests a connecting link between the two elements of village and chapel.

Bearing the foregoing in mind, the question arises of what choice of route was taken at the southeast corner of the village wall. Did one pass straight to the flight of stairs leading to the forecourt of the Main Chapel or did one veer slightly to the right and pass by basin T6 and enter the chapel via Annexe 450 (fig. 3)?[14] If we accept the route between the wall and the basins while entering the annexe, the vertical shaft of the basin would be faced, rather than the cross-bar, as was the case with the basins before the village. This suggests a change in purpose for the basins. If they all had the same intention, why did T6 not face the same direction as the other five, or the cross-bar lie to the west instead of to the east? Kemp has suggested that the basins were intended to be faced from the top of the **T** rather than the bottom, but in the case of T6 and the basin in Building 528, this suggestion does not hold.[15]

The route followed on informal occasions probably led directly to basin T6 before Annexe 450. The basin here could be symbolic of the chapel garden, where simple offerings or prayers could be made on behalf of the deceased. Its orientation to the east had the connotations connected with the solar idea. At the time of festivals, the main door to Chapel 561 was no doubt opened and the path taken would be that leading past the five basins on the village platform on the same axis as the steps leading into the chapel, which follows the parallel idea at Deir el Bahari. Whether an image of the deceased, a deity or a king was brought out at any of these festivals is impossible to confirm, but it is possible, if we rely on the Theban tomb paintings as evidence (see below, p. 110). If this were so, the exit route could have been through Annexe 450. Basin T6 would then have symbolized a small harbour to a temple or a lake upon which a boat containing a statue of the deceased king, deity or owner floated at certain occasions.[16]

The **T**-shaped basin in Building 528 (fig. 12), comprising the forecourt of Chapel 529, was oriented north to south, with the cross-bar lying to the north in the same way as the series of basins before the village wall. The basin had a small projection from the top of the centre of the cross-bar, which may have been a miniature quay, as the one in basin T6. As has already been described (Chapter 2, 20), the presence of alluvial mud suggests that a small garden surrounded the basin. Just beyond the basin to the north was a brick projection that had contained tiers, of which the topmost contained a receptacle for holding a jar. The type of jar was not described by Peet.[17] This basic composition is similar to the familiar scene of the funerary garden depicting the goddess Nut in the sycamore, from which she pours water from a jar, usually the *qbḥ* type vessel, onto the deceased or his Ba below (fig. 63).[18] Between them is often seen a **T**-shaped basin with the Ba bird perched on its edge. Could the unidentified jar situated in the brick projection have symbolized the jar from which Nut poured her life-giving waters to the Bas of the deceased below? The thought is tantalizing and, if so, we have here a unique physical depiction of the funerary garden represented in some of the Theban tomb paintings.

The remaining **T**-shaped basin from the Workmen's Village came from Chapel 525 (fig. 61b). It was cut out of limestone and placed in the inner hall of the chapel. When found, its orientation was from east to west with the cross-bar facing east. It is not known whether this was its original position, but it seems doubtful that it would have been moved from the outer court into the inner hall, since it was a substantial trough. Its placement within the interior of the chapel suggests that it was used for purification purposes during a ceremony.[19]

The Uses of the T-shaped Basin in the Main Settlement of El Amarna.

The **T**-shaped basin appeared in two specific ways at Amarna outside the Workmen's Village. One was as a unit within a complex of buildings devoted to a religious concept, and the other was seen within the garden of an estate. There is no evidence of its use in connection with the Great Temple to the Aten or the *Ḥwt* Aten.

Its use within the first type of structure was in an architectural scheme consisting of gardens, bodies of water and shrines called the Maru Aten (fig. 62). The plan consisted of a large enclosure with a small one abutting it to the south. Within the main enclosure, which is the one that concerns this discussion, was a lake with a quay lying on the longitudinal axis to the west. In the northwest corner of the enclosure was a single row of houses, and east of these and north of the lake was a temple, which could also have served as a palace for the king. Near the southeast corner of the enclosure was another building, consisting of a central portion flanked on either side by subsidiary rooms. A large rectangular tank lay to the north. The northeast corner of the enclosure contained a small complex of sacred buildings. Starting from the south was a temple oriented east to west in the typical Amarna plan of outer court, pronaos and hypaethral sanctuary. This fronted a kiosk, which was oriented north to south, and which was identified by Fairman as a sunshade temple. It stood on a square island, surrounded by water, beyond which lay a rectangular portion of ground devoted to flower beds, which were divided into eight rows. Beyond the flower beds to the north was an area called the Water Court. This contained eleven **T**-shaped basins set antithetically to one another to produce thirteen square bases within the resultant pattern. The series of basins were divided into a group of seven and a group of four. Alternatively, there may have originally been twelve basins, the missing one having been overlooked by the excavators. The space between the interval of the fourth and fifth basin in the plan could easily have accommodated another basin (fig. 62).

However, assuming there were eleven, Badawy has convincingly interpreted the symbolic role of this complex of buildings in the northeast corner.[20] He saw the eleven tanks as symbolizing the monthly festivals of the Aten called the 'Birth of the Aten'. He has described the kiosk as filling the role of the twelfth tank, which served for the initial feast. From the inscription of Amenhotep III about the Maru at Thebes,[21] Badawy saw the buildings and flower beds as the creative works of the Aten and the water in the pools and tanks as representative of Nun, the symbolic dwelling place of the Aten. These ideas sum up the interaction of the opposite polarities. In addition, Badawy remarked upon the conjunction of the east-west axis of the front temple to the long axis of the lake and suggested a connection with the viewing of the Aten during his diurnal and nocturnal course. The idea of the manifest and unmanifest world are contained in his observations.

Returning to the eleven basins and the kiosk with these points in mind, it is possible to see another geometrical relationship between this group, which could provide another rationale for the basins. These suggestions should be taken as tentative only and are offered as another approach. The axis of the kiosk is the line which divided the basins into two groups. By drawing an imaginary line from the altar to the outermost point of the basins lying to the east and a line from the southeast corner of the western garden plot to the westernmost basin, two right-angled triangles are produced. In Egypt, this was known as the triangle of Osiris and was the formula used when stretching a knotted cord to lay out a temple plan.[22] In the triangle to the right, the vertical line forming the 90° angle with the horizontal line stretching to the kiosk contained seven basins and in the case of the other, the line contains four. Seven was an important number in Egypt and it also symbolized the creative forces behind manifestation.[23] Four, such as the four corners of the universe, gave the idea of stability and the world of form. Here is another simple symbolism of the sun's creative activities through the agency of primordial matter. The vertical line oriented to the east and the rising sun conjoined with the horizontal line of the triangle oriented north to south and representative of Nun or the feminine attribute seen in the kiosk and the tanks. Between them lay the eight flower beds, the result of the creation. The Maru Aten and the Workmen's Village provide the most impressive and extended use of the **T**-shaped basin so far known in Egypt.

The second use of the **T**-shaped basin recorded in the main settlement of Amarna is represented in a relief from tomb no. 2 (fig. 64) of Meryre II, Royal Scribe, Overseer of the two Treasuries and Overseer of the Harem of the Great Royal Wife Nefertiti, from the northern group of tombs.[24] The basin was depicted on the east side of the south wall in the outer chamber of the tomb. Meryre, to the acclamation and praise of his servants, was shown entering his estate via a monumental gateway that led into a garden with a sizeable **T**-shaped basin. The cross-bar faced the gateway and the vertical shaft was bordered with sycamore trees. At the top of the garden was a row of sycamore trees alternating with date palms. Around the basins is what appears to have been a flower bed. The small rectangular projection from the top of the cross-bar must have been a small platform, since it is too far from the interior of the basin to represent a quay. In no other tomb does a **T**-shaped basin appear, nor does it appear in connection with any of the houses excavated so far in the southern city.[25] It seems curious that Meryre should be the only one to have had this type of basin in his garden, and that Panehesy and Pawah, who served the Aten, should not, unless the evidence is missing. The shape of garden pool was no doubt a matter of personal preference, rather than a choice for some esoteric reason.

The historical development of the T-shaped basin

From the evidence available, this basin did not appear in its fully developed form until the Eighteenth Dynasty. It seems unlikely that this type of basin should suddenly emerge without an anterior development of ideas. These primarily seem to arise from the simple stone offering table of the Old and Middle Kingdoms[26] and the pottery trays and soul houses of the First Intermediate Period. Other possible sources may have been the plans of funerary architecture and the garden pool.

The Offering Table

By the Fourth Dynasty, the importance of the offerings in the burial chamber were superseded by those at the false door.[27] With this incipient elaboration of the funerary cult, the stone offering table became a regular feature which represented in carved relief the simple offering of a *ḥtp* loaf, laid on a mat with a jug or basin.[28] The Old Kingdom offering table was almost always rectangular and the disposition of the elements carved into the stone could vary from a basic to a more complex composition. These elements included the loaf and mat, basins, jars, dishes and receptacles for holding food offerings and liquids.[29]

The central feature of the representation was the loaf on a mat, usually protruding into an interior shallow rectangular basin that sometimes contained a short channel forming the rudiments of a **T**.[30] When the libation was poured, it would have had to fall over the loaf into the basin, thus symbolically the two features were united. In some of the designs, the interior basin contained two small rectangular tanks set symmetrically on either side of the loaf. One type showed the loaf on its mat projecting outwards from the table and as a result forming a **T**, with the conical loaf acting as the vertical shaft. Another version was a table with a long rectangular portion containing a narrow tank. Abutting this was a semi-circular table, which acted as the shaft of the cross-bar (fig. 56b and c).

Basins appearing separate from the offering table during the Old Kingdom were either rectangular or square,[31] and some included flights of stairs. In the case of royal burial complexes, at least, the basins were found in the Valley and Mortuary Temples[32] and were used primarily during embalming rites and probably for purificatory purposes afterwards.[33] Smaller versions were found in corridors before mastabas, or in the offering chamber of the mastaba.[34]

With the decline of the Old Kingdom and the break-up of centralized government, a period of inferior craftsmanship ensued. At the same time, a new and more expansive world began to emerge for the ordinary man and in the case of cult objects this was expressed in a naive, but graphic, way in the crude provincial pottery offering trays and soul houses (fig. 65). Fine examples of these come from the cemeteries of Rifeh,[35] Armant,[36] Dendera[37] and Gurna.[38] These expressive objects are unequivocally the first to show the **T**-shape (fig. 66).

The overall shape of the trays from these sites can range from rectangular, square or oval. The projecting spout appeared for the first time during the First Intermediate Period and carried on into the latest dynasties. In the centre of the tray was either one rectangular tank, or two small tanks symmetrically placed, connected to a channel that passed through the spout. Meat and bread offerings were also included in the composition.

Unique examples come from Gurna. These date to the Eleventh Dynasty and were generally oval in shape. They differ from the others in their lack, in most cases, of models of offerings. Instead, the tray was divided into compartments by means of double-line crosses, or double-line T-crosses, or a stylized T-shape evolving into an *ankh* (fig. 66d).

The soul houses began to appear around the Eleventh Dynasty.[39] Those at Rifeh had the overall rectangular shape of the offering tray with its projecting spout, but the portico of a house rose to the rear of the rectangle (fig. 65b). In the courtyard, lying before the portico, was a large rectangular tank with a channel leading out through the spout. This suggests that the garden of the house of the owner had a pool that may have been T-shaped. It is difficult to determine at this period whether the connecting channel to the tank represented in the soul house was placed there for the convenience of draining off the libations, or whether it was a true representation of the owner's pool.

The stone offering tables of the Middle Kingdom (fig. 67) displayed more complexity of design.[40] The interior T-shape was now definitely established. The contents of offerings depicted on the surface of the table were ordered: the loaf, either with or without offerings and vases, often projected into the cross-bar of the T. Rectangular basins were usually arranged symmetrically on either side of the spout or vertical bar, although in some cases two Ts could succeed each other, and were connected by a vertical channel.

Innovations in the stone offering table increased from the New Kingdom onwards (fig. 67). One basin dating to the reign of Tuthmosis III showed the vertical shaft of the T bisecting a second *htp* loaf placed in the spout. The libation was poured over the first loaf, which lay on a mat with two vases and round loaves of bread on either side, and flowed into the inner T-shaped basin and out through the loaf depicted in the spout. The slicing of the *htp* loaf became common in the New Kingdom.

Finally, an example from the Twentieth Dynasty (fig. 67) showed an arrangement of three separate rectangular basins sunk into the surface of the table, framing a loaf within the overall design of the T-shape.

These examples show the gradual emergence of the T-shape and its significance in the offerings given to the *Ka*. This continued into the latest dynasties, but in the New Kingdom (or perhaps as early as the Middle Kingdom, if the T tanks in the gardens of the soul houses are acceptable proof) the T-shape divided itself from the offering table into a separate basin and was portrayed in scenes from New Kingdom tombs (to be discussed shortly) as part of a composition including the goddess Nut and the Ba bird. Therefore, these two uses of the T in an offering table and a basin suggest that it served two aspects of the deceased in the funerary cult.

The T-shaped Basin and its part in the Funerary Cult

As already mentioned, examples of the T-shaped basin in connection with the funerary cult come mainly from tomb paintings, but actual examples were found at Deir el Bahari, Deir el Medina and Amarna. The basin, as will be demonstrated below, was often depicted with the sycamore goddess and could also appear with Osiris and Hathor. It was represented either in a garden as a pool, or as an offering laid on top of an offering stand, with the deceased placed on one side opposite the deity. The T-shaped basin that finally appeared in the offering table may have become a type of sigil, or abbreviation of the tray, whilst the offerings that appeared on it in the form of bread and libations were transposed to the tree goddess. The elements of this composition may have started in the Eighteenth Dynasty.

One of the earliest paintings of the tree goddess near a pool is from the tomb of Sebekhotep (no. 63)[41] from the reign of Tuthmosis IV. The pond in this picture was rectangular. The tomb of Nebamun (no. 90),[42] from the same reign, showed a long rectangular garden with a large T-shaped pool at the end of a central path. Three sycamore trees were set on each side of the vertical shaft of the pool and the path was bordered with papyrus columns and trees from which a servant was gathering fruit.

The religious ideas behind these two representations can be traced to the Pyramid Texts and are later found in the Book of the Dead. Pyramid Text 574, lines 1485 and 1486 refer to the deity in the tree and the primordial waters, which Faulkner translated as 'Abyss':[43]

'Hail to you, you tree which encloses the god, under which the gods of the Lower Sky stand, the end of which is cooked, the inside of which is burnt, which sends out the pains of death: may you gather together those who are in the Abyss, may you assemble those who are in the celestial expanses'.

Several vignettes in Naville's *Todtenbuch* showed T-shaped basins.[44] One, from the Papyrus of Nebseni, depicts the deceased drawing water with his hands from a T-shaped basin. Another from the Papyrus of Nu shows the deceased kneeling before a rectangular pool at the side of which is a tree out of which the arm of the deity pours libation into the cup, which Nebseni holds. A vignette from the Papyrus of Ani[45] portrays the deceased by a pool adjacent to which grows a sycamore. Nut pours libations for Ani from the tree and offers him bread with her right hand. The intention behind these representations was that the deceased continued to receive the vital force symbolized by the water both in the basin and pouring forth from the vase of the goddess in the tree. The Abyss symbolized in the water in the basin and from which the tree could also draw and give forth by means of Nut created an unbroken life cycle.

These ideas were depicted in a fuller way in the tomb paintings dating to the Nineteenth and Twentieth Dynasties. Tomb 51 of Userhat[46] shows the deceased and his family before the goddess Nut, standing on a hieroglyph for the word *mȝˁt*. The main body of the sign is filled with the ripples of water, with the wedge part of the sign separated from the rest of the symbol by a vertical line forming a right-angled triangle. In her right hand is a vase and in her left are loaves of bread. Before her, and just above the sign for *mȝˁt*, is a T-shaped basin filled with water painted blue, indicative of Nun.[47]

At Deir el Medina, tomb 217 of Ipuy,[48] a sculptor of the Nineteenth Dynasty, shows a T-shaped basin on an offering stand. Here the water is red instead of blue. Bruyère suggested this colour represented the red Nile and the first fruits of the inundation.[49] Ipuy and his wife stand before the vertical shaft of the basin while, instead of Nut, Osiris and Hathor are before the cross-bar. The whole scene is fittingly placed on the west wall on the south side facing the western mountain.

Tomb 178 of Kenro,[50] also known as Neferronpe, shows the deceased and his wife in their garden drinking water from a T-shaped pool, which is depicted vertically with the cross-bar on top. The water in the basin is blue. Three date palms[51] and one palm without dates are painted on the right of the vertical branch of the T.

In the following two tombs the deceased is portrayed fishing instead of drinking from the T-basin. One is tomb 324 of Hatiay (fig. 68)[52] and the other is tomb 158 of Tjanefer,[53] third prophet of Amun. Two T-shaped basins are shown in this tomb. The first shows the more usual scene of the tree goddess pouring water into the hands of the Ba of the deceased and the deceased kneeling by the pool with his Ba perched on the side. Date palms surround the pool. The other basin shows the deceased with his wife. He holds two fishing rods, each with two lines. On one rod he has caught two fish, which he throws by means of the lines to his wife behind him. A parallel could be made between this scene and the spearing of the two fish represented in tombs from the Old Kingdom.[54] Junker discussed the 'Wasserberg'[55] or mound of water and its connection with the spearing scene. Although the fishing scene cited above in connection with the T-shaped basin would seem separate from the well-known spearing motif, I feel there could be a link between the two. This will be considered later in connection with Deir el Bahari.

Finally, an unusual representation of the T-shaped basin was recorded by Champollion from a Theban tomb (fig. 69). The basin is placed as an inverted T, within which are fish, ducks and lotuses. From the top of the vertical shaft emerges a sycamore with herons standing on either side. A goddess pours libations from the top of the tree onto the deceased couple, while offering them a sycamore fig.

In excavations at the sites of Deir el Bahari and Deir el Medina, T-shaped basins were revealed in connection with funerary gardens. These basins are the only ones so far located on the West Bank to be sunk into the ground (fig. 70).

The two **T**-shaped basins in the forecourt leading to the first terrace of the mortuary temple of Hatshepsut are the earliest known examples of this type of tank.[56] These basins, which were oriented north to south, had their cross-bars facing inwards towards the central avenue before the first ramp. Before them, to the east, were two recumbent lions and beyond them, to the west, were two tree pits on either side of the ramp. The basins were shallow and unlined, but were filled with mud in which papyrus had grown. Among them was a fowler's throw-stick. Winlock suggested that these two **T**-shaped papyrus pools played a part in the dedication ceremonies of the temple when birds were caught and papyrus cut. The idea of spearing the fish has been mentioned already in connection with the tombs of Hatiay and Tjanefer, and associated with this activity is the fowling of birds. The boomerang found in one of the **T**-shaped pools at Deir el Bahari fills the other part of the scene depicted in the above-named tombs. The mound of water could almost form a stylized **T**. Schäfer identified this mound as a bay of water.[57] By the New Kingdom, this 'hill of water' had acquired a red frame of zigzag lines, possibly representing the calyxes of the papyrus plant.[58] Tomb 69 of Menna shows a fine example of this (fig. 71). If these jagged lines represented the lower part of the papyrus plant, which in fact they seem to do upon close examination, the colour red in which they are depicted holds the potential of new life, as suggested by Bruyère (see above, p. 108). From this hill sprouts papyrus, the glyph of which, *w3ḏ*, means 'green', 'fresh', or 'to flourish'.[59] Further, the two Tilapia fishes in the mound have been interpreted as the rebirth of the dead by Moens.[60] Schäfer compared this scene with medieval representations of the baptism of Christ, where the water rises up similarly into a hill and a shaft of light containing a dove connects Christ and the hill with the sun.[61] Schäfer stated that the real meaning of these pictures is lost, but that artists recognized a mythical interpretation. The ideas of rebirth contained in this scene are, in my opinion, similar to some of those suggested by the **T**-shaped basin. Looking at Champollion's reproduction of the inverted basin (fig. 69), the whole idea of rebirth is portrayed in what could be called a stylized mound of water. Assuming that the 'hill of water' could be a type of **T**, the spiritual or transforming activities in most cases take place at the top end of the vertical shaft. More will be said of this later.

Only one **T**-shaped basin appeared at Deir el Medina. This was situated in dependency 1217, the garden to C.V. 1190 (fig. 19). The basin was oriented to the west, with the cross-bar facing that direction, and may have been dedicated to Osiris and Hathor, since this orientation was the same as that in Tomb 217 (Chapter 4, 43).

In contrast to Building 1217, basins which have been found dug into the courtyards of tombs at Deir el Medina were either rectangular or round. Tomb 216 of Neferhotep[62] had three rectangular basins contiguous to each other, reminiscent of the scene of two kites before four tanks[63] in a garden portrayed in tombs until the reign of Akhenaten. In the courtyard of tomb 291 of Nu and Nakhtmin,[64] which dates to the late Eighteenth Dynasty, was a large rectangular basin and in the courtyard of P 1097[65] was a circular basin.

Amongst the various funerary themes associated with the **T**-shaped basin, Nut was the most popular, and one of her more usual speeches as tree goddess was as follows: 'I have presented thee with this cool water that thy heart may be refreshed thereby — this water which comes from thy pool in the necropolis on the west of Thebes. Thou hast received dainty food in the fruit which springs from my limbs. Thy bird soul sitteth in my shade and drinks water to its heart's content'.[66]

The **T**-shaped Basin: its part in the Religious Ritual in the Temple

The **T**-shaped basin was not only featured in the funerary cult, but also played a part in offering scenes to the Triad of gods Amun, Mut and Khonsu. Unlike the tomb scenes, it is represented only as an offering on a stand or altar, or as part of a list of offerings in a register.

One of the earliest representations of the basins in this capacity dates to the reign of Tuthmosis III. It is seen in the temple of Karnak in the Hall of Annals as part of the offerings of the king to Amun depicted on the granite shrine. There are two **T**-shaped basins portrayed. In the second register from the top, the basin is described as made out of gold and in the ninth register from the top the other tank, framed by papyrus plants, is a bronze offering plate.[67]

The **T**-shaped basin surmounting an altar usually had libations poured into it or near it by the king. The basin was always situated between the king and the god (fig. 72). Usually the cross-bar faced the king, but this is not 'de rigeur'. Examples are found in the temples of Medinet Habu, the bark chapel of Seti II at Karnak, the Luxor temple, the temple of Mut, the temple of Amun at Karnak and the mortuary temple of Seti I at Gurna.[68]

An interesting example from this group is one from the Great Hypostyle Hall at Karnak.[69] This is situated on the east wall, south half, third register and shows Ramesses II pouring a libation on an offering table in the presence of Amun-Re and Amunet. The **T** and offering table are unusual. The table consists of a stand in the shape of an *ankh* with arms stretched upwards in the shape of a *Ka* holding a **T**-shaped basin or a solid **T** (fig. 73). The libations falls onto the cross-bar, which is positioned vertically or upright, instead of horizontally.

The **T**-shaped Harbour

The **T**-shape was not only confined to the small basin connected with tombs and temples, but also was greatly enlarged and converted into a harbour. Pictorial and archaeological evidence from the New Kingdom shows that these **T**-shaped harbours were associated with temples and in one known case with a royal palace. Whether or not the **T**-shaped harbour was employed before the New Kingdom is not established. In the opinion of Drioton, this type of harbour was associated with the purification tent to be discussed later.

The size of this type of harbour and quay was too small and its depth too shallow to accommodate large ships, for example, the great barges carrying granite blocks from the quarries in the time of Hatshepsut.[70] The use of these harbours was ceremonial: for the purpose of receiving ships carrying the statue of a god or king, or the reception of a king and his court upon an official visit.[71] The quay projected into the cross-bar of the **T** and was provided on either side with flights of stairs. The disembarking party would be greeted on the quay with altars of offerings and by the temple priests.

Archaeological remains of the **T**-shaped harbour are best exemplified at Medinet Habu and the Birket Habu connected with Malkata Palace. The harbour at Medinet Habu had a vast quay built of stone blocks, its platform being enclosed by a low wall (fig. 74).[72] Two flights of stairs set at right angles abutted three sides of the quay. At the summit of each staircase was another set of stairs leading to the top of the ramp, which lay parallel to the entrance to the temple. Leading from the top of the harbour was a long narrow canal. The harbour at Malkata was never completed; construction probably commenced around Year 30 of the reign of Amenhotep III, which would coincide with the king's first jubilee.[73] Huge earthen mounds from the digging out of the harbour surrounded the edges. O'Connor and Kemp believe this artificial harbour could have served in part of the king's jubilee celebrations, as well as for the purposes of the king's Maru to Amun.[74]

Pictorial evidence of temple harbours is best seen in three Theban tombs. Tomb no. 49 of Neferhotep[75] of the Nineteenth Dynasty shows the harbour and quay to the Temple of Karnak as it existed in the time of Amenhotep III. The area accommodating the harbour was later occupied by the forecourt and the pylon of Ramesses II. Sycamore trees and gardens lined the canal and boats are depicted plying the Nile. The other two examples depict harbours outside the mortuary temples of Amenhotep I and Tuthmosis III, found in the tombs of Amenmose (no. 19)[76] and Khonsu (no. 31), both dating to the Nineteenth Dynasty (see below, n. 16). The former shows altars with offerings on the quay and priests waiting to receive the statue. The second tomb shows a boat containing a statue of Tuthmosis III being towed by a warship. Khonsu is portrayed officiating as mortuary priest to the king.

The foregoing examples of the **T**-shape in the role of a harbour show that it served a practical purpose in religious and state ceremonies.

The Implications of the Use of the **T**-shape in Architecture

The **T** must have held some significance to the Egyptians, since besides its use in cult practices, it was incorporated into the architectural plan of funerary monuments. These plans can be easily traced to the Old Kingdom and are found in the Valley and Mortuary Temples of the pyramids, the purification tent and mastabas. By the New Kingdom, it was prominent as a plan in tomb chapels.

One of the earliest examples of the use of the **T** in architecture is in connection with the huge altar to the north of the Step Pyramid (fig. 75).[77] The altar was approached by steps and was oriented north to south. It was set within the framework of an elaborate **T**. The cross-bar formed the northern perimeter, while the vertical bar spanned a short distance and then formed a series of four right angles, two on either side, which marked out the area containing the altar.

The royal mortuary cult became modified during the reign of Sneferu, founder of the Fourth Dynasty.[78] The valley temple appeared for the first time, and the mortuary temple was placed on the east side of the pyramid, instead of the north. To the three chapels of Abydos, two more were added in the mortuary temple, symbolizing the king as Osiris united with Khentamenti.[79]

In most cases, a pillared hall preceded the inner chapel of three or five shrines and may be seen as an inverted **T** in echelon. The area in the pillared hall and directly in front of the passage leading to the inner chamber has been identified by Ricke as the *Gate of Nut*,[80] or in the case of the mortuary temple of Sahure, the *Gate of Nun*.[81] Examples of this are found in the mortuary temples of Khufu, Khephren, Menkaure (fig. 76) and Pepi II.[82]

The **T**-shape can be found in the plan of some of the valley temples. A classical example is the temple of Khephren (fig. 77).[83] This building acted as the *sḥ nṯr* and is believed to be the royal counterpart to the *ibw*, the private man's purification tent.[84] Here the rites of purification were performed subsequent to embalming in the mortuary temple. In both royal and private spheres, a plan of the **T**-shape was included.

The temple of Khephren was entered from a platform through doors on the north and south ends of the building, which joined two right-angled passages leading into a corridor. This in turn was connected by a short, centrally-placed passage to a large **T**-shaped chamber containing sixteen granite pillars, between which stood twenty-three diorite statues of Khephren.

However, Brovarski suggested that the royal purification tent was set up on the terrace before the Valley Temple and was also used by the private citizen.[85] Although this may be true, the ground plans of the examples provided from private tombs also show the use of the **T**. Earlier examples dating from the Fourth Dynasty, such as Debehen at Giza and Washptah of the Fifth Dynasty, have been disputed by Brovarski,[86] but succinct portrayals of the purification tent, or *ibw*, appear in the Sixth Dynasty tombs of Mereruka at Saqqara, Idu and Qar from Giza and Pepi-Ankh the Younger from Meir.[87] The temporary structure set up on a terrace formed a long narrow rectangle, with two doors at opposite ends approached by slipways. However, in all the representations, the central element to the *ibw* is the **T**-shape. From the centre of the tent, where the rites of purification were performed, projected a long covered channel. In the case of Qar's tent (fig. 78), this was matting, which connected with the water below, resulting in a **T**-shape.[88] During the Sixth Dynasty, the determinative for *ibw* changed from a booth to a **T** (⟨𓉽𓏤𓉺⟩).[89] This new form was used in the tombs of Mereruka, Qar and Idu. Grdseloff interpreted this sign as the shape of the tent, whereas Drioton saw it as the basin or harbour acting as a terminus before the tent.[90] In either case, both elements of tent/terrace and harbour form a **T**, since the link between them is the vertical shaft, which is shared in each case.

Brovarski noted the hieroglyph *pt* for 'sky', 'heaven' surmounting the representation of Mereruka's tent[91] and suggested that this and the two doors at either end of the rectangular structure symbolized 'the doors of heaven', *ꜥꜣwy pt*, which he traced to an ancient origin.[92]

In addition, Ricke suggested that the body of water before the structure was the 'Binsenfeld' or Field of Rushes.[93] Before the king could be united with Re, he had to pass through the two doors and be purified in the Field of Rushes as described in Pyramid Text 325: 'The doors of the sky (are opened), the doors of the firmament are thrown open at dawn for Horus of the Gods. He goes up into the Field of Rushes, he bathes in the Field of Rushes ...'.[94]

The use of the T shape, together with the elements just described for constituting the *ibw* and demonstrated by the foregoing passage, encompass the ideas of regeneration and reconstitution of the deceased, a primary role of the T-shaped basin appearing centuries later.

The T-shape seems to have been incorporated intentionally into the plan of many tomb chapels of mastabas of the Old Kingdom. This could have been mainly for a practical reason, but may also have been an attempt in miniature to preserve the broad and deep halls discussed by Ricke in connection with the mortuary temples of the kings. The essence of this idea was carried on into the New Kingdom and seen in many Theban and Amarna tombs. Sometimes the T could be reversed, with the cross-bar serving the most sacred area, but in most cases it was the vertical shaft and its junction between the two 'bars' which marked out the invisible world. The Old Kingdom mastaba will be considered first, followed by some examples from the New Kingdom.

The cruciform chapel developed its true form during the reign of Khasekhemwy and became the most frequent type of interior chapel during the Third Dynasty. A modified version of this type was produced by flattening out the west wall of the chapel, or its niche, resulting in a nearly perfect T-shape.[95] Both these variations of the cruciform chapel flourished at the same time.

With the extending of the southern niche on the eastern side of the mastaba, the simple niche was replaced, becoming the chief offering place and incorporating a false door. The rock tombs of Prince Duwanera (G5110); (fig. 79) and Rawer at Giza (fig. 80), tomb chapels Saqqara Fs 3030 and Saqqara-Mariette B4, and the mastaba of Abu Suten at Dendera present varied examples of this type.[96] In some of these examples, the T was 'upright', causing the cross-bar to be the sanctified area, but in the case of Rawer the elaborate vertical shaft assumed this role.

The T-shape or cruciform chapel is unmistakable in many of the Theban and Amarna tombs. The basic plan was an inverted T. The cross-bar was the broad hall, and the vertical the deep hall. In the Theban tombs the disposition of funerary scenes followed the general rule, where depictions of daily life were placed in the broad hall towards the outer entrance to the chapel, whilst the scenes pertaining to the afterlife and funerary gods were placed on the walls of the vertical passage. The concentration of offerings and representation of the gods was mainly centred near the end of the inner hall near the statue niche.[97] By analogy, attention is drawn to the reliefs of the king during the New Kingdom in the state temple: while making offerings to Amun, the vertical shaft of the basin was almost always facing the god (see above, p. 110).

The tombs of Rekhmire (100), Ramose (55), Sennufer (99) and Ptahemhet (77) provide good examples of the cruciform or T-shaped tomb chapel (fig. 81).[98] In many of the tombs at Amarna, the cross-bar has moved further to the interior and towards the niche at the end of the shaft. This is especially noticeable in the northern group. In fact, a true cruciform appears, or even a stylized *ankh*. Tombs 1 and 3 of Huya and Ahmose (figs 82, 83) are examples of this.[99] Perhaps the change in the funerary cult and the abolition of the doctrine of Osiris by Akhenaten was responsible for the shift of the cross-bar nearer to the statue niche. The darkness was replaced by light and the arduous trek through the *Duat* before reaching the Elysian Fields was no more.

Conversely, tomb no. 8 of Tutu still retained the Theban plan of the cross-bar or broad hall near the entrance.[100]

The Religious or Symbolic Significance of the **T**-shape

Was there any religious or symbolic significance to the **T**-shape, or was it a form which evolved through practical needs when planning temples and tomb chapels, or designing an offering table or basin? Of course, practical reasons must have been a factor in determining the shape of an object or plan of a building. For instance, a **T**-shape in a rock-cut tomb chapel would be a more practical proposition than undertaking a pentagonal shape. Nevertheless, a rectangular basin would be less difficult to make than a **T**-shape, in the case where no outflow is needed. The Egyptian favoured principally rectilinear lines in his structures and used these harmoniously, worked out to specific mathematical proportions, which have been studied by Badawy,[101] Ricke[102] and others.[103] Therefore, the idea of an accident of form is unlikely for the **T**-shape.

To enter a long discussion on the vast subject of symbolism and the Jungian permutations on the topic is not possible here, but suffice it to say that symbols are one of the oldest forms of the written language in man's attempt to synthesize his ideas about the universe and his environment. The original intent behind many of these symbols, such as the *cross*, the *ankh*, the *circle*, etc., may have become lost to the outer consciousness of the Egyptian during the passage of time, and he came to understand them as a tradition, and as shapes that were familiar and pleasing. A modern analogy is the Christmas tree. It is set up in many houses during Christmas as a tradition and part of the festival, but the true symbol and intent behind it has been lost to many.

It is doubtful, however, that the intention behind the iconography used in Egyptian architecture and art was lost to the inmates of the House of Life, who were well-schooled in the meaning behind their creations,[104] and whose archives were consulted by the Pharaoh and the chief architect. For instance, an architectural genius like Amenhotep, son of Hapu,[105] could never have designed the mortuary temple of Amenhotep III without knowledge behind his work. On the other hand, the inhabitants of the workmen's villages may have chosen their forms through tradition and for talismanic purposes. Returning to the original issue of a possible symbolic significance behind the **T**-shape, its form and way of use should be examined.

The **T** as a form of cross was used mainly as a basin. This has been suggested as a symbol of the water of Nun (see above, p. 108; below, n. 47). This, of course, can be extended to the rectangular basin. The distinguishing point, nevertheless, is the two intersecting bars, which suggest opposing forces (Nun and Naunet) as the underlying potential of creation, yet formless in the endless expanse of the primordial waters. On a cosmic scale, it is from these unordered realms in the twelfth hour that the newly created sun god emerges. As with Nun, *Qqw* (concentrated darkness) and *Ḥḥw* (the limitless flood), all are formless and, in a sense, are attributes of Nun.[106] They are subliminal to the orderly world of *mꜣꜥt*. Some of these ideas are reflected in the Papyrus of Nesi-Amsu, dating to about 305 B.C., in the section devoted to 'The Book of Knowing the Evolutions of Ra, and the Overthrowing of Apepi':

'I am he who evolved himself under the form of the god Chepera. I, the evolver of evolutions, evolved myself, the evolver of all evolutions after many evolutions and developments which came forth from my mouth. There was no heaven, there was no earth, ground — animals and reptiles were not then in existence. I constructed their forms out of the inert mass of watery matter, ... I developed myself from the primeval matter which I made, I developed myself out of the primeval matter ...'[107]

A connection between the **T**-shape and the *ankh* is possible. A stela from the Abydos tomb groups of the Thirteenth to the Seventeenth Dynasties shows the *ankh* as the central feature with the deceased couple on either side (fig. 84). The eyes of Horus are carved in the summit of the arc of the stela. These are separated from the *ankh* by a ripple of water. The *ankh* is clearly depicted as two elements. The egg shape or elliptical sphere is separated from the stem which forms a **T**. The ideas expressed above concerning the potential of creation in the **T** are further extended by the loop of the *ankh* suggesting a continuous state of being or immortality. This is demonstrated in the mythology of the sun disappearing into Nun while his mother, Nut, nourishes him as he performs his transformations to re-emerge from the abyss renewed as Khepera. Although immortal, the sun-god vanishes to reappear in accordance with immutable laws of rhythm and periodicity.

Finally, one of the amulets contained in the mummy wrappings of Tutankhamun was a **T** cut from gold sheet.[108] It was laid on the left side of the abdomen, or intestinal region. The intestines were one of the four organs preserved in the canopic jars, and it is in the viscera that food is broken down into its primal substance called 'chyle', which sustains the body. The analogy of this function with that already discussed above in connection with Nun is similar, and it would seem that the **T** represented the potential of the elements of the creative process before they were manifested into form.

Conclusion

The **T**-shape was primarily associated with the funerary cult, but in addition to this function, its use also extended into the daily religious life of the Egyptian. It may have been employed within a domestic context, as a garden pool, before the New Kingdom.

Its initial appearance was in funerary architecture of the Old Kingdom and, in a rudimentary form, in the simple offering table in the tomb chapel. It later emerged in the New Kingdom in a clearly recognizable form as a cult object. Coincident with this, it continued to develop clear lines within the confines of tomb chapel architecture and appeared in the form of a harbour, as an adjunct to the overall temple plan.

Ideas behind its symbolism encompassed the archetypal world of Nun or the creative elements of the life force as a continuous process. It served not only the hopes of the deceased in the afterlife, but also the prayers of the living, such as those performed in the state temples by the king.

Notes

1. W.B. Emery, *The Tomb of Hemaka* (Cairo, 1938), pl. 41. This same type of sign is cited by M.A. Murray as the determinative of festival. See Murray, *Saqqara Mastabas* I (London, 1905), pl. XLIII, second from bottom.
2. Griffiths, *The Origins of Osiris and His Cult*, 230-231.
3. Peet and Woolley, *COA* I, 103.
4. Kemp, *JEA* 69 (1983), 15.
5. Kemp, ibid. 67 (1981), 8.
6. Kemp, ibid. 66 (1980), 14, pl. II, 1.
7. Basins No. 1 and 2 (3) are those that conform the least to a proper **T**-shape and were added to the group later as it proceeded towards the west.
8. Nullifying the magical properties of an object was not an uncommon practice in ancient Egypt, and was done frequently to pots. East of the village wall, an intact jar with two holes bored into its side was found in the animal pens. See Bourriau, *Pottery from the Nile Valley before the Arab Conquest* (Cambridge, 1981), 113.
9. Kemp, *AR* I, 11, 13.
10. A. Badawy, *JEA* 42 (1956), 58-64.
11. H.W. Fairman in J. Pendlebury, *COA* III (1951), 206.
12. Badawy, *A History of Egyptian Architecture*, 61.
13. Bleeker, *Hathor and Thoth*, 89. The statue of Hathor was set in her kiosk on the roof exposed to the rays of the sun to which she was united.
14. C.V. 1222 has two entrances, a main one to the west and subsidiary one to the south with a *zir* near its entrance. This could very well have been the chosen entrance for informal visits to the chapel.
15. Kemp, *AR* I, 13.
16. G. Foucart, *Le Tombeau d'Amonmos*, Pt. 4 (Cairo, 1935), pl. XI A, B. This shows a boat containing a statue of Ahmose Nefertari being towed on a **T**-shaped lake from Tomb 19 of Amenmose. N. de G. Davies, *Seven Private Tombs at Ḳurnah* (London, 1948), pl. XV. A statue of Tuthmosis III in a boat is being towed either on a large lake or harbour from tomb 31 of Khonsu. N. de G. Davies, *The Tomb of Rekh-mi-re at Thebes* II (New York, 1943), pl. CX. A statue of Rekhmire is seen in a boat in a rectangular pond.
17. Peet and Woolley, *COA* I, 105.

18. A fine example of this is from the tomb of Tjanefer (no. 158). K.C. Seele, *The Tomb of Tjanefer* (Chicago, 1959), pl. 11.
19. Jéquier explains that the purpose of purifying the deceased or a god was to qualify him in a universal aspect. He states that at the beginning of a divine cult before entering a temple, the officiant was received in a special place by the two gods Horus and Thoth or Horus and Seth, who would pour onto his head the contents of two vases while he stood between them in a little basin. A modified version of this ritual could have been conducted in the chapels. G.M. Jéquier, *Les Frises d'Objets des Sarcophages du Moyen Empire* 47 (Cairo, 1921), 309, 312. If Chapel 525 follows the reconstruction by Newton (*COA* I, pl. XXVI) and no roof covered the inner hall, then the **T**-shaped basin could have represented a garden pool, but this is extremely doubtful, since a real or simulated garden is not found within the main structure of a chapel.
20. Badawy, op. cit.
21. Breasted, *Ancient Records of Egypt* II, 358: 887, 'Buildings near Luxor'.
22. A. Badawy, *Ancient Egyptian Architectural Design: a study of the harmonic system* (Berkeley, 1965), 3, 42-44; fig. 2. The right-angled triangles in the Water Garden have different units of measurement owing to the length of the vertical line thus forming a large and a small triangle.
23. Badawy, ibid., 58-62. Badawy's comments on the goddess Seshat and her relationship to both seven and to the moon's phases suggest the idea of growth.
24. N. de G. Davies, *The Rock Tombs of El Amarna* II (London, 1905), 37-38, pls XXXIII, XXXVI.
25. L. Borchardt and H. Ricke , *Die Wohnhäuser in Tell el Amarna* (Berlin, 1980). None of Ricke's over one hundred plans of the houses and larger estates in the Southern City contained this type of basin.
26. Badawy, *A History of Egyptian Architecture*, 495-496. In my opinion, Badawy is correct in his observations on the offering table incorporating the **T**-shape and a model of a pond with a vertical branch.
27. S. Hassan, *Excavations at Giza* VI, Part II (Cairo, 1948), 5-7.
28. Petrie found one of the earliest examples of a mat, dish and jug set before a false door at Deshasheh. W.M.F. Petrie, *Deshasheh* (London, 1898), 35.
29. L. Borchardt, 'Denkmäler des Alten Reiches' I, *Catalogue Général des Antiquités* (Berlin, 1937), 10-35, Blatt 4-7, nos 1323-1376.
30. Jéquier, *Les Pyramides des Reines Neit and Apouit*, 58, fig. 35. This example is from a private tomb. It is a rare example at this period of the spout piercing the outer edge of the table.
31. Borchardt, op. cit., nos 1323, 1325. C.S. Fisher, *Giza: The Minor Cemetery* I (Philadelphia, 1924), pl. 20: rectangular basin before single niche; pl. 21: square basin before niche.
32. Hassan, op. cit., IV (1943), pls XIV A, XXII. Khentkawes' basins are noted for their size.
33. Hassan, ibid., 87-98.
34. H. Junker, *Giza* V (Leipzig, 1941), Tàf. XI a, b. From the mastaba of *dtw*.
35. W.M.F. Petrie, *Gizeh and Rifeh* (London, 1907), 14-20, pls XIV-XXII.
36. R. Mond and O.H. Myers, *Cemeteries of Armant* I (London, 1937), 59; *II*, pl. XXII, 5, 6. Most of these trays are oval and have **T**-shaped basins in conjunction with offerings.
37. Petrie, *Dendereh* (1898), pl. XIX.
38. W.M.F. Petrie, *Qurneh* (London, 1909), pls XX, XXI.
39. Petrie, *Gizeh and Rifeh*, 14-20.
40. A. Bey Kamal, 'Tables d'Offrandes' I, *Catalogue Général des Antiquités* (Cairo 1909), 1-55, nos 23001-23064. Observe offering tables from other periods.
41. N de G. Davies, *Two Ramesside Tombs at Thebes* (New York, 1927), 15, n. 2. J. Spiegel 'Die Entwicklung der Opferszenen in den Thebanischen Gräbern', *MDAIK* 14 (1956), 190-207, Tafel XV.
42. N. de G. Davies, *The Tombs of Two officials of Tuthmosis the Fourth* (London, 1923), pl. XXX.
43. R.O. Faulkner, *The Ancient Egyptian Pyramid Texts* (Oxford, 1969).
44. E. Naville, *Das Aegyptische Todtenbuch: Der XVIII bis XX Dynastie* I (Berlin, 1886), pl. LXXII, Kapitel 62 A.a; pl. LXXIII, Kapitel 63A, P.d; pl. CLXXII, Kapitel 150 A.a.
45. E.A. Wallis Budge, *The Book of the Dead: Facsimile of the Papyrus of Ani* (London, 1894), Sheet 16, Ch. LIX.
46. N. de G. Davies, *Two Ramesside Tombs at Thebes*, frontispiece, pls IX, X.
47. The hieroglyphic texts carved in sunk relief in the Pyramid of Unas are painted in blue to designate the idea of Nun or the Primordial Ocean. See J. Baines, *Fecundity Figures* (Warminster, 1985), 194-195.
48. N. de G. Davies, *Two Ramesside Tombs at Thebes*, pl. XXIV.
49. B. Bruyère, *Tombes Thebaines de Deir el Médineh: à Décoration Monochrome* (Cairo, 1952), 26.
50. N. M. Davies, *Ancient Egyptian Paintings* II (Chicago, 1936), pl. XCIV.
51. Bruyère, *Rapport* II (1934-1935), I, t.XV, 108. Bruyère distinguishes between the symbolism of the dom and date palm: the former represents the vital masculine force, whilst the latter stands for the female principle.
52. N. de G. Davies, *Seven Private Tombs at Ḳurnah*, 45, fig. 7.
53. Seele, *The Tomb of Tjanefer*, pls 11, 15, 27, 36.

54. Junker, *Giza* IV (Vienna, 1940), Abb. 8; Abb. 8a.

55. Junker, ibid., 28-35.

56. H.E. Winlock, *Excavations at Deir el Baḥri* (New York, 1942), 90, pl. 44, fig. 12.

57. H. Schäfer, *Principles of Egyptian Art* (translated and edited by J. Baines, 1974), 240-244.

58. This was suggested to me by A. Boyce, artist for the E.E.S.

59. G(M 13); R.O. Faulkner, *A Concise Dictionary of Middle Egyptian* (Oxford, 1972), 55. Baines, *Fecundity Figures*, 142.

60. Moens, *OLP* 15 (1984), 48.

61. Schäfer, op. cit., 244, fig. 257.

62. Bruyère, *Rapport* (1928), pl. I.

63. Davies, *The Tomb of Rekh-mi-re at Thebes* II, pl. LXXIX.

64. Bruyère, *Rapport* (1928), pl. I.

65. Ibid.

66. N. de G. Davies, *Two Ramesside Tombs at Thebes*, 19.

67. W. Wreszinski, *Atlas* II. 1 (Leipzig, 1924-1935), Tafels: 33a, 33b.

68. H.H. Nelson, *Reliefs and Inscriptions at Karnak* I (Chicago, 1936), pls 56, 58, 68. H.H. Nelson, *Medinet Habu* IV (Chicago, 1940), pl. 241E. H. Chèvrier, *Le Temple Reposoir de Seti II à Karnak* II, (Cairo, 1940), pls VII, IX, X. W. Wreszinski, *Atlas* II.2, Tafel 198. H. Brunner, *Die Südlichen Räume des Tempels von Luxor* (Mainz, 1977), Tafel 163, XVIII/165. H.H. Nelson, *The Great Hypostyle Hall at Karnak* I, Part I (Chicago, 1981), pls 76, B117, 118; 218, B323-25; 226, B334. Petrie *Qurneh*, pl. XLV. At Deir el Medina, fragments of what may have been a pottery T-shaped basin from tombs nos 1153-5 were discovered. This may have rested on an altar. See Nagel *La Céramique du Nouvel Empire à Deir el Medineh* I, 61-63, fig. 44, 1; 212-213, fig. 186.

69. Nelson, *The Great Hypostyle Hall at Karnak*, pl. 102, B146.

70. B. J. Kemp and D. O'Connor, *The International Journal of Nautical Archaeology and Underwater Exploration* (1974), 103.

71. Kemp and O'Connor, ibid., 130-133. U. Hölscher, *The Mortuary Temple of Ramesses III* IV, Pt. II (Chicago, 1951), 12.

72. Hölscher, ibid., 13, figs 12, 13.

73. Kemp and O'Connor, op. cit., 129-130.

74. Ibid., 130-131.

75. N. de G. Davies, *The Tomb of Neferhotep at Thebes* I (New York, 1933), 32-33, pl. XLII.

76. This has been variously interpreted as a lake or harbour. See Hölscher, op. cit., 12, n. 32 on both tombs 19 and 31.

77. J. Ph. Lauer, *La Pyramide à Degrés: L'Architecture* II (Cairo, 1936), pl. III.

78. Vandier, *Manuel II, L'Architecture Funéraire* (Paris 1954), 144.

79. Vandier, ibid., 145.

80. H. Ricke, 'Bemerkungen zur Ägyptischen Baukunst des Alten Reichs II', *Beiträge zur Ägyptischen Bauforschung und Altertumskunde* 5 (Cairo, 1950), 'Tor der Nut' 60-83; 'Breite Halle and Tiefe Halle' 112-114. The conjunction of the broad hall usually abutting a large pillared hall and the deep hall mark the gate of Nut which opens into the vertical passage leading to the chapels and the sacred area. The significance of this symbolism is apparent when what has been discussed already concerning the tree goddess's link with the T-shaped basin is taken into account. In this case, it is an architectural T-plan.

81. Ricke, ibid. See 'The Mortuary Temple of Sahure', 72, Abb. 28. The same consideration in n. 95 applies to Nun here.

82. Ricke, ibid., Khufu, 37, Abb. 10; Khephren, 49, Abb. 16; Menkaure, 57, Abb. 22; Pepi II, 81, Abb. 35.

83. Ricke, ibid., Valley Temple of Khephren, 88, Abb. 37.

84. Hassan, op. cit., IV, 69-70.

85. E. Brovarski, *Orientalia* 46 (1977), 113.

86. Brovarski, op. cit., 110-111. Hassan, op. cit. IV, 69-70.

87. Hassan, ibid., 79-80, figs 35, 36, 37, 38.

88. Ibid. Compare tents of Mereruka and Idu: 79, figs 35, 37.

89. B. Grdseloff, *Das Ägyptische Reinigungszelt* (Cairo, 1941), 8.

90. E. Drioton, *ASAE* 40 (1940), 1011.

91. Brovarski, op. cit., 107, fig. 1.

92. Ibid., 107.

93. Ricke, op. cit., 93, Abb. 39, 40: the tents of Qar and Idu. The water before the structures is labelled *Binsenfeld*.

94. Faulkner, op. cit., Utterance 325: 525.

95. G.A. Reisner, *The Development of the Egyptian Tomb Down to the Accession of Cheops* (Cambridge, Mass., 1936), 263-283.

96. G.A. Reisner, *A History of the Giza Necropolis* I (Cambridge, Mass., 1942), 249, fig. 152; 234, fig. 138. Reisner, *The Development of the Egyptian Tomb*, 273-278, figs 167, 168. Petrie, *Dendereh*, pl. XXVIII.

97. N. de G. Davies, *The Tomb of Rekh-mi-re at Thebes*, see plates. This tomb provides one of the most complete repertoires to tomb scenes.

98. PM I¹, Compare the various tomb plans as shown.

99. N. de G. Davies, *The Rock Tombs of El Amarna* III (London, 1905), pls I, XXVI.

100. N. de G. Davies, ibid. VI (London, 1908), pl. XI.

101. Badawy, *Ancient Egyptian Architectural Design*. See above, n. 22.

102. Ricke, op. cit.

103. E.C. Kielland, *Geometry in Egyptian Art* (London, 1955).

104. S. Sauneron, *The Priests of Ancient Egypt* (New York, 1980), 135-170.

105. D.H. Wildung, *Egyptian Saints* (New York, 1977), 83-109.

106. S. Morenz, *Egyptian Religion* (London, 1973), 167-182.

107. E.A. Wallis Budge, *The Hieratic Papyrus of Nesi-Amsu, a scribe in the Temple of Amen-Ra at Thebes about B.C. 305* (Westminster, 1891), 48, Col. XXVI, 22; Col. XXVIII, 21.

108. Desroches Noblecourt, *Tutankhamun*, 226, fig. 139; 235.

Appendix

The Ḥnw

Whether there was a specific word for the private chapel is uncertain, but the word *ḥnw* may have referred to them in some cases. *Ḥnw* (⬭) was generally used to signify a chapel or shrine and appeared in various contexts, to be discussed below. It is formed from the root *ḥnỉ*, a verb meaning 'to alight', 'stop', 'halt', which can be traced back to the Old Kingdom.[1] The noun *ḥnw* appears in the Eighteenth Dynasty and has the overall sense of a 'resting-place' or 'abode'. It is used to refer to a temple/chapel, a tomb, possibly a house, a magazine or a warehouse.[2]

The following examples show its use in connection with some of the royal monuments. In the Hathor Chapel at Deir el Bahari, part of an inscription from an address given by the Hathor Cow to Queen Hatshepsut says: *ḥtp kwỉ m mnw·t ỉpn ḥnw nfr ỉr·n·t n ỉỉ n m P šm n Dp*. 'I rest in this your monument, the beautiful chapel which you made for (me) to come from Pe and to go to Dep'.[3] *Ḥnw* in this context stands for a small chapel which may have housed a statue of the Hathor Cow originally, and part of a complex forming a royal mortuary temple.

Another example comes from the inscription on the Stela of Tuthmosis III from the great temple of Amun-Re at Gebel Barkal.[4] The excerpt reads: *ỉr·tw n·f ḥnw n nḥḥ dr ntt sꜥꜣ n·f nḥtw ḥm(ỉ) r nsw nb ḥpr*. 'There was made for him a *ḥnw* of eternity because he had made great the victories of My Majesty more than any king who existed'. This passage implies that a chapel was erected within the precincts of the main temple as a specific thanks offering to the god Amun for granting the king victories in battle. Once again, *ḥnw* may have contained a statue to the god and if so, it would have been in recognition of a divine gift, with no funerary connections.

The Great Limestone Stela[5] from the cult temple of Amenhotep II at Giza refers to *ḥnw* several times. In one passage in the text, Amenhotep II stops at the *ḥnw* of *Ḥr-m-ꜣḫt* to observe it for some moments. This is what today is known as the Temple of the Sphinx, which forms part of the pyramid complex of Khephren and Khufu. Later, this sanctuary became a centre of pilgrimage.[6] From the text we gather that out of respect for the early kings, who probably by the New Kingdom were surrounded by legend, Amenhotep II was inspired to erect a small cult temple (*ḥnw*) in honour of *Ḥr-m-ꜣḫt*. This complex, although associated with a mortuary cult of the Old Kingdom, also had a specific identity as a sanctuary of a god, in this case *Ḥr-m-ꜣḫt*.[7]

A sandstone block[8] from the temple of Amun-Re at Karnak, dating to Tuthmosis III and found near the main central sanctuary of the temple, is inscribed: *r ḏd ḥnw pw w swꜥb n ḥm·f ꜥš*: 'saying that it is a sanctuary, a place of purification of His Majesty with cedar (oil)'.[9] This passage may refer to a small chapel in the area of the main sanctuary and the Hall of Annals.

In the goldmining area some 35 kilometres east of Edfu in the Wadi Abbad at Kanais,[10] Seti I built a settlement with a small sanctuary for the goldminers, who worked for the Abydos temple.[11] The deities represented in the sanctuary were Amun, Re, Ptah, Osiris, Horus, Isis and Menmaatre (Seti I). Seti I's proposal for building this temple is contained in his inscription from Year 9 from Kanais.[12] The excerpt reads *ky sp nfr iw r ib·i ḥr wḏ nṯr m rdi grg niwt iw ḥnw m-ḥnw·s špssy dmit ḥr ḥwt-nṯr iw·i r qd ḥnt m st tn ḥr rn wr itw nṯrw*; 'another good thing has come to my heart upon the god's command, consisting of causing the establishment of a town. A temple/chapel will be in it. A place is august which possesses a temple. I will build a temple/chapel in this place with the Great Name of "Father of the Gods" '.

The word *ḥnw* was used with various meanings in connection with the lives of the workmen at Deir el Medina. A hieratic ostracon from Deir el Medina is inscribed with the following phrase: 'The scribe Amennakht: likewise the jars of wine which I told you were in the *ḥnw* of Amenhotep (l.p.h.)'.[13] This clearly refers to one of the votive chapels at Deir el Medina dedicated to the deified king, Amenhotep I. There must have been storage chambers attached to it, which stored the jars of wine mentioned on the ostracon.

Papyrus Salt 124 (BM 10055)[14] is concerned with charges brought against a man called Paneb of Deir el Medina. This dates from the Nineteenth to the Twentieth Dynasty or the first half of the reign of Ramesses III. A workman called Amennakht accuses Paneb of causing him to swear not to go to the *ḥnw* of his mother and father, and that no member of the family of the chief workman Nebnefer, to whom Amennakht was related, should be acknowledged when they brought offerings to their god Amun.[15] Černý believed that in this context *ḥnw* may refer to the chapel of the family god.[16] Amun figures frequently in many of the private chapels at Deir el Medina and his name has already been noted in connection with the chapels at El Amarna. Amennakht also could have been prevented from attending to the offices associated with the family ancestor cult, which could have been carried on in his parents' *ḥnw*.

An ostracon belonging to the Hood Collection[17] describes the giving to another the property of a man named Telmonth, which consists of *pr*, *ḥnw*, *ꜥt* and *mꜥḥꜥt*.[18] Gardiner believes that *pr* probably meant the estate as a whole. That being the case, he assigns *ḥnw* as the dwelling place or house of Telmonth with the tomb, *mꜥḥꜥt*, distinct from it. However, if *pr* were to be interpreted as the house of Telmonth, then *ḥnw* would become the chapel of Telmonth.

Gardiner and Blackman refer to Ostracon BM 5637, vs. 4,[19] with an inscription including the word *ḥnw* in the sense of a house or dwelling place, instead of its other meaning of a *chapel* or *shrine*. The text on the ostracon concerns the robbing of the plaintiff's warehouse while participating in a festival of the deified king Amenhotep I, and while all the villagers were busy celebrating. The line, vs. 4, 'while I was in the house (*ḥnw*) of my father' has been interpreted by Blackman in the following quote,[20] 'no doubt after the procession the holiday-makers returned home to feast'. In my opinion, it seems more likely that the villagers were observing the festival in the various private chapels,[21] of which many were dedicated to Amenhotep I, or at least included him amongst other dedicatees.

The noun *ḥnw* from a text on Ostracon BM 5625 has been translated as 'house' by Blackman (Chapter 5, 72; 79, n. 103) and 'chapel' by Janssen and Černý.[22] Kenna, a workman, is prevented from living in a ruined chapel/house (*ḥnw*). If the building was a house, it may have been a small enclosure connected to a private chapel.

The subject of inheritance of real estate is taken up in Papyrus Bulaq X, verso.[23] The real estate of the workman, Huy, has been left to his children, part of which includes 'the dwelling place which is beside the *ḥnw* of Huy ...'.[24] Kemp suggests that *ḥnw* may refer to the type of enclosure attached to a tomb that possesses cooking facilities.[25] The sense here seems to refer to a complex such as C.V. 1190 and 1218 and other similar instances cited in Chapter 5. It could also refer to the type of tombs that had attached enclosures containing evidence of domestic activities (Chapter 5, 76). It is clear in the text that the word *ḥnw* signifies a structure different from the dwelling place and, in my view, would refer to a private chapel and its dependencies, or a tomb chapel with a dependency.

The textual evidence provided above has demonstrated that in most cases the word *ḥnw* refers to a chapel or shrine, with or without a funerary purpose, that could be dedicated to one or more gods, a deified king or possibly an ancestor cult. The *ḥnw* could include domestic facilities in its complex, such as a magazine or small dwelling. The two cases where it could be interpreted as a house are open to argument, and need more qualification.

Notes

1.   *Wb* III, 287-288.
2.   Ibid., 288. L.H. Lesko, *Dictionary of Late Egyptian* II, 179.
3.   *Urk* IV, 237, 5-8.
4.   Ibid. IV, 1228, 13-14.
5.   Ibid. IV, 1282, 20; 1283, 10-14.
6.   S. Hassan, *The Sphinx — Its History in the Light of Recent Excavations* (Cairo, 1949), 43-47.
7.   C.M. Zivie, *Giza au Deuxième Millénaire* (Cairo, 1976), 286-288.
8.   G. Legrain, *ASAE* 2 (1901), 228.
9.   *Urk* IV, 736, 16; 737, 1.
10. J. Baines and J. Malek, *Atlas of Ancient Egypt* (Oxford, 1980), 71.
11. B. Gunn and A.H. Gardiner, *JEA* 4 (1917), 242-245; 245, see n. 4, 'a stopping place used both for the dwellings of men and the chapels of gods'.
12. *KRI* I, 'Seti I, Kanais, Great Inscription Yr. 9 I' (Oxford, 1975), 66, 15-16.
13. J. Černý, *Ostraca Hieratiques non Littéraires de Deir el Médineh* IV (Cairo, 1939), No. 248, recto.
14. J. Černý, *JEA* 15 (1929), 243-258.
15. Ibid., 246.
16. Ibid., 250, n. 47.
17. A.H. Gardiner and K. Sethe, *Egyptian Letters to the Dead* (London, 1928), 24; VI, 23.
18. Ibid.
19. Ibid.
20. A.M. Blackman, *JEA* 12 (1926), 184 top of page.
21. K.A. Kitchen, *Pharaoh Triumphant* (Warminster, 1982), 169; compare Kitchen's description of the Feast of the Valley and how the workmen of Deir el Medina celebrated it in their chapels.
22. R.J. Demarée and J.J. Janssen, *Gleanings from Deir el Medina* (Leiden, 1982), 118-119; 129, n. 69. See also S. Allam, *Hieratische Ostraka und Papyri aus der Ramessidenzeit* (Tübingen, 1973), 46-7, no. 21.
23. J.J. Janssen and P.W. Pestman, *JESHO* 11 (1968), 147, (b) 4, (b) 9.
24. Ibid.
25. B. J. Kemp, *ZÄS* 105 (1978), 130, n. 41.

Addendum

Before going to press, information arose significant to the discussion of Level VII Temple at Bethshan and the Egyptian private chapels (Ch. 6), and which merited inclusion in this publication.

The excavations of the University of Arizona in 1985 at Tell el-Hayyat east of the Jordan river and some 15 to 20 kms southeast of Bethshan exposed a series of four superimposed temples (phases 5-2) dating from Middle Bronze Age IIA-C. These structures underwent successive rebuilding and alterations and served an essentially agricultural community. All four maintained an east/west orientation. The earliest temple (phase 5) was the "migdal" type with dimensions of 7.6 × 7.6m and walls 70 cm thick of mudbrick and puddled mud. Buttresses were on either side of the main entrance to the east. Inside, a mudbrick platform or altar was set into the northeastern corner, and a brick bench lined the opposite wall.

During phase 4 the temple was enlarged to 8 × 8m. Mudbrick pilasters were set on the exterior northern and southern walls, and a forecourt was added containing six upright stones (75-100 cm. high). In the interior the brick altar was still retained, but the bench was extended around all walls.

Little remained of the interior of the phase 3 temple. During phase 2 the temple was increased to 11 × 10 m. and plastered on the exterior and the interior. In the courtyard a basalt column drum was set in the centre of the rear wall. Within the temple a niche 2 × 1m. was set in the centre of the rear wall. There was no evidence of benches in this phase. The excavators believed that, if present, they would have been removed because of the extensive pitting of the walls.

The Tell el-Hayyat temple plans suggest an early prototype of the Late Bronze Age Temple at Bethshan (Level VII). Other temples of the same layout and period as those at Tell el-Hayyat have been found in the neighbouring vicinity at Tell Kittan and Kfar Rupin. These Middle Bronze Age structures help to provide evidence for a continuity and development of Syro/Palestinian religious architecture leading to the Late Bronze/Iron Age. They also emphasize the suggestion of a possible Near Eastern influence or derivative in the architecture of various private chapels at Amarna (525, 529, 571 and the Northern Group) and Deir el Medina (Chapelles B, C, D).

Bibliography

Falconer, S., and Magness-Gardiner, B., "Tell el-Hayyat, 1985: Report to the Department of Antiquities", Jordan.

Khouri, Rami G., "The Antiquities of the Jordan Rift Valley", (Amman, Jordan, 1988).

Bibliography

Adam, S. 'Report on the Excavations of the Department of Antiquities at Ezbet Rushdi', *ASAE* 56: 207-226, 1959.

Aharoni, Y. *The Archaeology of the Land of Israel*. London, 1982.

Aldred, C. *Egyptian Art*. Second edition 1986.

Allam, S. *Hieratische Ostraka und Papyri aus der Ramessidenzeit*: 46-7, no. 21. Tübingen, 1973.

Amiran, R. *Early Arad: The Chalcolithic Settlement and Early Bronze City I: first-fifth seasons of excavations 1962-1966*. The Israel Exploration Society: Jerusalem, 1978.

Andrae, W. *Die archäischen Ischtar Tempel* Berlin 1922; reprinted Osnabrück 1970.

Anthes, R. *Die Felseninschriften von Hatnub*: 36-37; GR. 16, 6. Leipzig 1928; reprinted Hildesheim 1964.

Arnold, D. *'Der Tempel Qasr el-Sagha'*. Mainz, 1979.

Badawy, A. *Ancient Egyptian Architectural Design: a study of the harmonic system*. Berkeley, 1965.

— *A History of Egyptian Architecture: The Empire*. Berkeley, 1968.

Baines, J. 'Practical Religion and Piety', Abstracts of Papers, *International Association of Egyptologists*: 4-7. Munich, 1985.

— Fecundity Figures. Warminster, 1985.

— 'Practical Religion and Piety', *JEA* 73: 79-98, 1987.

Baines, J. and Malek, J. *Atlas of Ancient Egypt*. Oxford 1980, reprinted 1983.

Baraize, E. 'Compte Rendu des Travaux Exécutés à Deir el Médineh', *ASAE* 13: 19-42, 1913.

Barnett, R.D. 'The Sea Peoples', *CAH II, Pt. 2, The Middle East and the Aegean Region c. 1380-1000 BC*: 359-378. Cambridge, 1975.

Bienkowski, P. *Jericho in the Late Bronze Age*. Warminster, 1986.

Bietak, M. *Avaris and Piramesse*, Proceedings of the British Academy 65, published separately (London), reprinted with a revised Postscript and Bibliography (1986), 1979.

— 'Problems of Middle Bronze Age Chronology: New Evidence from Egypt' *AJA* 88: 471-485, 1984.

— *Eine Palastanlage aus der Zeit des späten Mittleren Reichs und Andere Forschung-*

sergebnisse aus dem östlichen Nildelta (Tell el-Dab'a 1979-1984). Österreichischen Akademie der Wissenschaften: Wien, 1985.

Blackman, A.M.   'Oracles in Ancient Egypt', *JEA* 12: 176-185, 1926.

—   'Preliminary Report on the Excavations at Sesebi, Northern Province, Anglo-Egyptian Sudan 1936-1937', *JEA* 23: 145-151, 1937.

Bleeker, C.J.   *Hathor and Thoth*. Leiden, 1973.

Bonnet, C. and Valbelle, D.   'Le Village de Deir el-Médineh: Reprise de l'étude archéologique' *BIFAO* 75: 429-446, 1975.

—   'Le village de Deir el-Médineh: Etude archéologique'. *BIFAO* 76: 317-342, 1976.

Borchardt, L.   *Denkmäler des Alten Reiches, Catalogue Général des Antiquités Égyptiennes du Musée du Caire* I. Berlin, 1937.

Borchardt, L. and Ricke, H.   *Die Wohnhäuser in Tell el Amarna*. Berlin, 1980.

Bourriau, J.   *Pottery from the Nile Valley before the Arab Conquest*, Fitzwilliam Museum. Cambridge, 1981.

Breasted, J.H.   *Ancient Records of Egypt*, II. Chicago, 1906.

Brovarski, E.   'The Doors of Heaven', *Orientalia* 46: 107-115, 1977.

Brunner, H.   *Die südlichen Räume des Tempels von Luxor*. Mainz, 1977.

Bruyère, B.   *Les Fouilles de Deir el Médineh*: 1922-23. Cairo, 1924.

—   *Les Fouilles de Deir el Médineh*: 1924-25. Cairo, 1926.

—   *Les Fouilles de Deir el Médineh*: 1926-27. Cairo, 1927-8.

—   *Les Fouilles de Deir el Médineh*: 1928. Cairo, 1929.

—   *Les Fouilles de Deir el Médineh*: 1929. Cairo, 1930.

—   *Les Fouilles de Deir el Médineh*: 1930. Cairo, 1933.

—   *Les Fouilles de Deir el Médineh*: 1931-32, t. X. Cairo, 1934.

—   *Les Fouilles de Deir el Médineh*: 1933-34, t. XIV. Cairo, 1937.

—   *Les Fouilles de Deir el Médineh*: 1934-35, t. XV. Cairo, 1937.

—   *Les Fouilles de Deir el Médineh*: 1934-35, t. XVI. Cairo, 1939.

—   *Les Fouilles de Deir el Médineh*: 1935-40, t. XX. Cairo, 1948.

—   *Les Fouilles de Deir el Médineh*: 1945-47, t. XXI. Cairo, 1952.

—   *Les Fouilles de Deir el Médineh*: 1948-51, t. XXVI. Cairo, 1953.

—   *Tombes Thébaines de Deir el Médineh: à Décoration Monochrome*. Cairo, 1952.

Budge, E.A. Wallis.   *The Hieratic Papyrus of Nesi-Amsu, a scribe in the Temple of Amen-Ra at Thebes about B.C. 305*. Westminster, 1891.

—   *The Book of the Dead: Facsimile of the Papyrus of Ani in the British Museum*. Second Edition. London, 1894.

Calverley, A.M., Broome, M.F. and Gardiner, A.H.,   *The Temple of King Sethos I at Abydos*, III. London and Chicago, 1938.

Caminos, R.   'Surveying Kumma', *Kush* 13: 74-77, 1967.

Carless Hulin, L.   'Pottery Cult Vessels from the Workmen's Village', in Kemp, B.J., *AR* I: 165-177.

Caskey, J.L.   'Excavations in Keos 1963', *Hesperia* 33: 314-335, 1964.

Cauville, S.   'Une règle de la Grammaire du Temple', *BIFAO* 83: 51-84, 1983.

Černý, J.   'Papyrus Salt 124 (British Museum 10055)', *JEA* 15: 243-258, 1929.

—   *Catalogue des Ostraca Hiératiques non Littéraires de Deir el Médineh*, IV, Documents de Fouilles de l'Institut Français d'Archéologie Orientale de Caire III, IV, VII. Cairo, 1939.

—   in Parker, R. A., *A Saite Oracle Papyrus from Thebes in the Brooklyn Museum, Papyrus Brooklyn 47.218.3*: 35-48. Providence, R.I, 1962.

Chèvrier, H.   *Le Temple Reposoir de Seti II à Karnak*. Cairo, 1940.

Davies, N. M.   *Ancient Egyptian Paintings* II. Chicago, 1936.

Davies, N. de G.   *The Rock Tombs of El Amarna* II, III, VI. London, 1905-08.

—   *The Tombs of Two Officials of Tuthmosis the Fourth*, Theban Tomb Series III. London, 1923.

—   *Two Ramesside Tombs at Thebes* V. Metropolitan Museum: New York, 1927.

—   *The Tomb of Neferhotep at Thebes*, I. New York, 1933.

—   *The Tomb of Rekh-mi-re at Thebes* II. Metropolitan Museum of Art Egyptian Expedition. New York, 1943.

—   *Seven Private Tombs at Kurnah* (London, 1948.

Demarée, R.J.   *ȝḥ iḳr n Rꜥ-Stelae*, on Ancestor Worship in Ancient Egypt. Leiden, 1983.

Demarée, R.J. & Janssen, J.J.   *Gleanings from Deir el Medina*. Leiden, 1982.

Desroches-Noblecourt, C.   *Tutankhamen*. London, 1969.

Dothan, T.   *Qedem* Monographs of the Institute of Archaeology, The Hebrew University of Jerusalem 10, 1979.

—   *Philistines and Their Material Culture*. Israel Exploration Society: Jerusalem, 1982.

Dreyer, G.   in Kaiser, W., Dreyer, G., Grimm, G., Haeny, G., Jaritz, H., Müller, C., 'Stadt und Tempel von Elephantine, Fünfter Grabungsbericht', *MDAIK* 31: 51-58, 1975.

—   in Kaiser, W., Dreyer, G., Gempeler, R., Grossman, P., Haeny, G., Jaritz, H., Junge, F., 'Stadt und Tempel von Elephantine, Sechster Grabungsbericht', *MDAIK* 32: 75-87, 1976.

Dreyer, G. and Kaiser, W.   in Kaiser, W., Dreyer, G., Gempeler, R., Grossman, P., Jaritz, H., 'Stadt und Tempel von Elephantine, Siebter Grabungsbericht', *MDAIK* 33: 68-83, 1977.

Drioton, E.   'Bernhard Grdseloff — Das ägyptische Reinigungszelt' (Études égyptiennes, premier fascicule) *ASAE* 40: 1007-1014, 1940.

Dunham, D. and Janssen, J.M.A.   *Semna, Kumma* I. Museum of Fine Arts: Boston, 1960.

Emery, W.B.   *The Tomb of Hemaka*. Cairo, 1938.

—   *Great Tombs of the First Dynasty*, I. London, 1949.

Erman, A.   *Life in Ancient Egypt*. First edition 1894. New York, 1971.

Erman, A. and Grapow, H.   *Wörterbuch der Aegyptischen Sprache* III. Leipzig, 1951.

Fairman, H.W.   'Preliminary Report on the Excavations at 'Amarah West, Anglo-Egyptian Sudan 1938-1939', *JEA* 25: 139-144, 1939.

—   'The Inscriptions, 3. The Nature of the Sunshades', in J.D.S. Pendlebury, *COA* III: 203-208. London, 1951.

—   '*Worship and Festivals in an Egyptian Temple*', *Bulletin of the John Rylands Library* 37. Manchester, 1954.

Faulkner, R.O.   *A Concise Dictionary of Middle Egyptian*. First edition 1962, reprinted Oxford 1972.

—   *The Ancient Egyptian Pyramid Texts*. Translated into English. Oxford, 1969.

Faulkner, R.O., Wente, E.F., & Simpson, W.K.   *The Literature of Ancient Egypt*. New Haven and London, 1973.

Fisher, C.S.   *The Minor Cemetery at Giza*. Philadelphia, 1924.

Foucart, G.   *Tombes Thébaines: Nécropole de Dirâ' Abû' N-Naga*. Cairo, 1932.

—   *Le Tombeau d'Amonmos* Pt. 4. Cairo, 1935.

Frankfort, H.   *Kingship and the Gods*. First edition 1948. University of Chicago, 1978.

—   *The Art and Architecture of the Ancient Orient*. First edition 1954. Harmondsworth, 1979.

Friedman, F.   'On the Meaning of Some Anthropoid Busts from Deir el-Medina', *JEA* 51: 82-97, 1985.

Gardiner, A.H.   *Egyptian Grammar*. Third edition. London, 1969.

Gardiner, A.H. and Sethe, K.   *Egyptian Letters to the Dead Mainly from the Old and Middle Kingdoms*. London, 1928.

Garstang, J.   'Jericho: City and Necropolis', *LAAA* 23, 1936.

Giveon, R.   *The Impact of Egypt on Canaan: iconographical and related studies*. Orbis biblicus et orientalis vol. 20. Freiburg Schweiz Universitätsverläg, 1978.

—   'Resheph in Egypt', *JEA* 66: 144-150, 1980.

Goedicke, H.   'Abi-Sha(i)'s Representation in Beni Hasan', *JARCE* 21: 203-210, 1984.

Goyon, G.   'Le Papyrus de Turin dit 'Des Mines d'or' et le Wadi Hammamat', *ASAE* 49: 337-392, 1949.

Grdseloff, B.   *Das Ägyptische Reinigungszelt*. Cairo, 1941.

Grébaut, E.   *Le Musée Égyptien*. Recueil de Monuments et de Notices sur les Fouilles d'Égypte I. Cairo, 1890-1900.

Griffiths, J. Gwyn   *The Origins of Osiris and His Cult*. Leiden, 1980.

Gunn, B. and Gardiner, A.H.   'New Renderings of Egyptian Texts', I. *The Temple of the Wady Abbad*; JEA 4: 241-251, 1917.

Hassan, S.   *Excavations at Giza: 1932-1933* IV. Cairo, 1943.

—   *Excavations at Giza* VI Part II. Cairo, 1948.

—   *The Sphinx — Its History in the Light of Recent Excavations*. Cairo, 1949.

Hayes, W.C.   *A Papyrus of The Late Middle Kingdom*. Brooklyn Museum, 1955. Reprinted 1972.

—   *The Scepter of Egypt* II. First printed 1959. Metropolitan Museum of Art, 1978.

Hecker, H.   'Excavation of floor (873) in the Main Chapel', in Kemp, B.J., *AR* III: 80-89.

Helck, W.   *Urkunden der 18 Dynastie* V Heft 17. Berlin, 1955.

—   'Zum Auftreten fremder Götter in Ägypten', *Oriens Antiquus* 5: 1-14, 1966.

—   *Die Bezeihungen Ägyptens zu Vorderasien im 3, und 2. Jahrtausend v. Chr.* First published 1962. Wiesbaden, 1971.

—   *Die Bezeihungen Ägyptens und Vorderasiens zur Ägais bis ins 7 Jahrhundert v. Chr.* Darmstadt, 1979.

Hölscher, U.   'The Mortuary Temple of Ramesses III', *The Excavation of Medinet Habu* IV parts I and II. Chicago, 1951.

Hornung, E.   *Conceptions of God in Ancient Egypt; the one and the many*. Translated by J. Baines. Great Britain, 1983.

James, F.   *The Iron Age at Beth Shan*. Philadelphia, 1966.

Janssen, J.J.   'Eine Beuteliste von Amenophis II und das Problem der Sklaverei im alten Ägypten', *JEOL* 17: 141-147, 1963.

Janssen, J.J. and Pestman, P.W.   'Burial and inheritance in the community of the necropolis workmen at Thebes', *JESHO* 11: 137-170, 1968.

Jéquier, G.M.   *Les Frises d'Objets des Sarcophages du Moyen Empire*. Mémoires publiés par les membres de L'Institut Français d'Archéologie Orientale du Caire 47. Cairo, 1921.

—   *Les Pyramides des Reines Neit et Apouit*. Cairo, 1933.

Junker, H. *Giza* IV. Wien, 1940.

—   *Giza* V. Leipzig, 1941.

Kamal, Ahmed Bey   'Tables d'Offrandes', *Catalogue Général des Antiquités Égyptiennes de Musée du Caire* I. Cairo, 1909.

Keimer, L.   'Jeux de la Nature', *Études d'Égyptologie*, Fascicule II: 1-21. Cairo, 1940.

Keith-Bennett, J.L.   'Anthropoid Busts II: Not from Deir el Medineh Alone', *Bulletin of the Egyptological Seminar* 3: 43-72, 1981.

Kemp, B.J.   'The Harim-Palace at Medinet el-Ghurab', *ZÄS* 105: 122-133, 1978.

—   'Preliminary Report on the El-'Amarna Survey, 177', *JEA* 64: 22-34, 1978.

—   'Preliminary Report on the El-'Amarna Expedition, 1979', *JEA* 66: 5-16, 1980.

—   'Preliminary Report on the El-'Amarna Expedition, 1980', *JEA* 67: 5-20, 1981.

—   'Preliminary Report on the El-'Amarna Expedition, 1981-2', *JEA* 69: 5-24, 1983.

—   *Amarna Reports* I-IV, 1984-7.

Kemp, B.J. and Merrillees, R.S.   *Minoan Pottery in Second Millennium Egypt, Deutsches Archäologisches Institut Abteilung Kairo*. Mainz am Rhein, 1980.

Kemp, B.J. and O'Connor, D.   'An Ancient Nile Harbour, University Museum Excavations at the Birket Habu', *The International Journal of Nautical Archaeology and Underwater Exploration* 3: 101-136, 1974.

Kielland, E.C.   *Geometry in Egyptian Art*. London, 1955.

Kitchen, K.A.   *Ramesside Inscriptions* I. Oxford, 1975.

—   *Pharaoh Triumphant, the Life and Times of Ramesses II*. Warminster, 1982.

Köhler, U.   *Das Imiut*, Göttinger Orientforschungen IV Reihe: Ägypten 4 (Teil A, B). Wiesbaden, 1975.

Krauss, R.   *Sothis und Monddaten*. Hildesheim, 1985.

Lacovara, P.   *Deir el-Ballas 1985*. Preliminary report issued to the Visiting Committee of the Department of Egyptian and Ancient Near Eastern Art. Boston, 1985.

Lauer, J. Ph.   *La Pyramide à Degrés: l'Architecture* II. Cairo, 1936.

Leahy, M.A.   'The hieratic labels, 1979-82', in Kemp, B.J., *AR* II: 65-109.

Legrain, G.   'Mémoire sur la Porte Située au Sud de l'Avant-Sanctuaire à Karnak et sur son Arche Fortuite' *ASAE* 2: 223-229, 1901.

Lesko, L.H.   *A Dictionary of Late Egyptian*. Providence, Rhode Island, 1984.

Lichtheim, M.   *Ancient Egyptian Literature I: The Old and Middle Kingdoms*. Berkeley and Los Angeles, 1973.

Loat, L.   *Gurob* part volume with M.A. Murray, *Saqqara Mastabas* I. London, 1905.

Loukianoff, G.   'Le Dieu Ched: l'évolution de son culte dans l'Ancienne Égypte', *Bulletin de l'Institut d'Égypte* 13: 67-83, 1931.

Lucas, A. and Harris, J. R.   *Ancient Egyptian Materials and Industries*. First published 1924, 4th Edition. London, 1962.

Matthiae, P.   *Ebla: An Empire Rediscovered*. G. Einaudi, 1977. English translation London 1980.

McGovern, P. E.   *Late Bronze Palestinian Pendants*. Sheffield, 1985.

Moens, M.F.   'The Ancient Egyptian Garden in the New Kingdom, a study of Representations', *OLP* 15: 11-53, 1984.

Mond, Sir R. and Myers, O. H.   *Cemeteries of Armant* 2. London, 1937.

Montet, P.   *Les Reliques de l'Art Syrien dans l'Égypte du Nouvel Empire*. Paris, 1937.

Morenz, S.   *Egyptian Religion*. London, 1973.

Murray, M.A.   *Saqqara Mastabas* I. London, 1905.

Nagel, G.   *La Céramique du Nouvel Empire à Deir el Médineh*. Cairo, 1938.

Naville, E.   *Das Aegyptische Todtenbuch: Der XVIII bis XX Dynastie* I. Berlin, 1886.

Nelson, H.H.   *Reliefs and Inscriptions at Karnak, Ramesses III's Temple* I. Chicago, 1936.
—   *Medinet Habu, Festival Scenes of Ramesses* III, IV. Chicago, 1940.
—   *The Great Hypostyle Hall at Karnak* I, Part I, O.I.P.: Chicago, 1981.
Oren, E.D.   *The Northern Cemetery of Bethshan*. Leiden, 1973.
Paton, L.B.   'Survivals of Primitive Religion in Modern Palestine', *The Annual of the American School of Oriental Research in Jerusalem*: 51-65. New Haven, 1920.
Peet, T.E. and Woolley, C.L.   *The City of Akhenaten* I. London, 1923.
Petrie, W.M.F.   *Kahun, Gurob, and Hawara*. London, 1890.
—   *Deshasheh*. London, 1898.
—   *Dendereh*. London, 1900.
—   *Abydos* II. London, 1903.
—   *Gizeh and Rifeh*. London, 1907.
—   *Qurneh*. London, 1909.
Piankoff, A.   *The Tomb of Ramesses VI*. New York, 1954.
Porter, B. and Moss, R.L.B.   *Topographical Bibliography of Ancient Egyptian Hieroglyphic Texts, Reliefs, and Paintings: I The Theban Necropolis, Part I: Private Tombs; Part II: Royal Tombs and Smaller Cemeteries*. Oxford, 1960, 1964.
Posener, G., Bottero, J. and Kenyon, K.M.   'Syria and Palestine, c. 2160-1780 B.C.', fascicle 29, *CAH* II². Cambridge, 1965.
Randal-MacIver, D. and Woolley, C.L.   *Buhen*. Philadelphia, 1911.
Redford, D.B.   'A Gate Inscription from Karnak and Egyptian Involvement in Western Asia during the Early 18th Dynasty', *JAOS* 99: 270-287. New Haven, 1979.
—   *Akhenaten, the Heretic King*. Princeton, 1984.
Reisner, G. A.   *The Development of the Egyptian Tomb Down to the Accession of Cheops*. Cambridge, Mass., 1936.
—   *A History of the Giza Necropolis* I. Cambridge, Mass., 1942.
Renfrew, C.   *The Archaeology of Cult: the Sanctuary at Phylakopi*. London, 1985.
Renfrew, J. M.   'Preliminary report on the botanical remains', in Kemp, B.J., *AR* II: 175-190.
Reymond, E. A. E.   *The Mythical Origin of the Egyptian Temple*. Cambridge, 1969.
Ricke, H.   'Bemerkungen zur Ägyptischen Baukunst des Alten Reichs II', *Beiträge zur Ägyptischen Bauforschung und Altertumskunde* 5. Cairo, 1950.
—   *Ausgrabungen von Khor-Dehmitt bis Beit el Wali* OINE II. Chicago, 1967.
Robins, G.   'The hieroglyphic wall plaster from Chapel 561', in Kemp, B.J., *AR* II: 110-132.
Rose, P.J.   'Pottery from the Main Chapel', in Kemp, B.J., *AR* III: 99-117.
Rowe, A.   *The Four Canaanite Temples of Bethshan* II Part I. Philadelphia, 1940.
Rutkowski, B.   *The Cult Places of the Aegean*. New Haven and London, 1986.
Sauneron, S.   *The Priests of Ancient Egypt*. First published 1960. New York, 1980.
Schäfer, H.   *Principles of Egyptian Art*. English translation by J. Baines. Oxford, 1974.
Seele, K.C.   *The Tomb of Tjanefer*. Chicago, 1959.
Sethe, K.   *Urkunden der 18 Dynastie* I. Leipzig, 1906.
—   *Urkunden der 18 Dynastie* III. Leipzig, 1907.
Shaw, I.M.E.   'Ring bezels at el-Amarna', in Kemp, B.J. *AR* I: 124-132.
Smith, W.S.   *A History of Egyptian Sculpture and Painting in the Old Kingdom*. First published 1946, second edition. Boston, 1949.
—   *The Art and Architecture of Ancient Egypt*. First edition 1958. Harmondsworth, 1981.

Spencer, A.J.   *Brick Architecture in Ancient Egypt*. Warminster, 1979.

Spiegel, J.   'Die Entwicklung der Opferszenen in den Thebanischen Gräbern', *MDAIK* 14: 190-207, 1956.

Steindorff, G. and Wolf, W.   *Die Thebanische Gräberwelt*. Hamburg, 1936.

Strabo   *The Geography of Strabo* VII, English translation by H.L. Jones. London and New York, 1930.

Taylor, J.H. and Boyce, A.   'The late New Kingdom burial from beside the Main Chapel', in Kemp, B.J. *AR* III: 118-146.

Thausing, G. and Goedicke, H.   *Nofretari, Queen of Egypt*. Graz, 1971.

Ussishkin, D.   'The Ghassulian Shrine at En-gedi', *Tel Aviv* 7: 1-44, 1980.

Valbelle, D.   '*Les Ouvriers de la Tombe: Deir el-Médineh à l'Époque Ramesside*'. Cairo, 1985.

Vandier, J.   *Manuel d'Archéologie Égyptienne II. Les Grandes Époques: l'Architecture Funéraire*. Paris, 1954.

—   *Manuel d'Archéologie Égyptienne. II. Les Grandes Époques: l'Architecture Religieuse et Civile*. Paris, 1955.

Weinstein, J.M.   '*The Egyptian Empire in Palestine: A Reassessment*', *BASOR* 241: 1-28, 1981.

Wildung, D.H.   *Egyptian Saints*. New York, 1977.

Wilkinson, Sir J.G.   *Manners and Customs of the Ancient Egyptians* I. New edition revised 1878. London, 1841.

Winlock, H.E.   *Excavations at Deir el Baḥri: 1911-1931*. New York, 1942.

Wreszinski, W.   *Atlas zur altaegyptischen Kulturgeschichte* II.1, II.2. Leipzig, 1924-1935.

Wright, G.R.H.   *Ancient Building in South Syria and Palestine*. Leiden-Köln, 1985.

Yadin, Y.   *Hazor*. The Schweich Lectures (1970), published for the British Academy. London, 1972.

Yeivin, Sh.   'Canaanite Ritual Vessels in Egyptian Cultic Practices', *JEA* 62: 110-114, 1976.

Zivie, C.M.   *Giza au Deuxième Millénaire*. Cairo, 1976.

Index of Egyptian words and phrases

General Index

A

Abi Shai
 See Asiatics
Abydos 72
 early temple 82
 temple of Seti I 86, 120
 three chapels 111
 tombs 113
 See also Khentamenti
Abyss 107-108
Acacia 12
 pods 61
Adam, Shehata 86
Aegean 81, 93
 aegeans in Egypt 95
 cult buildings 81, 93-94
 pottery 96
 temple of Ayia Irini 94
 temple of Phylakopi 67, 94
Aharoni
 See Bethshan, chronology
Ahmose Nefertari
 ancestor cult 58, 69-72, 75-76
 chapel of 49
 statuary 50
Ahmose, son of Abana 95
Ahmose, tomb of (3), Amarna 95, 112
Ai, acropolis temple 87
Akhenaten 63, 66, 68, 74, 92, 112
 jar dockets 7
 military presence 95
 ring bezels 7, 96
 Workmen's Village 7, 36
 See also Gurob
Akhetaten 3
Altars 28, 48, 64, 67, 71, 82, 86, 91-92, 94, 97,
 105, 109-111
Amara West, temple of
 See Nubia, temples
El Amarna 1, 7, 88
 Great Wadi 3
 Main City 5, 66, 68
 royal tomb 96
 Royal Wadi 3, 58, 96
 Stone Village 96
 tombs 63-64, 105, 112
 Workmen's Village 1-3, 5, 7, 24, 35-36, 59, 66,
 96
 See also Chapels, Amarna

See also Walled Village
Amenemhat I 94
 cult temple of 85
Amenemhat III 83
Amenhotep I
 cartouches 42, 73
 cult of 49, 54, 58, 69-72, 75-76, 120
 mortuary temple of 110
 oracle of 72
 statuary 50
Amenhotep II 75, 83, 85, 95, 119
 cult of 69
 temple of 84, 119
Amenhotep III 75, 83, 89, 110
 Bethshan, mortuary temple of 89, 92
 cartouches 90
 inscriptions 105
 mortuary temple of 113
 ring bezels 96
Amenhotep, son of Hapu 113
Amenmopet, Deir el Medina 70
Amenmose, tomb of (19) 110
Amennakht, foreman 49, 72
Amennakht, scribe 120
Amennakht, workman 120
Amiran, R. 88
Amorites 87
Amulets 61, 77, 90, 114
Amun
 See Gods, Egyptian
 temple of 47, 52-53, 69, 71, 83
Amun criocephalus
 See Gods, Egyptian
Amun-Re
 See Gods, Egyptian
 sandstone block 119
 temple of 119
Amunet
 See Goddesses, Egyptian
Anat
 See Goddesses, Asiatic
Ancestor busts 64-65, 68-70, 72, 74
Ancestor cults 57-58, 68-69, 71-72, 74, 76, 121
 origin of (Horian) 74
 private 68-69, 73-74, 76, 120
 royal 68-70, 72-74, 76
Andrae, W. 88
Ani, Papyrus of 108
Animals
 enclosures 4, 34

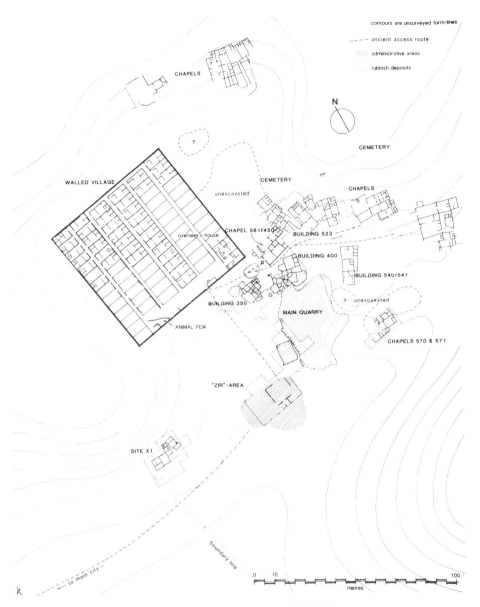

N

CHAPELS

CEMETERY

WALLED VILLAGE

?

CEMETERY

unexcavated

CHAPELS

overseer's house

CHAPEL 561/450

BUILDING 523

BUILDING 400

BUILDING 540/541

BUILDING 350

? unexcavated

MAIN QUARRY

ANIMAL PEN

CHAPELS 570 & 571

"ZIR"-AREA

SITE X1

boundary line

to main city

.0   10   100

metres

k

1   The Workmen's Village: excavations of 1921-22 and 1978-83.

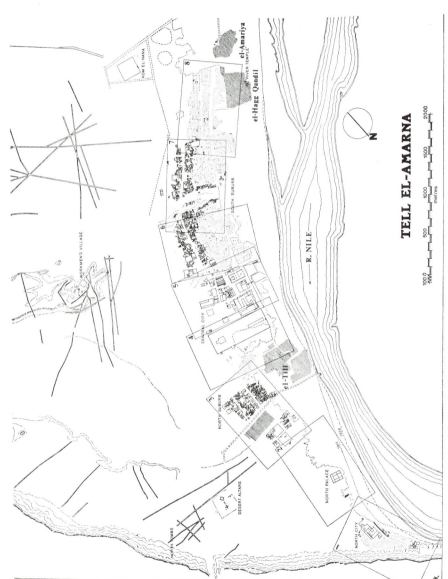

TELL EL-AMARNA

KOM EL-NANA

el-Amariya

RIVER TEMPLE

el-Hagg Qandil

WORKMEN'S VILLAGE

8

7

6

SOUTH SUBURB

5

CENTRAL CITY

4

el-Till

3

NORTH SUBURB

NORTH TOMBS

DESERT ALTARS

2

NORTH PALACE

WADI ABU HASAH EL-BAHRI

1

NORTH CITY

R. NILE

N

100.0
MM

500   1000   1500   2000

metres

2   The Main City.

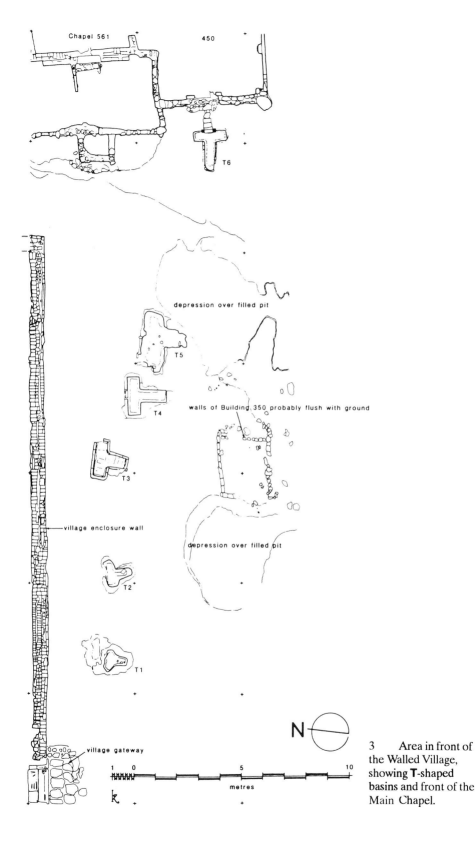

Chapel 561   450

T6

depression over filled pit

T5

T4

walls of Building 350 probably flush with ground

T3

village enclosure wall

depression over filled pit

T2

T1

N

village gateway

1 0   5   10

metres

3   Area in front of
the Walled Village,
showing **T**-shaped
basins and front of the
Main Chapel.

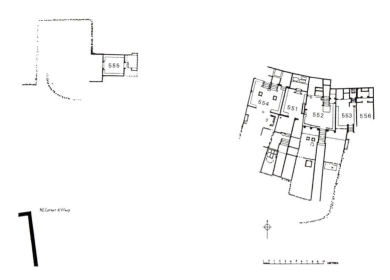

4   Chapels (northern group) 555, 554, 551, 552, 553, 556.

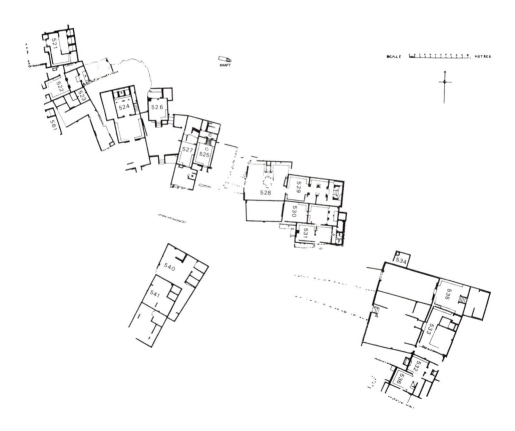

5   Chapels (southern group) 521, 522, 523, 561, 524, 526, 527, 525, 540, 541, 528, 529, 530, 531, 534, 535, 533, 532, 536.

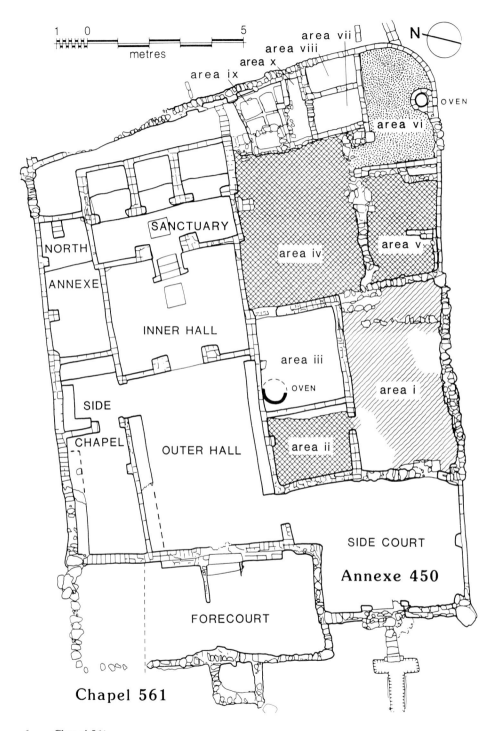

6   Chapel 561.

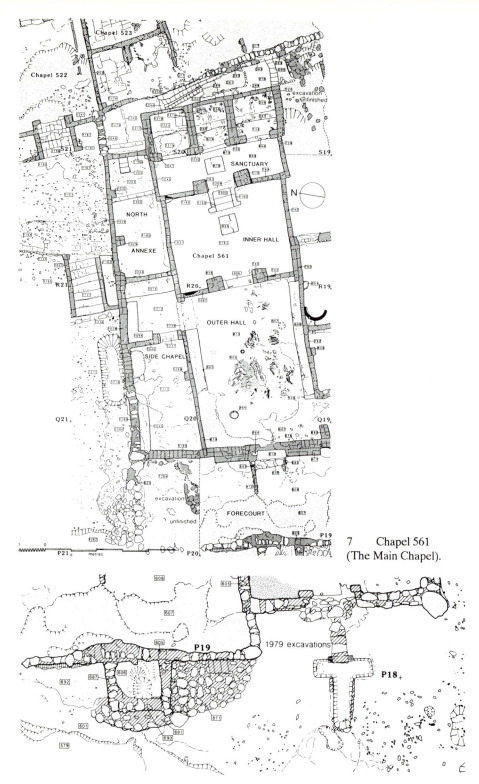

7   Chapel 561
(The Main Chapel).

7a   Chapel 561 (western end).

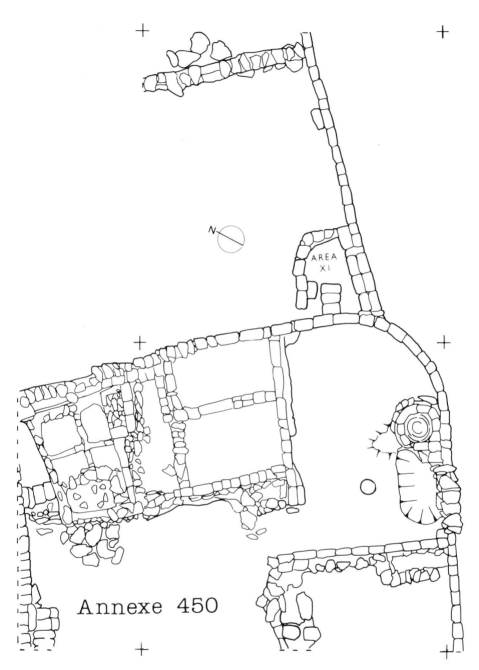

AREA
XI

Annexe 450

8   Eastern Sector of Annexe 450 showing Area XI.

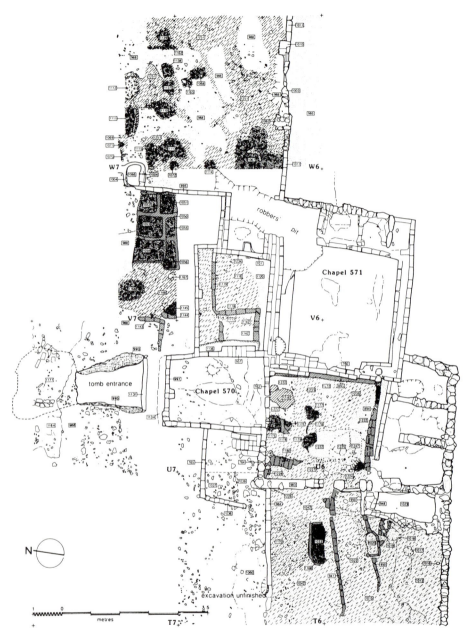

W7

W6

robbers' pit

Chapel 571

V7

V6

tomb entrance

Chapel 570

U7

U6

N

excavation unfinished

metres

T7

T6

9   Chapels 570 and 571.

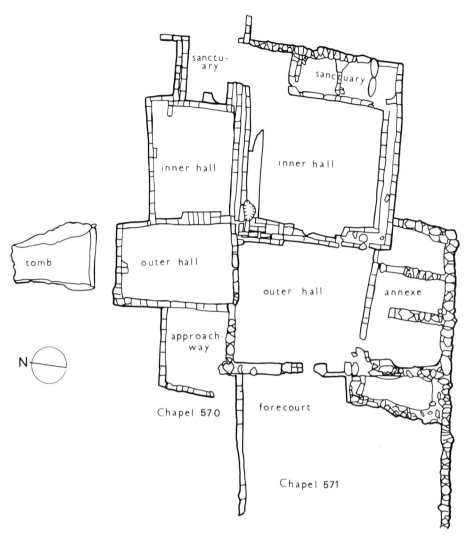

sanctu-
ary

sanctuary

inner hall

inner hall

tomb

outer hall

outer hall

annexe

N

approach-
way

Chapel 570

forecourt

Chapel 571

9a   Chapels 570 and 571. Diagram of areas.

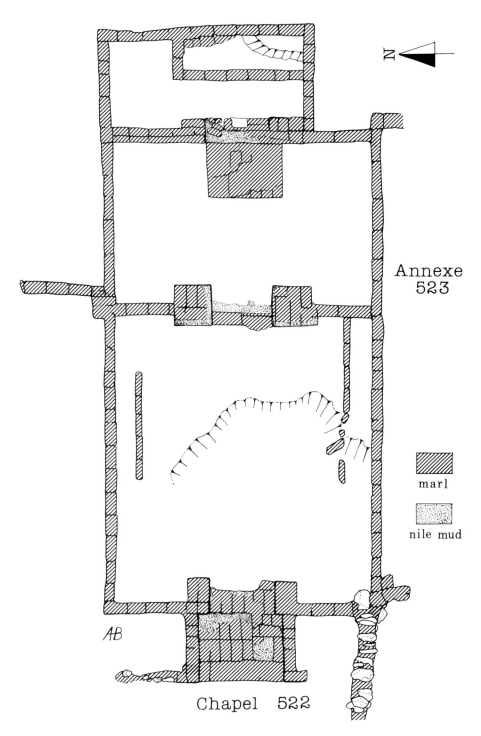

N

Annexe
523

marl

nile mud

AB

Chapel 522

10   Chapel 522.

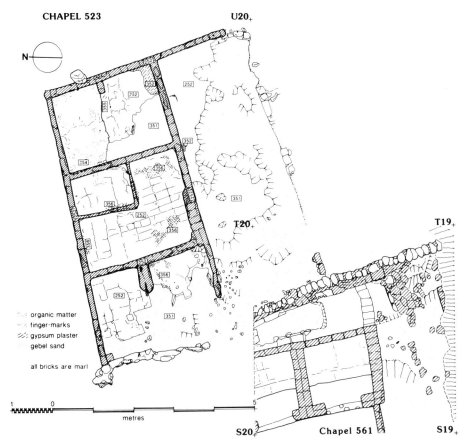

CHAPEL 523

U20₊

N

352
252
352
351
252
351
356
254
356
252
356
356
356
351
252
351

T20₊

T19₊

organic matter
finger-marks
gypsum plaster
gebel sand

all bricks are marl

1   0   5

metres

S20₊   Chapel 561   S19₊

11   Annexe 523.

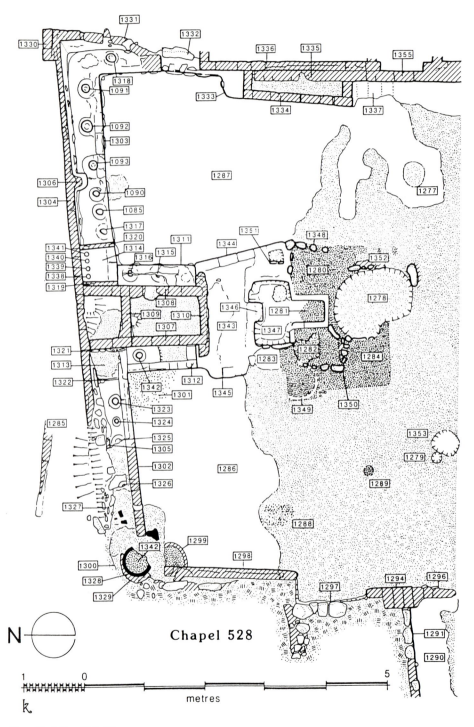

Chapel 528

N

metres

12   Building 528 (Chapel 528).

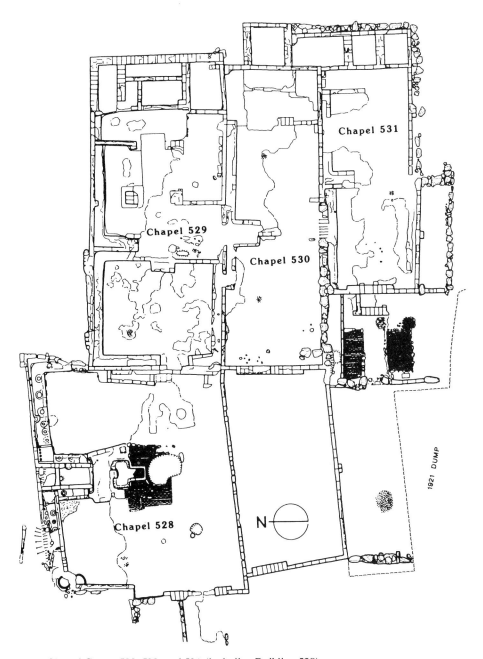

13   Chapel Group 529, 530, and 531 (including Building 528).

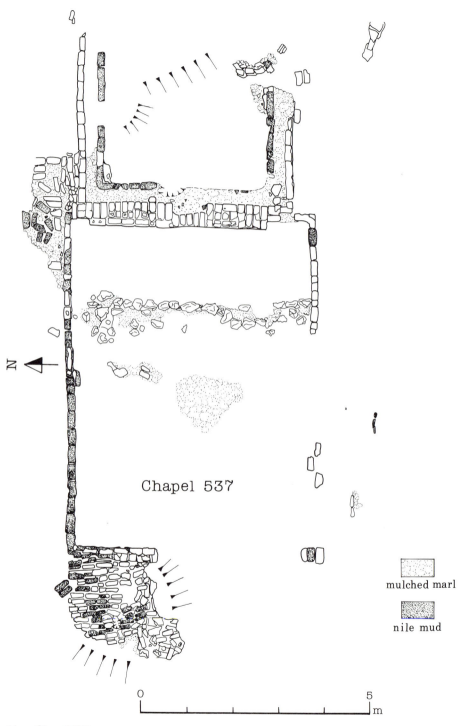

N

Chapel 537

mulched marl

nile mud

0 _____ 5
m

14   Chapel 537.

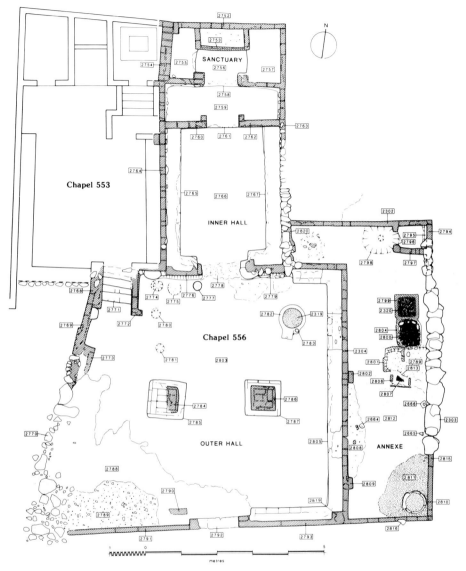

15   Chapel 556 by B. J. Kemp and outline plan of Chapel 553 by F. Newton.

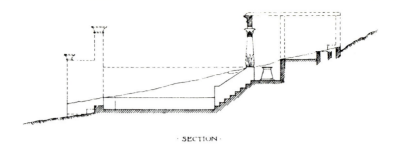

· SECTION ·

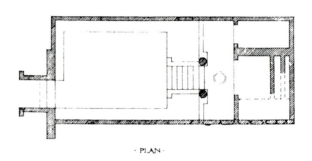

· PLAN ·

16   Section and plan of Chapel 525.

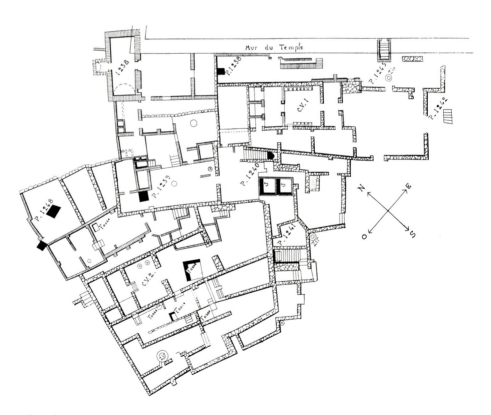

17   C.V. 1 and 2.

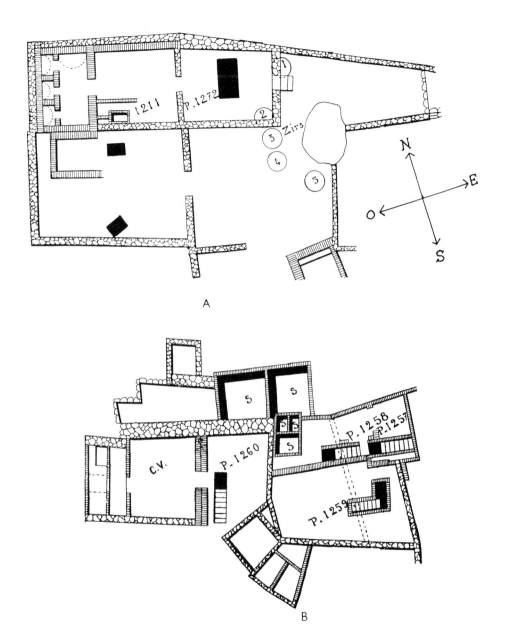

18   a) C.V. 1211; b) C.V. (no number).

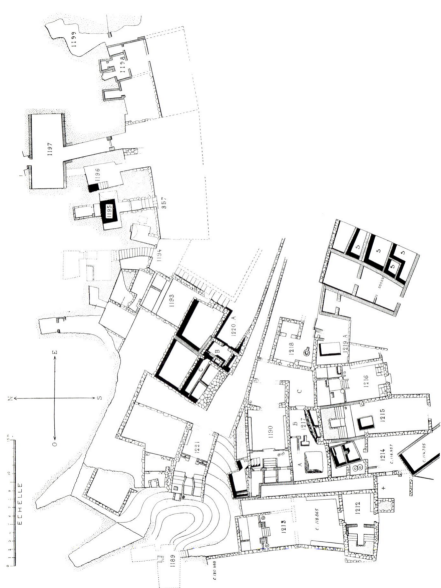

19   C.V. 1212, 1213, 1215, 1216, 1190, 1221, 1193, 1198.

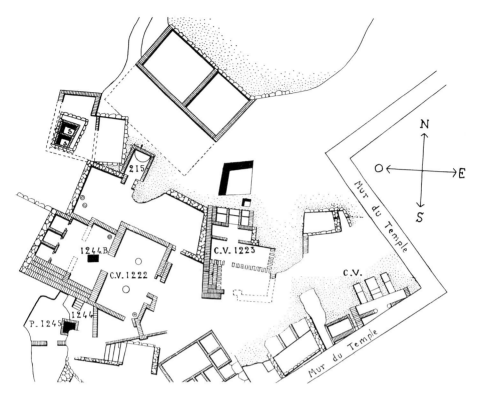

20   C.V. 1222 and 1223.

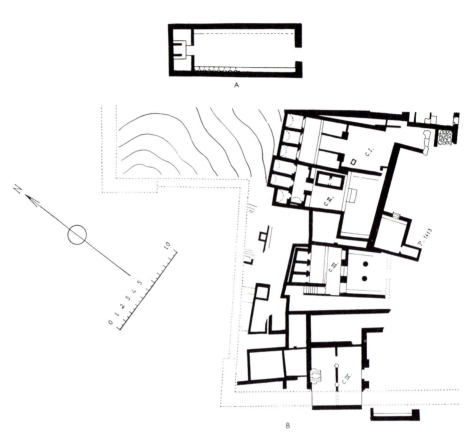

21   a) Chapel Northeast of Village Enclosure Wall.
      b) Chapelles 1, 2, 3, and 4.

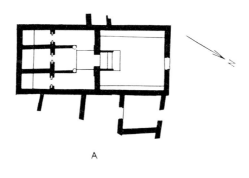

A

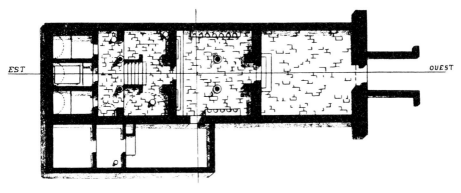

EST   *OUEST*

B

22   a) Small Ramesside Chapel.
      b) Temple of Amun of Ramesses II.

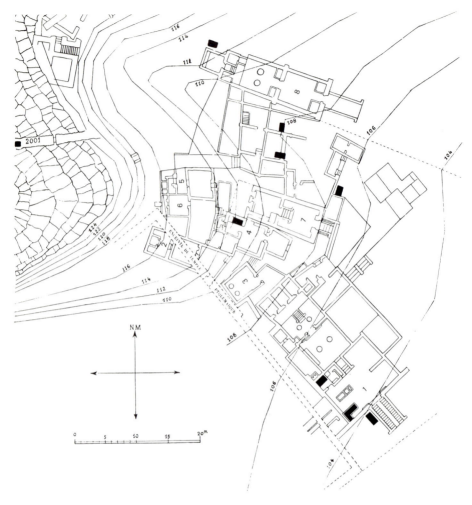

23   1) Chapel of Hathor of Seti I;   2) Chapel E,   3) Chapel A,   4) Chapel B,
5) Chapel C,   6) Chapel D,   7) Chapel F,   8) Chapel G.

(a)

(b)

24 a) Hemispherical bread moulds, Chapel 556, El Amarna.
    b) Lotus goblets from Deir el Medina.

25   Plan of Deir el Medina showing the layout of some of the chapels outside the Temple Enclosure Wall and the four Chapelles within (9, 10, 11, 12). Note no. 6, bottom left.

26   *3ḥ iqr n Rꜥ* stela of *Ḥꜥpy-ꜥꜣ* from C.V. 1215, Deir el Medina.

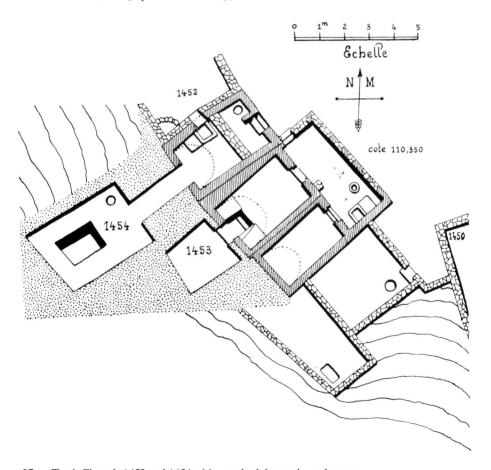

27   Tomb Chapels 1453 and 1454 with attached domestic enclosures.

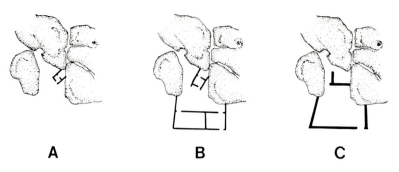

A   B   C

28   The development of the early Satis Temple at Elephantine: a) First and Second Dynasty, b) Third Dynasty, c) Sixth Dynasty.

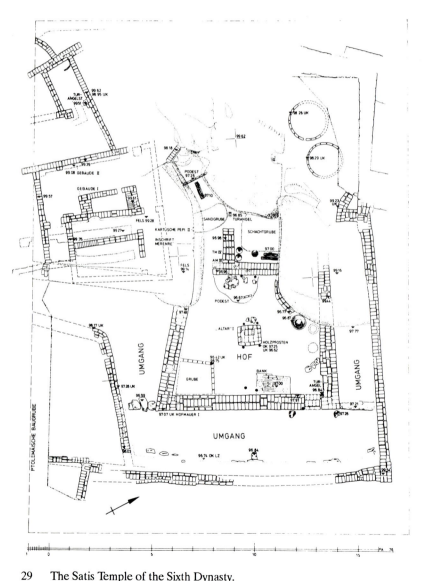

29   The Satis Temple of the Sixth Dynasty.

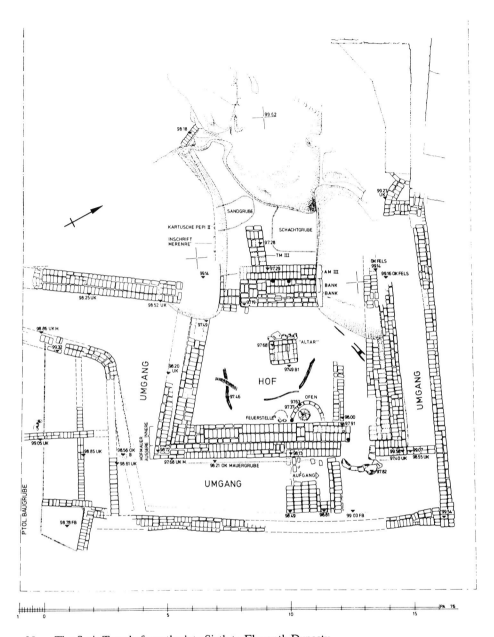

30 The Satis Temple from the late Sixth to Eleventh Dynasty.

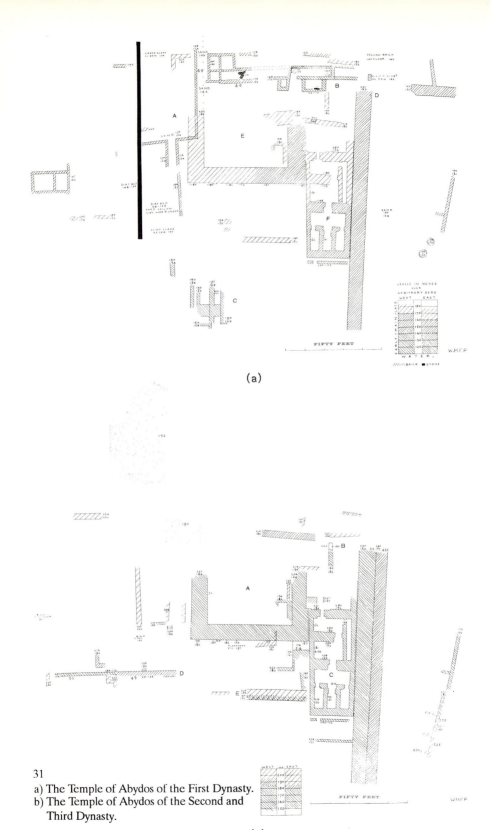

31

a) The Temple of Abydos of the First Dynasty.
b) The Temple of Abydos of the Second and
   Third Dynasty.

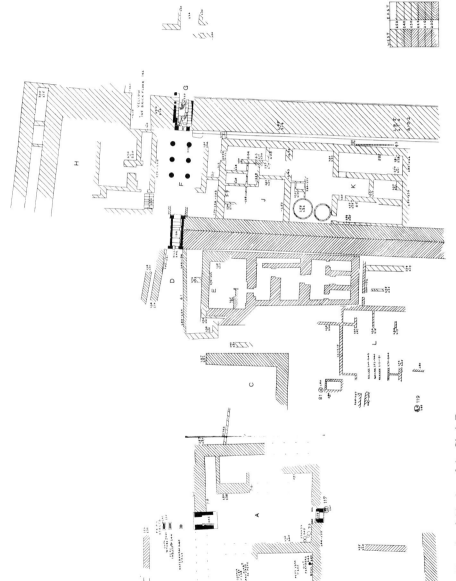

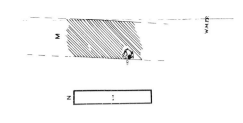

32   The Temple of Abydos of the Sixth Dynasty.

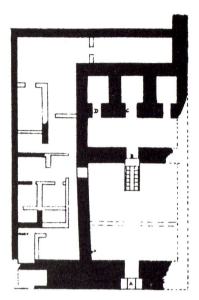

34   The Mortuary Temple of
       Wadjmose on the West Bank,
       Thebes.

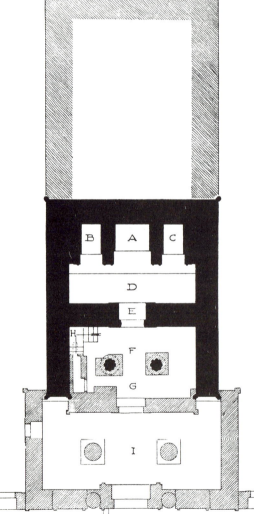

33   The Temple of Amenemhat III and Amenemhat IV
      at Medinet Ma'adi.

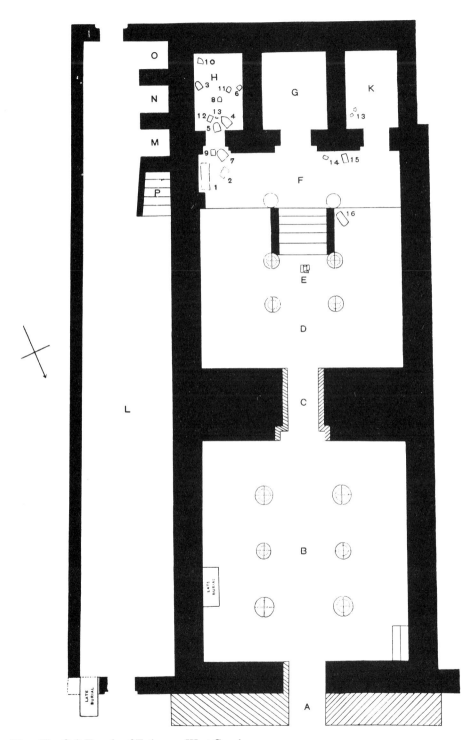

35   The Cult Temple of Tuthmose III at Gurob.

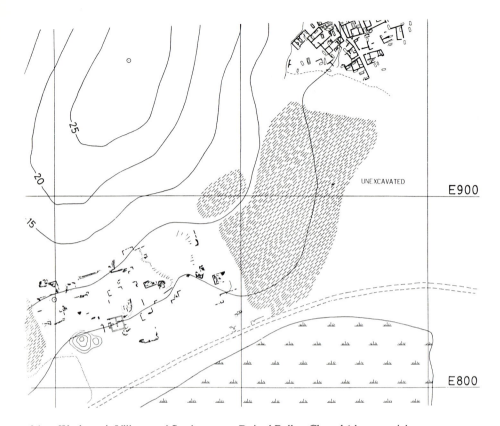

UNEXCAVATED

E900

E800

36   Workmen's Village and Settlement at Deir el Ballas: Chapel 1 bottom right.

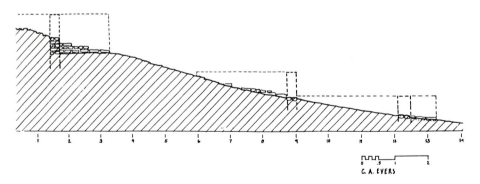

G.A. EVERS

37   Chapel 1 - Deir el Ballas.

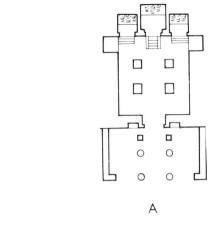

A

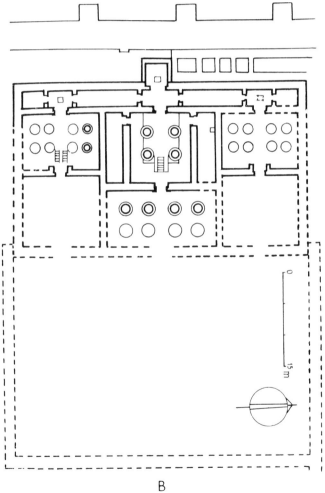

B

38   a) The Temple of Seti I at Wadi Mia.
       b) The Aten Temple at Sesebi.

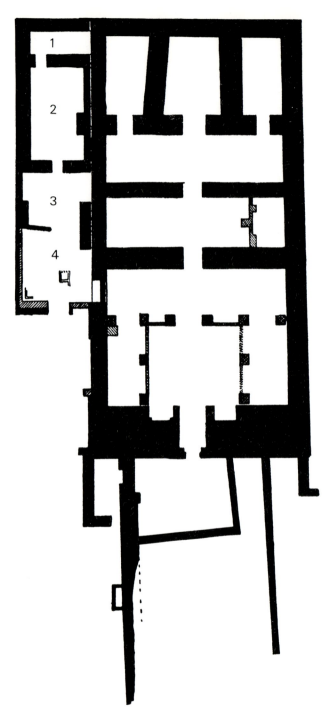

39　The Temple of Amenhotep II at Buhen.

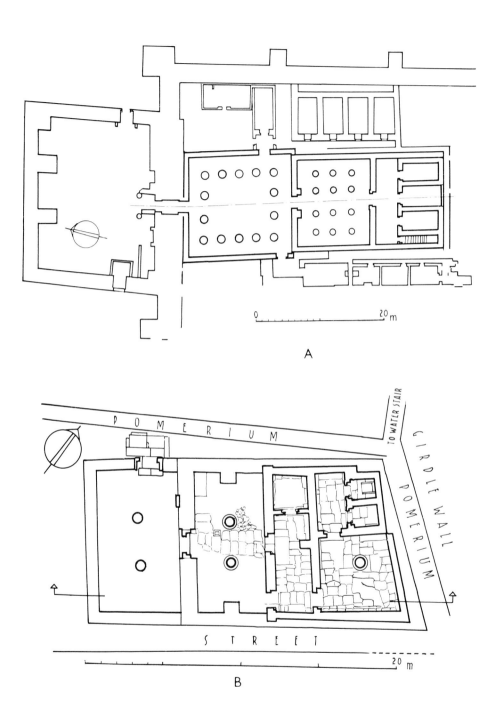

A

B

40   a) The Temple of Ramesses II at Amara West.
       b) The Temple at Kumma.

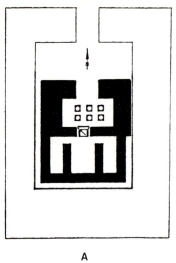
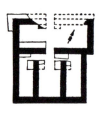
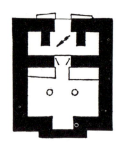

A   B   C

41   a) The Temple of Amenemhat I at Ezbet Rushdi.
       b) Mortuary temple I at Tell el Dab'a, Str. E/2-1.
       c) Temple at Hazor from area H.

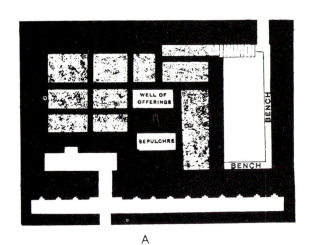

A

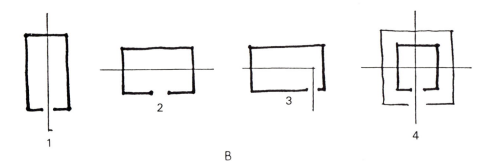

B

42   a) Mastaba of Prince Mena at Dendera.
       b) 1. Langbau, 2. Breitbau, 3. Knickachse, 4. Centralized Square Plan.

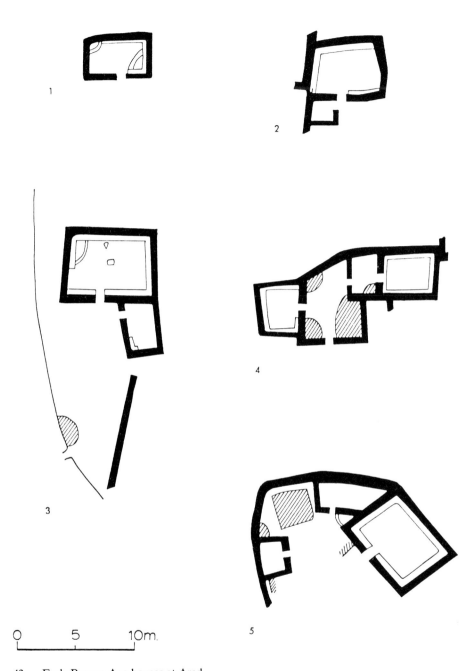

1

2

3

4

5

0   5   10m.

43   Early Bronze Age houses at Arad.

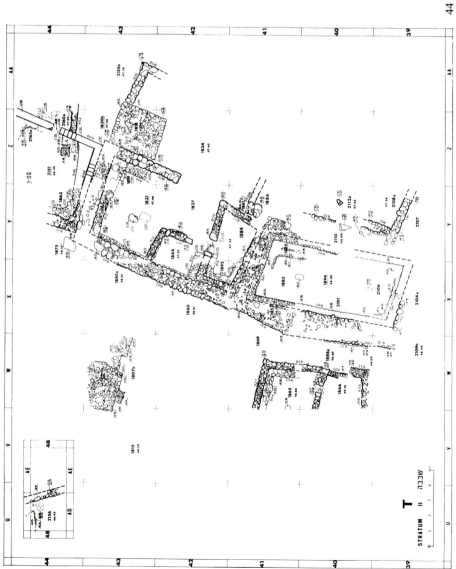

STRATUM II שכבה

45   The cult room of the Ishtar Temple at Assur.

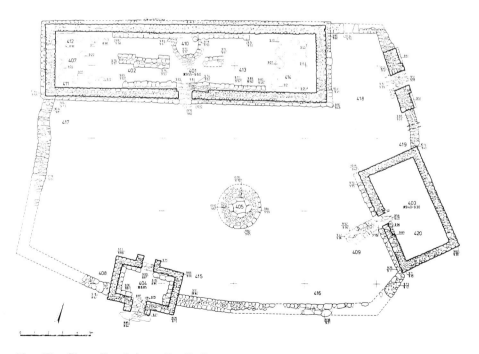

46   The Ghassulian shrine at En-Gedi.

47   Jericho, the Early Bronze Age I Sanctuary from Level VII.

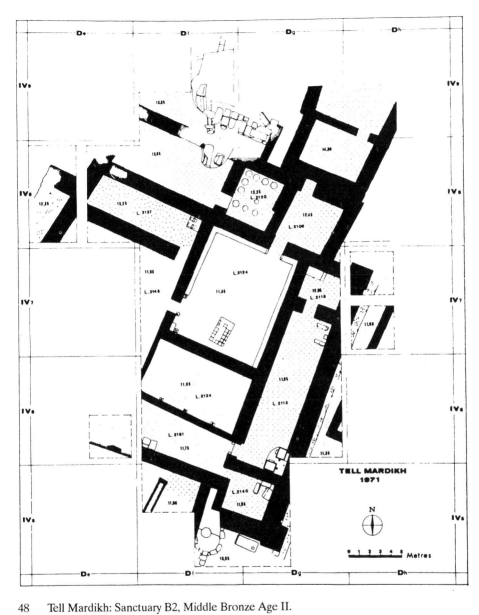

48   Tell Mardikh: Sanctuary B2, Middle Bronze Age II.

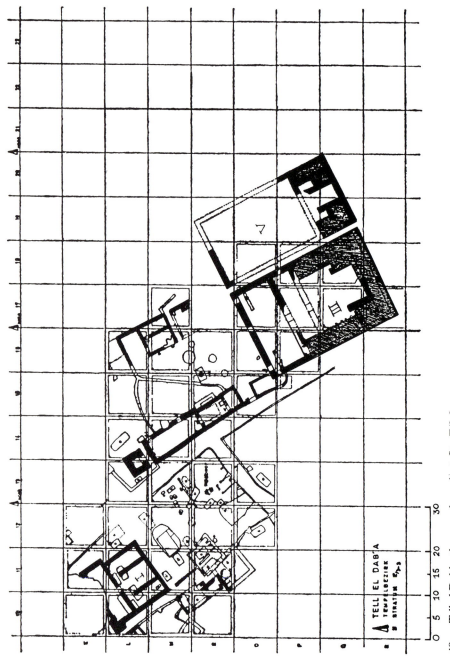

49   Tell el Dab'a, the sacred precinct, Str. E/3-2.

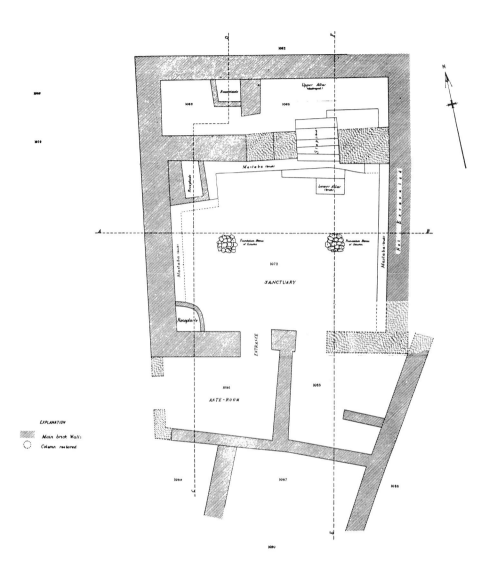

1062

1069

1070

Upper Altar
(destroyed)

Receptacle

1068

1066

Step platform

Mastaba (brick)

Lower Altar
(brick)

Receptacle

Mastaba (brick)

Mastaba (brick)

A

B

Foundation Stones
of Column

Foundation Stones
of Column

1072

SANCTUARY

Receptacle

ENTRANCE

1086

1065

ANTE-ROOM

1064

1067

1068

1090

EXPLANATION

Main brick Walls

Column restored

TEMPLE OF AMENOPHIS III

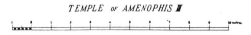

50   Bethshan: The temple from Level VII (Seti I). Originally attributed to
      Amenhotep III.

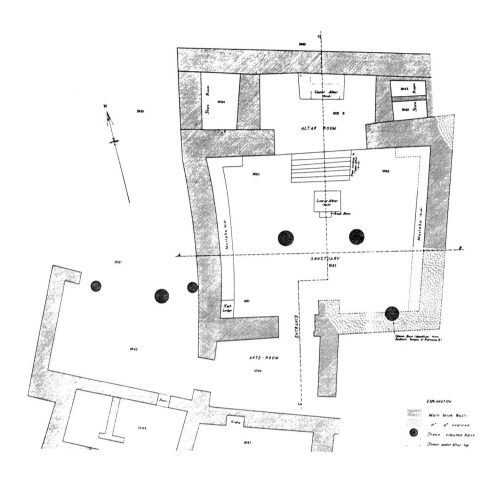

TEMPLE of SETI I

51   Bethshan: The temple from Level VI (Ramesses III). Originally attributed to Seti I.

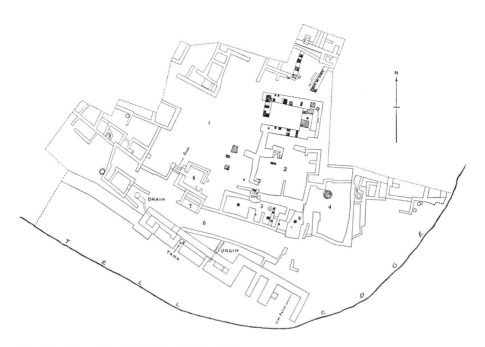

52   Bethshan: The Mekal Temple: Level IX.

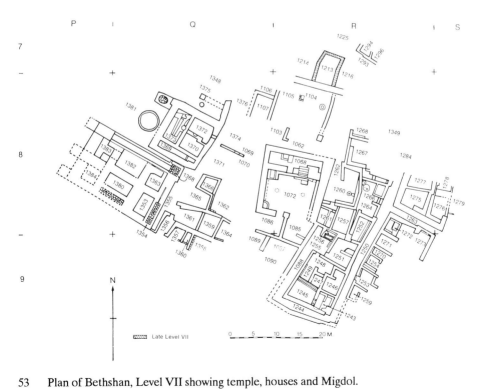

53   Plan of Bethshan, Level VII showing temple, houses and Migdol.

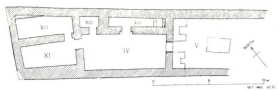

54   The Bronze Age Temple of
      Ayia Irini in Keos.

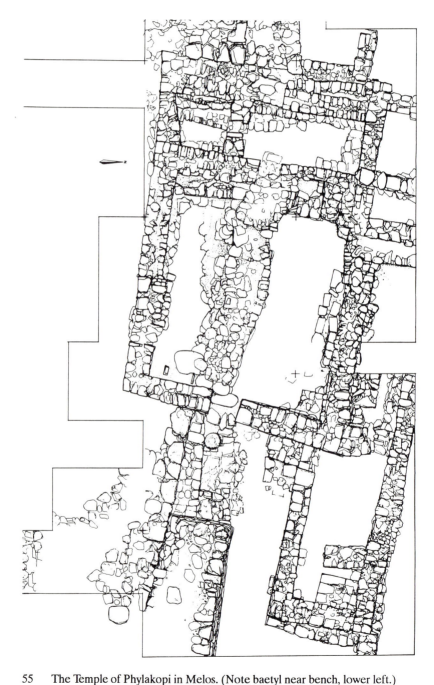

55   The Temple of Phylakopi in Melos. (Note baetyl near bench, lower left.)

56   a) Pot marks from the Tomb of Hemaka.
b) & c) Offering tables from the Old Kingdom.

(a)

(b)

1358

(c)

1366

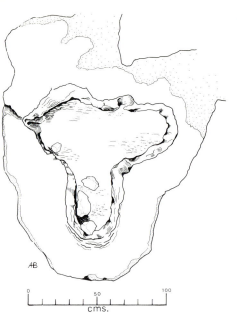

57   Basin T1: Workmen's Village,
      El Amarna (1981).

58   Basin T2: Workmen's Village, El
      Amarna (1981). A superimposition
      of basins: 1) the earliest,
      2) a superimposition of another basin,
      2a) re-siting of next basin,
      3) final basin.

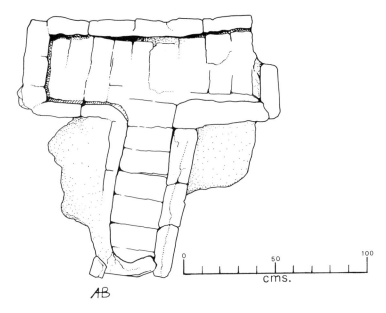

59   Basin T3: Workmen's Village, El Amarna (1981).

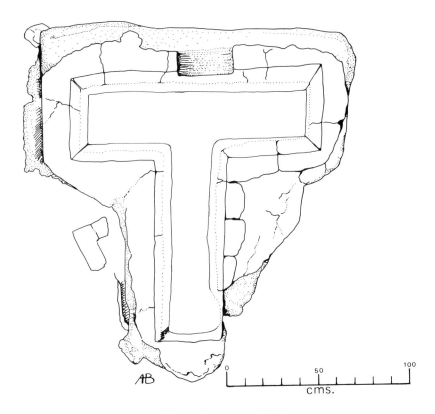

60   Basin T4: Workmen's Village, El Amarna (1981).

(a)

(b)

61   a) **T**-shaped basin T6 before Annexe 450.   b) **T**-shaped basin in Chapel 525.

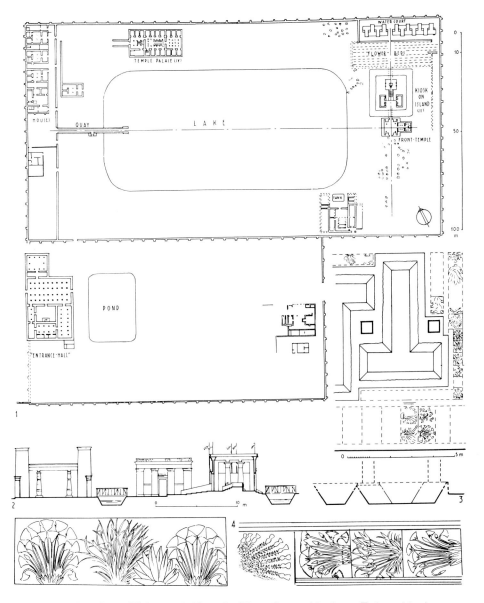

62   The Maru Aten (El Amarna). Note the Water Court with eleven **T**-shaped basins
in top left corner.

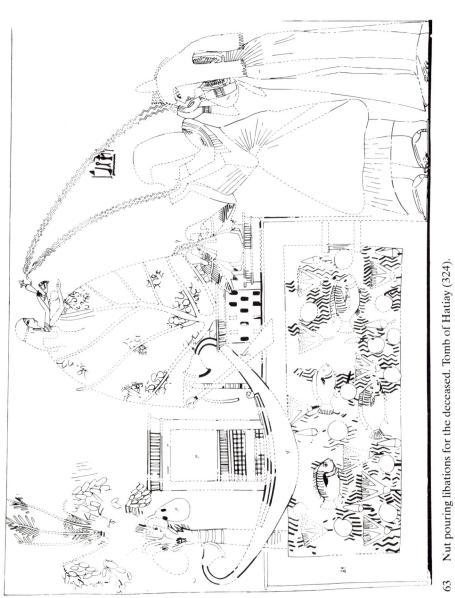

63   Nut pouring libations for the deceased. Tomb of Hatiay (324).

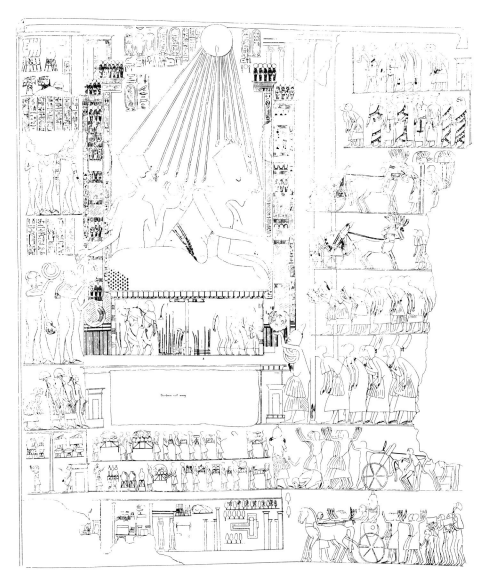

64   The Tomb of Meryre II (2), showing **T**-shaped basin, El Amarna.

(a)

(b)

65   a) Rifeh: pottery offering trays, Dynasty VI-XI.
        b) Rifeh: pottery soul houses, Dynasty IX-XII.

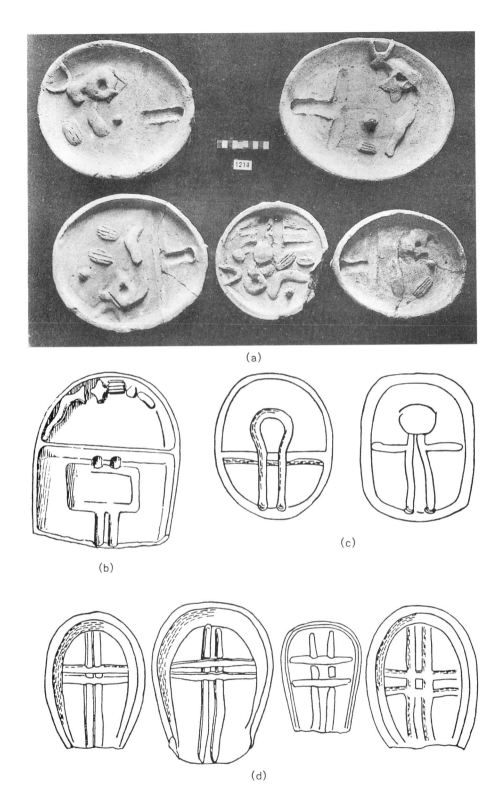

66   Pottery Offering Trays from: a) Armant, b) Dendera, c) and d) Gurna.

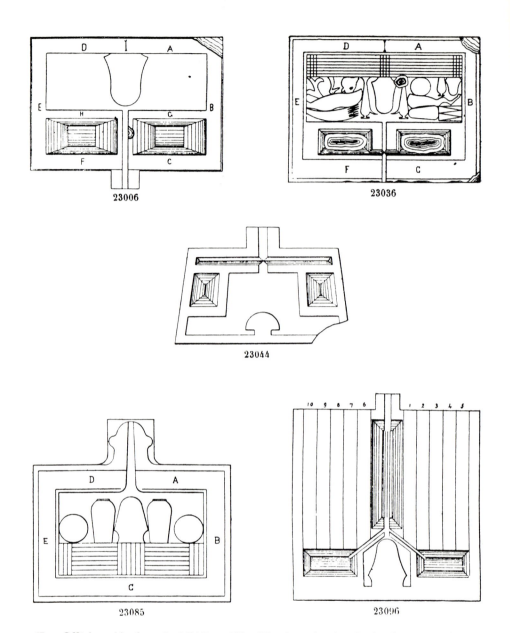

67   Offering tables from the Middle and New Kingdoms showing the development and variations of the **T**-shape. Middle Kingdom: 23006, 23036, 23044; Eighteenth Dynasty: 23085; Twentieth Dynasty: 23096.

68   Hatiay fishing in a **T**-shaped basin. Tomb of Hatiay (324).

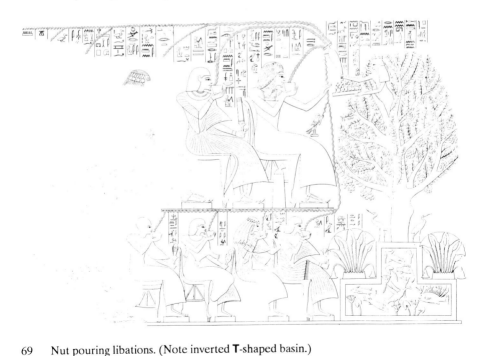

69   Nut pouring libations. (Note inverted **T**-shaped basin.)

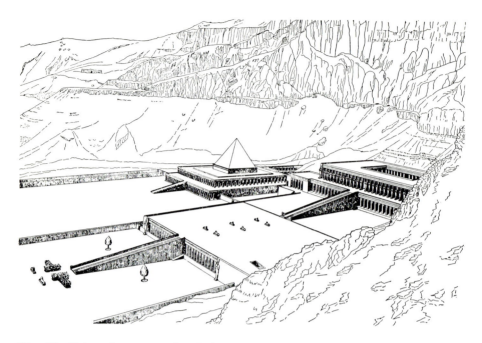

70   The **T**-shaped papyrus pools at Deir el Bahari.

71   Fowling and spearing fish in the marshes. The hill of water in the centre is enclosed by red zigzag lines. (Tomb 69, Menna.)

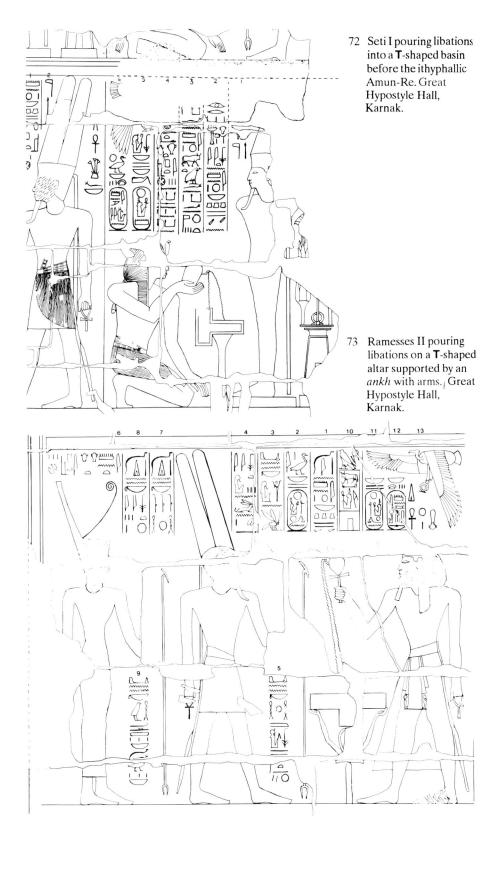

72 Seti I pouring libations into a **T**-shaped basin before the ithyphallic Amun-Re. Great Hypostyle Hall, Karnak.

73 Ramesses II pouring libations on a **T**-shaped altar supported by an *ankh* with arms. Great Hypostyle Hall, Karnak.

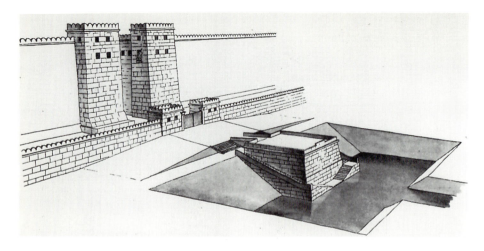

74   The harbour and quay to the Temple of Medinet Habu.

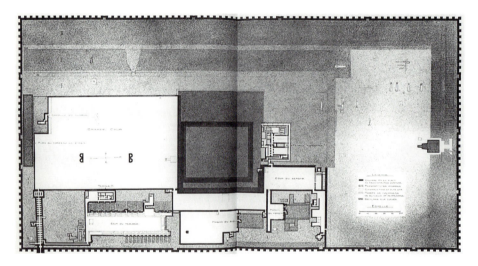

75   The Great Altar to the north of the Step Pyramid.

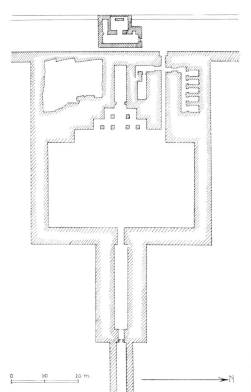

76   The Mortuary Temple of Menkaure.

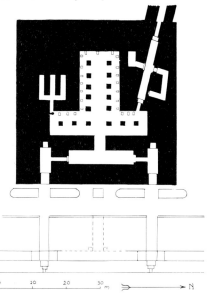

77   The Valley temple of Khephren.

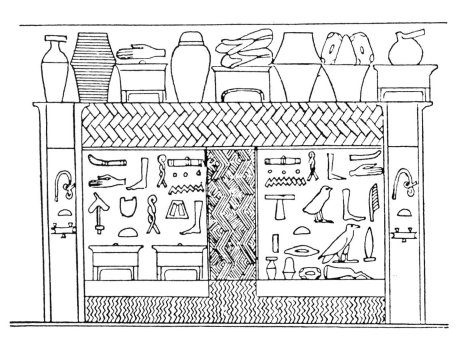

78   The purification tent of Qar from Giza (G 7101), Sixth Dynasty.

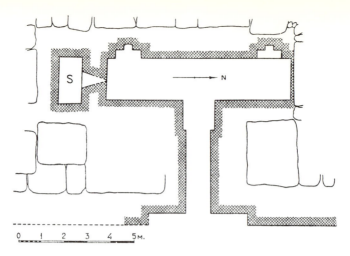

79   Tomb G5110 (Prince Duwanera), Giza.

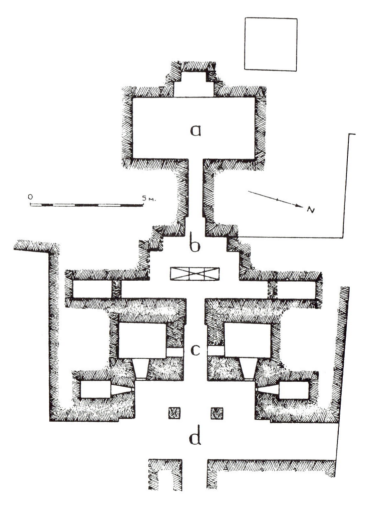

80   Tomb of Rawer, Giza.

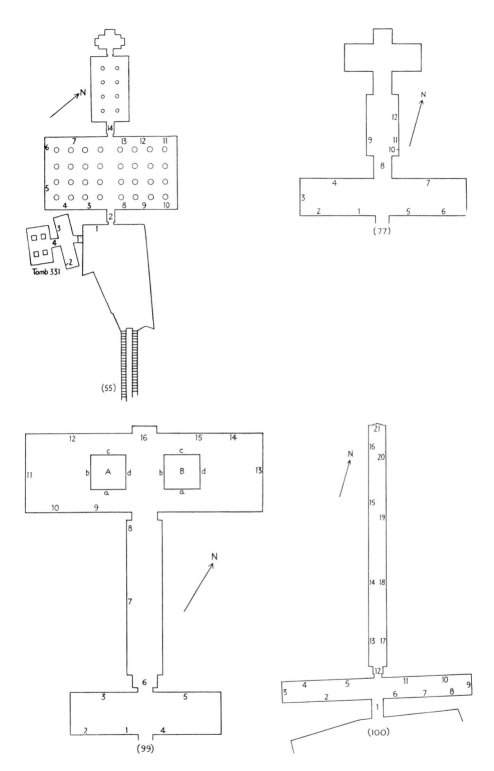

81   Tombs: 55 (Ramose), 77 (Ptahemhet), 99 (Sennufer), 100 (Rekhmire).

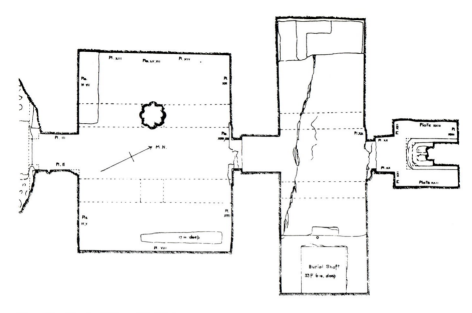

82   The Tomb of Huya (1), El Amarna.

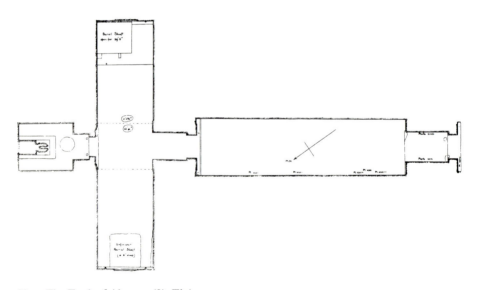

83   The Tomb of Ahmose (3), El Amarna.

84   Stela showing the *ankh* with separation of loop and **T**.

DATE DUE

HIGHSMITH 45-220